Introduction to the
Study of Religion

Introduction to the
Study of Religion

T. WILLIAM HALL

General Editor

with RONALD R. CAVANAGH

Contributors

ALAN L. BERGER
RONALD R. CAVANAGH
T. WILLIAM HALL
JAMES W. KARMAN
RICHARD B. PILGRIM
MILTON C. SERNETT
MICHAEL W. SEXSON
HUSTON SMITH
GABRIEL VAHANIAN
JAMES B. WIGGINS
JAMES G. WILLIAMS

1817

Published in San Francisco by HARPER & ROW, PUBLISHERS

New York / Hagerstown / San Francisco / London

INTRODUCTION TO THE STUDY OF RELIGION. Copyright © 1978 by T. William Hall. All rights reserved. Printed in the United States of America. No part of this book may be used or reproduced in any manner whatsoever without written permission except in the case of brief quotations embodied in critical articles and reviews. For information address Harper & Row, Publishers, Inc., 10 East 53rd Street, New York, N.Y. 10022. Published simultaneously in Canada by Fitzhenry & Whiteside Limited, Toronto.

FIRST EDITION

Designed by Jim Mennick

Library of Congress Cataloging in Publication Data
Main entry under title:

Introduction to the study of religion.

  Bibliography
  1. Religion—Addresses, essays, lectures.
I. Hall, Thomas William, 1921–   II. Cavanagh,
Ronald R. 1938–   III. Berger, Alan L., 1939–
BL48.I56 1978   200'.7   78-4427
ISBN 0-06-063572-X

78 79 80 81 82 10 9 8 7 6 5 4 3 2 1

Contents

Preface

This introduction to the study of religion is unique in both its conception and its aims. It is a basic text for the introductory course in religion that is intended to be fully adaptable to the many ways in which such courses are taught. In addition, it is a workbook, providing teacher and student with questions for discussion, suggested projects, selected bibliography, and a broad range of material for study, but also allowing the freedom for a great variety of concrete courses. In fact, this balancing of structure, substance, and freedom is integral both to religious studies and to religious life itself.

Over the past quarter-century, and especially the past decade, the study of religion has burgeoned into a well-developed academic field. There are strong undergraduate and graduate programs in colleges and universities throughout North America, and the number of religious-studies courses in junior colleges and high schools is growing rapidly. The professional societies of religious-studies teachers are among the most active, innovative, and loyally supported in academia.

There is a maturing conviction that religion is a vital dimension of human life and society and that to neglect its study is to be cut off from many of the most important and fascinating questions that human existence poses. Concomitantly, it is becoming clear that the study of religion can be as academically responsible—neither proselytizing nor debunking—as any other branch of the human sciences, while addressing issues that lie at the heart of culture and of every student's quest for value and meaning. Religious questions—and the religious quest—are becoming an increasingly dominant part of North American life, from evangelical Christians and Catholic Charismatics to Hare Krishna devotees and followers of esoteric teachings. Just as the types of religious expression seem to multiply, so do controversial issues.

However, as the study of religion has become a prominent academic discipline, no clear consensus has emerged about precisely what religious studies is and what approach should be taken in teaching it. No one approach or methodology predominates. Rather, there is a remarkable—and rich— diversity.

In the case of the introductory course, it almost seems that there are as many styles for teaching religion as there are teachers. Some courses emphasize philosophical issues, others adopt a historical perspective; some are based on a phenomenological method, others are more theological; sometimes stress is laid on "primitive" traditions, sometimes on Eastern religions, while in other cases the Western tradition is accented. The world of religious tradition and experience, as reflected in our college catalogs, is truly a "many-splendored thing."

There is little wonder, then, that no one standard text has emerged in the field of religious studies. For the most part, introductory texts in religion have chosen to adopt one or another emphasis and method (e.g., history of religions, theology, philosophy of religion, phenomenology of religion, etc.) and to pursue it vigorously. This is certainly one option, but even within these widely adopted approaches there is great diversity among actual course curricula that use the same method—one teacher stresses primary texts; another, secondary, interpretive work; still another, contemporary literature.

There seems, then, a clear call for the sort of text presented here. *Introduction to the Study of Religion* aims to be as flexible in its potential uses as religious studies is richly varied in its methods and subject matter. It offers a variety of approaches, a broad range of topics, and emphases on different religious traditions in different chapters. The chapters can be used in any order, and teachers and students may stress the chapters that suit the needs of a particular course of study or range of interests. Further, the text is designed to be supplemented by outside readings—paperbacks, articles, notes—and films tailored specifically to the approach of particular teachers and students.

Thus it is our intention to offer an introductory text that responds explicitly to the healthy diversity in the field of religious studies while at the same time providing a solid underpinning for any introductory course and interesting and instructive reading for individual students. Each teacher is invited to use this book as a basic resource for developing his or her own individual introductory course, and students are encouraged to use it independently as well, as an introduction to various dimensions of the world of religion and as a guide to more in-depth study.

This book has grown out of an experimental introductory course developed by the faculty of the Department of Religion at Syracuse University. In the early 1970s, with over 600 students each semester enrolled in an introductory course, it became clear that we had to create an entirely new basic course in religion. That new course, we were convinced, must be both academically rigorous and intellectually seductive as it introduced students to the fascinating study of religion. In addition, the course content and structure must provide maximum flexibility, so that each faculty member might teach in his or her own area of greatest expertise, along with varied options for students to explore different academic and personal interests in religion.

We decided to create a course that would examine a variety of the key expressions of religion (myth, ritual, scripture, art, etc.) as well as major problems or issues in religion and religious thought (death, evil and suffering, God, etc.), and to explore several different methods available for the study of religion. Thus three categories—expression, issue, and method—became the organizational model for the course and hence for this book.

The contributors to this book were involved in the creation and teaching of that new Syracuse University introductory course. Essays originally prepared for the course have been revised so that in their present form they are the most effective way of ushering students into a scholar's way of studying religion. Chapters 8 and 14 were added in order to provide a more comprehensive book.

In recent years several different ways of organizing our introductory course have been used successfully. In the structure for which these materials were originally designed, the entire group of students first spends a few days in independent study on Chapters 1 and 2, "the Term *Religion*" and "Religion as a Field of Study." All students are then invited to participate in two seminars in which the issues of definition are discussed.

Each student then chooses several four-week units or modules. A single chapter provides the outline of study, questions for discussion, and written or oral projects. Paperback books, tapes, and films selected by the teacher give his or her distinctive flavor to the module. Thus during a single semester a student may elect up to six different modules, earning one semester credit for each such unit of study.

In a second pattern used by the editor and several contributors, a two-semester sequence was developed utilizing a selection of chapters each term. During the first two weeks of the first semester we focus on Chapters 1 and 2, concentrating on problems of definition and methods of inquiry. Selected readings from other introductory texts are used to show the diversity of approaches to the study of religion.

During the next four weeks of the course, two "forms of religious expression" from Part II are selected for study, such as ritual and belief, or myth and scripture. Special readings are added that the teacher believes are also important. Next the class focuses on two or more of the "issues" in Part III, such as evil and suffering and paths of salvation, or the problem of God and death and eschatology. To supplement the chapters selected, novels, films, and projects used inside and outside of class time make stimulating units of study.

The first semester of the two-term sequence concludes with a brief reflection on several methods of study based on reading of the final chapter. During the second semester other chapters not previously read are utilized, along with collateral reading. For both semesters the course unity is maintained by the logical progression of "expression, issue, and method" as developed in the organization of the book.

A third way of using this book as a text is to develop the first term around Parts I and II and the second term around Parts III and IV. As in other organizational structures, the questions for discussion at the end of each chapter are helpful in stimulating class participation. Moreover, the projects may be chosen for independent study and research papers. In experimenting with this third format, each teacher selects supplementary readings to provide illustrative material from varied historical religious traditions or from secular culture.

These materials have been utilized in still other ways in selected New York State high school courses in religion, in community colleges, and in adult continuing-education courses. The experience thus far suggests that there are any number of different styles of teaching to which this book may be adapted.

As the editor of this book, I wish to acknowledge the distinctive contribution of two people—Ronald R. Cavanagh and Robert M. Diamond. Dr. Cavanagh, associate professor of religion at Syracuse University, worked closely with me in revising our introductory course. As the first coordinator of the new course, he guided the planning and encouraged other faculty in the preparation of teaching materials that were first drafts of most of the chapters included in this book. Since January 1975, when he became chairman of the Department of Religion, he has given constant support to the improvement and continued modification of the course that he earlier directed. Chapters 1, 2, and 4, which he wrote, demonstrate his scholarship and his commitment to the project.

Second, Robert M. Diamond and the staff of the Center for Instructional Development (CID) at Syracuse University have made an important contribution to this book. The Center's staff members were creative critics in the development of the structure of the course. Most of the chapters included were first published by CID, and in a number of cases they were revised several times in accordance with student evaluation.

As chairman of the Department of Religion when we began this experimental course and as a continuing member of the faculty for the course, I have derived tremendous satisfaction from working with my colleagues. In addition to the authors of the fifteen chapters, H. Katherine Havice, Jared Massanari, David L. Miller, Amanda Porterfield, Patricia Cox, and D. B. Robertson have participated in the teaching of Religion 105. In one way or another, each has contributed to the course development and to this book. We have shared in intellectual dialogue and in the joys and woes of teaching.

Finally, I wish to express my appreciation to the students at Syracuse Uni-

versity who for over five years have been participants with us in the introductory course known as Religion 105. We have wanted the course to be the
best possible one for students who might not have another formal class in
religion. At the same time, we have hoped that it would whet the intellectual
appetite of our students to do further study while it provided a background
for that future enterprise. These students have at times been harshly critical,
and we have learned from them. At other times they have been generous in
their praise, and for that we are grateful. I continue to hope that the students
with whom I work each semester, and all the others who use this book, will
become both informed and excited about the study of religion.

T. WILLIAM HALL, 1978

Contributors

ALAN L. BERGER, assistant professor of religion at Syracuse University, is a specialist in Jewish religion and culture with a special interest in Jewish mysticism.

RONALD R. CAVANAGH, a theologian and philosopher of religion, is an associate professor and chairman of the Department of Religion at Syracuse University.

T. WILLIAM HALL, the editor of this volume, is a philosophical theologian. Formerly chairman of the Department of Religion, he is now a professor in that department.

JAMES W. KARMAN completed his Ph.D. in religion at Syracuse University and in 1977 joined the faculty of religious studies at the State University of California at Chico.

RICHARD B. PILGRIM, a specialist in Japanese religions and in the history of religions, is an associate professor offering courses in Buddhism and Japanese religions. His area of research and writing is Japanese religion and the arts.

MILTON C. SERNETT, a historian of the Black Church, is an associate professor of Afro-American studies at Syracuse University.

MICHAEL W. SEXSON received his Ph.D. in religion at Syracuse University in 1976. In September 1976 he returned to his position as assistant professor in the Department of English at Montana State University at Bozeman.

HUSTON SMITH, author of *The Religions of Man* and other books, a philosopher of religions, and for fifteen years professor of philosophy at Massachusetts Institute of Technology, is the Jeanette K. Watson Professor of Religion and an adjunct professor of philosophy at Syracuse University.

GABRIEL VAHANIAN is the Thomas J. Watson Professor of Religion at Syracuse University. Author of *The Death of God* and other volumes and formerly director of graduate studies in religion, he continues teaching and writing about theology.

JAMES B. WIGGINS, a historian of Christianity and an author in the fields of Christian history and religion as story, is a professor of religion and director of graduate studies in religion at Syracuse University.

JAMES G. WILLIAMS, a historian of scriptures and religions with specialization in Old Testament studies, is an associate professor of religion at Syracuse University.

Part I

DEFINITION AND
FIELD OF STUDY

Whenever most of us begin studying something, we already know what we are going to study and why we want to do it. We first suppose that the same understanding is true in the study of religion, but is it? A brief survey of religious writings, or even a few moments of introspection into our own unexamined thoughts, may provide a hint that there is no easy way to define religion. Nor is it self-evident why one might wish to study religion.

The purpose of Chapter 1 is to help you confront the question, What is religion? While the chapter does not presume to reach a simple, "true" definition of religion, the author proposes a functional definition that is believed to be useful for the academic study of religion as well as a working hypothesis for this volume.

Chapter 2 makes clear that there are various motivations for engaging in religious studies. Some people may study religion in search of information to be used in converting nonbelievers to a particular religion. Others may study religion in order to reinforce their own prejudices. In Chapter 2, however, these inadequate reasons are repudiated and more appropriate motivating principles for a critical inquiry into the phenomena of religion are set forth.

Chapters 1 and 2 are written in a programed style that will encourage deliberate and intense independent study. The writing format will encourage you to understand a question, give your answer, and then check the adequacy of your answer.

It is recommended that you study all of Part I before reading later chapters. From time to time it may be valuable to return to Chapters 1 and 2 for a review and, if you wish, to develop your own definitions and reasons for the study of religion.

CHAPTER 1

The Term Religion

RONALD R. CAVANAGH

The term *religion* means many things to many people. We will consider some of the ways the term has been used and, in the process, generate a definition that will be useful in this study.

This chapter and the next are presented in a programed format. At times, depending on your specific answer to a question, you will be sent to different pages, so please follow directions carefully.

As a start, let us see what the term *religion* means to you. Which one of the following statements would you say is closer to your own definition?

1. "Religion is a belief in an invisible superhuman power together with the feelings and practices that flow from such a belief."
2. "Religion is the quest for the values of the ideal life, and for the means of achieving them, and includes a world view that relates this quest to the surrounding universe."

If you selected the first definition, that "religion is a belief in an invisible superhuman power . . . together with the feelings and practices that flow from such a belief," you chose a definition similar to the one you will find in Webster's *Third New International Dictionary.*

If, on the other hand, you selected the second alternative, that "religion is the quest for the values of the ideal life and for the means of achieving them, etc.," you are more in agreement with a definition found in the *American College Dictionary.*

Obviously, both definitions are useful, and yet they differ in their basic approach: The first emphasizes belief while the second stresses the concept of a quest for value.

The term *religion* is, in fact, highly ambiguous; that is, it is used to mean a variety of things to different people. In this chapter we will discuss some of the definitions that have been used and, in the process, assist you in recognizing some of the key characteristics that separate one emphasis from another.

To help you become more sensitive to these differences in emphasis, we are going to look at eight characteristics that appear in various definitions of the term *religion*. We will refer to them as "distinguishing characteristics."

DISTINGUISHING CHARACTERISTICS OF DEFINITIONS OF RELIGION

To help you identify these characteristics within a definition of religion, we will begin by introducing you to three of the eight characteristics and then give you an opportunity to identify them within a given definition.

It is not important that you know the names of the individuals associated with a particular characteristic. It is necessary, however, that you become aware of the wide range of characteristics in use and that you be able, when you see a definition, to identify the particular approach that is being taken.

1. FEELING

First we will consider the characteristic of feeling.

Friedrich Schleiermacher, an important nineteenth-century German theologian and philosopher, defines religion as "the feeling of absolute dependence." Notice the emphasis on feeling or emotion rather than knowing or doing. Here the definition of religion is based on the person's feeling and intuition that he or she is completely dependent on God, the Infinite, or the Eternal. In this approach any beliefs and practices of religion must be understood as expressions of this unique feeling of absolute dependence. Schleiermacher also says that "true religion is sense and taste for the Infinite."

2. RITUAL ACTIVITY

Now let us consider another important characteristic of definitions of religion, that of ritual activity.

Contemporary anthropologist Anthony Wallace defines religion as "a set of rituals, rationalized by myth, which mobilizes supernatural powers for the purpose of achieving or preventing transformations of state in man or nature."

Notice the emphasis on organizing, doing, or acting—"achieving or preventing transformations." This definition emphasizes the performance of specific acts that are established by the religious community.

A similar emphasis is described by Winston King, who says, "So it is with the Catholic, at the moment when the priest's blessing is changing the Sacred Host [the communion wafer] into the body of Christ. So it is with the Quaker when the holy silence is broken by words growing out of a true illumination by the Inner Light."

3. BELIEF

Third, let us consider belief as a characteristic of definitions of religion.

One of the basic definitions of the term *religion* given in the *Universal Dictionary of the English Language* is that it is a "specific system of belief in God, including a group of doctrines concerning Him, and His relations to man and the universe."

Notice that the stress is on the intellectual act of affirming doctrines rather than on the performance of any actions. In this approach all activities and feelings that are a part of the religion are supportive of a belief rather than, as in the previous example, the other way around.

Consent to such dogmas as the Nicene Creed (ca. 325) has long been important in the Christian Church. The candidate for confirmation is asked to say, "I believe in one God, the Father Almighty . . . and . . . in one Lord Jesus Christ . . . and I believe in the Holy Spirit, the Lord and Giver of Life . . ." to indicate that he or she affirms the universal truth of the Christian message.

We have just looked at three different definitions of religion and classified each according to its crucial or defining characteristics. These characteristics are the following:

FEELING—an emphasis on a distinct emotional state.
RITUAL ACTIVITY—an emphasis on the performance of patterned actions.
BELIEF—an emphasis on the intellectual act of thinking affirmatively.

If you are not completely sure of the differences among the three defining characteristics just outlined, reread paragraphs 1, 2, and 3 on feeling, ritual activity, and belief.

Now let us see if you can recognize these different characteristics in context. Which one of the three—feeling, ritual activity, or belief—do you think best describes the emphasis of the following definition of religion?

Religion is the consent of thought to particular ideas expressing the relation of humanity to the powers that rule the universe.

If you identified the distinguishing characteristic as belief, you are correct. The crucial phrase in this definition is "consent of thought," which stresses the intellectual operation of the mind in giving assent to certain ideas or to a particular view.

This definition could not be characterized as emphasizing feelings because it does not mention any particular emotional state. Neither could it be characterized as emphasizing ritual activity because there is no mention of the performance of any standardized or patterned action. Now let us try another question.

Which of the three characteristics—feeling, ritual activity, or belief—do you think best describes the emphasis of the following definition?

Religion is the immediate affective experience of a tremendous mystery that both awes people and fascinates them.

If you said "feeling," you are correct. The key phrase in this definition is "affective experience," which stresses the emotional responses to the mysterious. Nothing is said about the mystery or about the performance of any particular act in response to the experience.

Let us try one more before we examine five additional characteristics. Which of the three—feeling, ritual activity, or belief—do you think best describes the emphasis of the following definition:

Religion consists essentially in the performance of a regular order of procedures laid down by a community to set the sacred powers in motion for the benefit of humanity.

We hope that by now you are able to see clearly that the emphasis is on ritual activity.

The phrase "performance of a regular order of procedures" stresses human doing or performing for a specific purpose that has been standardized by the community. We could not characterize the definition either by belief or by feeling because neither the assent of the mind to certain ideas nor the existence of a particular emotional state is mentioned. Belief and feeling will certainly be part of religious ritual activity, but they are not the crucial defining characteristics that we may encounter in definitions of the term *religion*.

4. MONOTHEISM

The fourth characteristic of definitions of religion is *monotheism,* a term that emphasizes the crucial relationship between humanity and the one God. St. Thomas Aquinas (1225–1274), one of the most important theologians in the history of Roman Catholic thought, says that the term *religion* "denotes properly a relation to God." His definition excludes any other object except the one God as appropriate for religious relations. Judaism expresses this notion in its great *Shema:* "Hear O Israel, the Lord our God, the Lord is One." Islamic scripture (the *Koran*) states that "your God is one God . . . There is no God but He—the living, the Eternal." Thus the faithful are called to prayer five times a day by the *muezzin,* who cries out, "There is no God but God!" (*Laa ilaaha illa llah.*)

Neither humanism nor communism nor any feeling, ritual activity, or belief that does not express a relationship to this monotheistic God is properly religious, according to this emphasis, because religion is essentially a relationship to one God who is conceived of as the only divine being.

5. THE SOLITARY INDIVIDUAL

Another characteristic that recurs in definitions of religion is a reference to the solitary individual, which is our fifth emphasis.

One definition given to the term *religion* by Alfred North Whitehead, a prominent English-American philosopher of this century, is, "Religion is what the individual does with his own solitariness; and if you were never solitary, you were never religious." This definition emphasizes the individual involved in an intimate personal dialog with himself or herself. For Whitehead, the essence of religion lies in humanity's confrontation with "the awful ultimate fact, which is the human being, consciously alone with itself, for its own sake." We need to keep in mind, however, that it is possible for a person to be solitary in this sense while he or she is actually with other people; the solitariness is an inward state, not a public one.

6. SOCIAL VALUATION

Now let us consider a sixth emphasis in definitions of religion—the characteristic of social valuation.

Two anthropologists, William Lessa and Evan Vogt, give the following definition of religion in a recent work on comparative religion: Religion is "a system of beliefs and practices directed toward the 'ultimate concern' of a society."

It is important to recognize that in this definition it is society and not the individual that provides the center for religious valuation. Religious beliefs, practices, and attitudes are directed toward the expression of what a society of people holds to be of central importance. Contrast this with Whitehead's definition, which stresses the solitary individual as the center of religious valuation.

7. ILLUSION

A seventh characteristic that is sometimes emphasized in defining religion is illusion.

Karl Marx, a nineteenth-century social philosopher whom you have probably heard of as the father of communism, defines religion this way: "Religion is the sigh of the oppressed creature . . . It is the opium of the people . . . Religion is only the illusory sun which revolves around man as long as he does not revolve around himself."

Marx's definition describes religion as primarily something that misinterprets reality. According to this definition, all the beliefs, practices, and attitudes of religion reflect a distorted and essentially immature response to the universe as it actually is.

8. ULTIMATE REALITY AND VALUE

The eighth characteristic we are concerned with considers religion as the true focus on ultimate reality and value.

John B. Magee, the author of *Religion and Modern Man*, offers the following definition: "Religion is the realm of the ultimately real and ultimately valuable." Here religion is defined as the true and ultimate measure of people's existence, the final test of life's meaning. This is in direct contrast to Marx's view of religion as an illusion.

Notice that this definition of religion as concerned with ultimate reality does not tell us whether the religious experience is monotheistic or solitary or social or whether it is best characterized by belief, ritual activity, or feeling. It does, however, emphasize that religion deals with ultimate reality and value.

Now let us see if you can recognize the five characteristics we have considered when you meet them in the following definitions. Using scrap paper, match the letter of one of the five characteristics—(A) monotheism, (B) the solitary individual, (C) social valuation, (D) illusion, (E) ultimate reality and value—with the definition that best reflects it. You will find the answers in the paragraphs that follow this list.

1. "Religion is the rationalization of human deceptions, the insistent but unrealistic wishes of humankind. It is the universal obsessional neurosis of humanity."
2. "Religion, as it is expressed in belief and practice, is essentially the conveyor of the collective ideals or central value of society."
3. "Religion is the dimension of human experience in which humanity encounters what is authentically real and unconditionally important."
4. "Religion is that which binds us to one almighty God."
5. "Religion consists of the acts and experiences of individuals in their solitude, so far as they understand themselves in relation to what they regard as divine."

If you said that definition (1) emphasizes illusion, (D), you are correct. It stresses the deceptive character of religious ideas and suggests that religion is a sickness brought on by failure to recognize a distinction between impossible wishes and the way things really are. It contradicts definition (3), which states that through religion humanity encounters that which is authentically real and unconditionally important. If you were mistaken in your identification, reread Karl Marx's definition of religion, which emphasizes the illusionary characteristic of religion.

If you recognized that definition (2) stresses social valuation, (C), you must have been paying close attention. The key phrase is "central values of a society." This definition does not distinguish between the real and the illusory characteristics of these central values. Nor does it contend that they are monotheistic. It does, however, specifically contradict the assertion that religion is characterized primarily by the solitary individual.

If you did not answer correctly, reread the description of the social-valuation characteristic.

If you recognized that the emphasis of definition (3) is on ultimate reality and value, (E), you are correct. The definition states that religion expresses the "authentically real and unconditionally important," which is what we mean by ultimate reality and value. Note that this definition is a direct contradiction of definition (1).

If you missed the correct answer, carefully reread the material on ultimate reality and value.

If you said that definition (4) emphasizes the characteristic of monotheism, (A), you are correct. The definition states that it is humanity's relationship to one almighty God that distinguishes religion. Note that the definition does not say whether this relationship is primarily individual or social, or illusory or real, only that it stresses monotheism.

If you missed this one, read the section on monotheism again.

Were you able to see that definition (5) emphasizes the solitary individual, (B)? The key phrase in this definition is "individuals in their solitude." It rejects any emphasis on the centrality of social valuation and locates the religious dimension completely within the experience and action of the solitary individual. The definition does not state whether such experience is illusory or real. Neither does it specify that the divine must be understood as the one God in relation to humanity, as the monotheistic type of definition does.

If you were in error, reread the material carefully.

DEFINING THE TERM

You should now be able to see that the term *religion* is ambiguous to the extent that (1) it is actually defined in a number of ways; (2) these definitions emphasize several distinguishing characteristics; and (3) some of them are in conflict with some others. You should now be able to recognize eight basic emphases in definitions presented to you for analysis.

Recognizing that the term *religion* has been defined in a number of different ways and is therefore ambiguous, we still need a specific definition as a starting point for our study of religion. This is so for the following reasons:

1. Without a specific definition to clarify and stabilize the meaning of religion, it will be impossible to know precisely what it is that we intend to study.
2. In order to decide how we will go about studying religion, it is necessary to know specifically what the term *religion* will mean for us.
3. Without a definition specifying clearly what religion is and how we are going to study it, we cannot evaluate either the goals proposed for the study or the conclusions of the study. We need a specific defini-

tion so that we may know when we have adequately completed our study of religion.

In other words, our definition must help us answer three questions: What? How? When?

Let us consider the nature and purpose of a definition. All definitions are products of human decision; they are rules laid down by people for the purpose of establishing clear and precise meaning. When a term is clarified by definition, the possibility of communicating it successfully is increased. Thus we may say that a definition is a rule set down for the purpose of fostering clear communication. A definition is judged by the criteria of clarity and utility. In choosing or developing a definition, we must answer the following questions: Is it clear or is it confusing? Is it helpful or is it useless?

It is important to remember that we do not choose or construct a definition in a vacuum. We always have some purpose in mind, and we may—as we do in the case of religion—have examples of previous usage. The objectives of this chapter and the actual definitions of religion we have already presented will influence our final decision on a specific definition.

Let us consider the following question: How shall we define the term *religion?*

Among the following responses, indicate on a scrap paper the one you feel best represents your judgment at this time.

"We should choose one of the definitions that has already been given and stick with it." (See paragraph A.)
"We should construct a definition of our own and stick with it until we see whether it works." (See paragraph B.)
"It does not make any difference how we define it, for some other group of students will come along and define it in a different way." (See paragraph C.)

A. You said, "We should choose one of the definitions that has already been given and stick with it." A definition is a rule that is freely established by people and reflects a decision to standardize the use of a term in a particular way. We could choose to use a rule that has already been decided on by somebody else.

But what definition is best for our present inquiry? If one definition is better than another, there must be some criteria or standards of judgment by which we come to prefer one definition to another. Let us consider these criteria before making a decision. We will call them our "predefinitional priorities."

B. You said, "We should construct a definition of our own and stick with it until we see whether it works." You have an adventurous spirit. You recognize that all definitions are rules made by humans and represent a particular person's decision to use a particular term in a precise way. There is no necessity for us to agree with any one of the actual definitions of religion that have been put forth.

But where shall we begin to construct our own? There must be some criteria against which we can measure the defining characteristics we will choose for our definition. Let us turn to a consideration of these criteria before we make any decisions. We will call them our "predefinitional priorities."

C. You said, "It does not make any difference how we define it, for some other group of students will come along and define it in a different way." You recognize rightly the possibility that another group of students might decide to define religion in a way different from ours, no matter how we choose to define the term. A definition is a rule made by people and represents somebody's decision to use a certain term in a specific way. There is no necessity for anyone else to be bound by our definition.

Is there, however, one definition that is best suited to our purposes? Let us turn to a consideration of some of the criteria or standards of judgment that make it clear that not all definitions are as good as others. We will call these criteria "predefinitional priorities."

PREDEFINITIONAL PRIORITIES [1]

In this chapter we are responsible for ensuring that our definition of the term *religion* is both clear and useful. In order to construct such a definition, we are setting certain predefinitional priorities. We must avoid the following features:

Vagueness
Narrowness
Compartmentalization
Prejudice

We must achieve the following features:

Specificity
Inclusiveness

In the following pages we will identify and give examples of each of these features. Then we will ask you to evaluate several actual definitions in terms of these criteria.

Definitional Features to Be Avoided

Vagueness

Following are three characteristic definitions of religion often offered by university freshmen:

"Religion is life."
"Religion is the history of the human race."
"Religion is the quest for true knowledge."

These definitions are not impossible, but they are not very useful either because each fails to differentiate religion from other aspects of life, history, or the pursuit of knowledge. If we look at the third statement, we see that it does not help us distinguish religion from the pursuit of truth in the arts, sciences, or philosophy. A definition is vague when it does not clearly distinguish its subject matter from other subject matters; a responsible definition must avoid such vagueness.

Narrowness

We have already considered Aquinas's definition that religion "denotes properly a relation to God." Since this definition is broadly monotheistic, it may seem quite liberal to Westerners, but its scope is not adequate for our study because it excludes both nontheistic forms, such as some forms of Buddhism, and polytheistic forms, such as those found in ancient Mesopotamian culture.

We have said that we must avoid a vague definition because it is overly inclusive and does not clearly discriminate its subject matter from others. We now say that a narrow definition must be avoided for the opposite reason: because it is overly exclusive and does not allow consideration of the entire subject. For example, a definition such as "Religion consists of the institutionalized thoughts and practices that relate humanity to a god or gods" excludes consideration of all forms of noninstitutionalized phenomena and does not allow us to consider such questions as "Was there a religious dimension to the Woodstock festival?" or "Might there be a religious dimension to some drug experiences?" This narrowness is inadequate, since our definition must serve as the basis for a comprehensive study of religion.

Compartmentalization

Although it is very similar to narrowness, compartmentalization in a definition suggests an even greater limitation of interests or concerns that can be addressed. Compartmentalization is to be avoided because it signifies a reductionist view of the religious person. Definitions with this feature reduce religion, or the religious dimension of human experience, to one single, special aspect of the human self such as emotion, thought, or action.

Some examples of definitions exhibiting compartmentalization are the following:

"Religion is the feeling of absolute dependence" (emotion).
"Religion is a specific system of belief in God" (thought).
"Religion is a set of rituals" (prescribed action).

The essays in this volume provide a study of religion in relation to the whole of human experience. Therefore a definition of religion in this context must avoid any compartmentalization that would limit our view of religion to one aspect of human experience.

Prejudice

Definitions that include blanket evaluations of religion as "true" or "false," "good" or "bad," "relevant" or "irrelevant" are not helpful for the purposes of a critical course of study. Defining religion at the outset as either "a set of false beliefs constructed by a neurotic mind suffering infantile delusions" or "humanity's encounter with and response to that which is ultimately real and valuable" does not permit open, critical consideration of religious experience and beliefs.

An inquiry like ours must avoid a dogmatic (i.e., prejudiced) definition, either negative or positive. Our definition of religion, although specific and inclusive, must be as unprejudiced as possible in order to allow us to critically examine all phenomena.

DEFINITIONAL FEATURES TO BE ACHIEVED

Specificity

This criterion includes the features of clarity as well as distinctiveness. Our definition of the term *religion* must indicate clearly what religion is and how it is to be differentiated from the things to which it is most closely related. It is crucial that we avoid both vagueness and overinclusiveness, which would blur the differences between, for example, religion and history, psychology, ethics, and so forth. Thus when Paul Tillich says that "religion, in the largest and most basic sense of the word, is ultimate concern," he identifies religion with human concern and also differentiates religious concern from all other human concerns by including the specific word *ultimate*. The qualifier *ultimate* rescues the definition from vagueness and achieves specificity because only one concern can be ultimate (i.e., most important), automatically relegating other concerns to less importance.

For our definition we must choose specific characteristics that both clearly distinguish religion from everything else and indicate precisely how it is distinctive.

Inclusiveness

The criterion of inclusiveness is not a contradiction to the criterion of specificity. On the contrary, inclusiveness requires that a definition clearly state the scope or limitations of its use in such a way that narrowness, compartmentalization, prejudice, and vagueness are avoided.

To apply the criterion of inclusiveness to our definition of religion, we should answer the following questions:

Does it include the whole of human life or is it restricted to one aspect of it such as thinking or feeling, or old age or adolescence?
Does it apply equally to all people, primitive and contemporary, individual and institutional?
Does it include that which may be true or false, helpful or harmful, or of great or little social consequence?

Although we could ask other questions, it is important only that we recognize that, as definition makers, we must consciously think about this criterion in order to avoid vagueness, narrowness, compartmentalization, and prejudice.

Read each of the following definitions carefully and, using the predefinitional priorities we have established, decide on the acceptability of each in terms of its specificity and inclusiveness and its avoidance of vagueness, narrowness, compartmentalization, and prejudice. After you have made each decision, use scrap paper to record your impression and then turn to the section indicated to see if you decided correctly.

1. "Religion is a set of beliefs binding the human mind to the one supernatural being."
2. "Religion is what the individual does with his or her own solitariness; if you were never solitary, you were never religious."
3. "Religion is the realm of the ultimately real and the ultimately valuable."

If you said definition (1) was not acceptable, you showed good judgment. The definition is not inclusive enough; it fails because of its compartmentalization and narrowness. First, we should remember that definitions that stress one part or compartment of human experience, such as belief or feeling or ritual activity, are not sufficiently comprehensive for our purposes. Second, we should remember that the phrase "one supernatural being" refers to God in the monotheistic sense and therefore excludes from our consideration all phenomena that are not monotheistic. In other words, we could not study Buddhism, mysticism, ancient Greek religion, or some of the contemporary counterculture's expressions of religiousness. Because of its narrowness, a monotheistic definition of religion is not useful to us.

If you missed these points, return to the relevant section and read it again. If you answered correctly, continue reading and check your answer for the second definition.

If you recognized that (2) also fails as a useful definition for us, you are correct. By stressing the individual as separate from any social influence, it narrows the scope of our interest too much to be useful for the study of religion. We wish to study the relationship of religion to the whole of human life. If we find that social or public influence is not relevant to religion, then we will have to modify our definition on the basis of our findings. However, given our concern for breadth, we should not begin with a definition that exhibits such narrowness.

If you evaluated this one correctly, check your response to definition (3).

If you said definition (3) was not acceptable, you judged correctly. It fails to be useful for us because it exhibits prejudice. The definition describes religion as an unquestionable good for humanity; it is made the standard for judging what is real as opposed to what is trivial. This assumption certainly is open to critical questioning, and thus we must reject the definition for our study. The same criticism of prejudice can be used against Marx's definition, "Religion is only the illusory sun which revolves around man as long as he does not revolve around himself." Here, by definition, religion is made an unquestionable hindrance to people's development.

If your answer was not correct, return to the section on prejudice. If you responded to all three definitions correctly, you should be able to evaluate an appropriate definition of religion.

TESTING THE DEFINITION

Let us now consider a specific definition. We will test it against our established criteria and, if we find it appropriate, accept it as long as it proves useful. We do not claim that it is the only possible definition; new definitions are always possible. We do, however, claim that it is useful for our purpose.

Our definition is as follows:

Religion is the varied, symbolic expression of, and appropriate response to, that which people deliberately affirm as being of unrestricted value for them.

Now let us examine our definition first in terms of features to be achieved and then in terms of features to be avoided.

Is This Definition Iinclusive?

The answer is yes. Why? Because the definition opens religion to all humans regardless of sex, age, education, politics, economic status, or geographic, cultural, or chronological location. The definition includes the possibility of both institutional and noninstitutional symbolic expression and response. By identifying religion as "the varied, symbolic expression of, and appropriate response to . . . ," the definition assures us that religious phenomena must show or reveal themselves as conveyors of human significance. Symbolic expression and response represent human intent. These phenomena, then, may be critically assessed in several ways: as to their truth or falsity, their helpfulness or harmfulness to humanity, or their great or little historical, cultural, or social consequence. The definition is appropriate for our purposes, using the criterion of inclusiveness, because it allows us to consider the broad scope of religious phenomena in terms appropriate to university study.

IS THIS DEFINITION SUFFICIENTLY SPECIFIC?

It meets our criterion of specificity if it indicates clearly what religion is and how it is distinct from everything else.

Our proposed definition has two distinguishing characteristics. The first, "the varied, symbolic expression of, and appropriate response to . . . ," emphasizes that religion is a human mode of expression and response that may be conveyed in a variety of ways. In other words, people have used, and continue to use, many different symbols to represent and affirm the meaning of their religious experience. Once affirmed, these symbols become guides for appropriate religious response.

The second distinguishing characteristic, "that which people deliberately affirm as being of unrestricted value to them," clearly differentiates religious valuation from all other (i.e., nonreligious) valuation by emphasizing the idea of ultimate importance. As a result all of humanity's other experiences of value will be considered less important than its religious experiences. Wherever you find symbols representing people's affirmation of something that is of unrestricted value for them, you have an example of religious phenomena.

Human beings alone deliberately discriminate and choose their own values (e.g., good–bad, beautiful–ugly, significant–insignificant, purposeful–purposeless). When such human judgment is further specified to be of ultimate and unrestricted value (e.g., supremely, unconditionally, without qualification), it enters the domain of the religious. What distinguishes unrestricted valuation from all other forms of valuing is that its object is valued equally in all situations and is not restricted by the specific conditions of any situation; therefore it can be said to apply comprehensively. It is also the last value that would be sacrificed or given up by an individual because it is regarded as being of primary importance to the whole of human life.

Thus a religious obligation takes precedence over all other obligations, or, in other words, a religious good that is ranked as a highest good would not ideally be given up in favor of any nonreligious good.

By the criterion of specificity, then, our definition is appropriate because it discriminates the religious from the nonreligious by indicating precisely the difference between the two.

DOES THIS DEFINITION AVOID VAGUENESS?

The answer to this question is yes. This does not mean that no one will have questions about the precise meaning of some of the terms in the definition. Words such as *unrestricted, value, symbolic,* and *expression* may have to be further qualified, but this is a standard expectation with any definition. However, the issue under this criterion is whether or not the definition has the power to discriminate religion from other forms of human valuation. We believe that it does differentiate and that this definition is appropriate.

DOES THE DEFINITION AVOID NARROWNESS?

Yes, our definition avoids overexclusiveness in its scope. For example, it does not limit religious valuation to monotheism or Christianity or institutionalized forms. It is conceivable under the present definition that certain atheistic phenomena could be considered religious if they function for their valuers as objects of unrestricted valuation. Thus under certain circumstances communism could be viewed as a religious alternative; under other circumstances democracy could be so considered. Certainly no particular religious tradition serves as the sole source of our definition.

Our definition makes no choice between institutionalized and noninstitutionalized forms of symbolic expression and response. The decision as to which forms actually do, or do not, reflect the religious is not mandated by the definition but, rather, is left to critical interpretation in each individual case.

DOES THIS DEFINITION AVOID COMPARTMENTALIZATION?

Yes, the definition specifically seeks to avoid compartmentalization (i.e., the focus on some special aspect of a person's being) by emphasizing the process of valuation that encompasses all aspects of human experience. Such specialized activities as thinking, feeling, or doing presuppose the general dimensions of human preference, attention, and interest. Our definition, by stressing unrestricted valuation, allows us to consider all or any of the aspects of a person's being as a potential source of religious data.

The definition not only avoids compartmentalization but is defined in direct contrast with it. Since the process of human valuation is the most primitive or general activity that all the more specialized ones presuppose, our definition requires us to study the expression and response of human thought as well as emotion and action.

DOES THE DEFINITION AVOID PREJUDICE OR PREJUDGING THE TRUTH OR FALSITY, HELPFULNESS OR HARMFULNESS, IMPORTANCE OR TRIVIALITY OF RELIGION TO THE INDIVIDUAL OR SOCIETY?

Yes. This does not mean that there is no value judgment involved in the construction of this definition; every definition involves value judgments in the selection of defining characteristics that will best explain the term. In this case we began, through our predefinitional priorities, with the conscious intent of constructing a definition that would serve our purpose of admitting a wide range of religious phenomena that can be critically studied in this book.

We believe that we have successfully achieved an unprejudiced definition because we have avoided the kinds of judgments that would more appropriately follow rather than precede the study of religion.

In summary, our definition is as follows:

Religion is the varied, symbolic expression of, and appropriate response to, that which people deliberately affirm as being of unrestricted value for them.

It meets the test of our specified criteria, or predefinitional priorities. It avoids vagueness, narrowness, compartmentalization, and prejudice, and it achieves specificity and inclusiveness. In addition, it permits critical consideration of a wide range of religious phenomena.

Our definition fulfills our requirements and can function as a basis for the consideration of religion as a field of study. You will need to be alert to discover whether subsequent chapters presuppose the definition proposed here or another one.

NOTE

1. This discussion of predefinitional priorities employs the categories set forth by Frederick Ferré in *A Basic Modern Philosophy of Religion* (New York: Scribners, 1967).

CHAPTER 2

Religion as a Field of Study

RONALD R. CAVANAGH

This is the second of two programed chapters on religion. You should already have completed the first chapter, which discussed some of the ways the term *religion* has been defined and also provided a functional definition of religion. Now we turn to the complex issues surrounding religion as a field of study. These issues include definition of a field of study, identification of appropriate data for the study, and reasons for studying religion.

The phrase "a field of study" denotes an identifiable sphere of intellectual activity. Any field of study implies specialized subject matters, specific methods for interpreting them, and individuals who are concerned with particular kinds of questions for which they seek appropriate and critical answers.

In this sense religion as a field of study can be conceived of in different ways, depending on how the term *religion* is defined. As you proceed through this chapter, remember that the definition being used is not the only one that could be used. Our definition of religion as

> the varied, symbolic expression of, and appropriate response to, that which people deliberately affirm as being of unrestricted value for them

is one we find reasonable and useful in our attempt to approach this field of study.

The task before us now is to ask and answer the question, What is the field of study of religion? To answer this question we must address ourselves to four more specific questions:

1. *What* is being studied?
2. *Who* is studying it?
3. *How* is it being studied?
4. *Why* is it being studied?

If we answer these specific questions in terms of the field study of religion, we can then answer our larger question.

WHAT IS BEING STUDIED?

In many fields of study, when we ask what is being studied we are asking, What are the generally accepted data of the field? By *data* we mean "the things that can be denoted or specified by some perspective of thought or speech." Data can include such things as ideas, ideals, individuals, feelings, man-made objects, and natural and social phenomena. Data are classified as religious if they can be identified from the perspective of religion.

Before we can identify any particular datum as religious, however, we must consider the specific circumstances surrounding it in relation to our definition. Specifically, we must know whether the significance or meaning or human value attached to it is of an "unrestricted" nature before we can judge whether or not it is an appropriate datum for our study. We must do this because there is no such thing as a religious datum per se, that is, in and of itself. Something becomes a datum only when a perspective of thought or speech identifies it as such. Data qualify as religious only if they meet the criteria that have been set by our definition. Let us look at some specific examples.

Consider a cross. Is a cross a religious datum? From what we have just learned about religious data, we would have to say that we do not have enough information to answer either yes or no. To a Roman Catholic a cross might represent the crucifix, which symbolizes the redemptive sacrifice of Jesus. To a truck driver a cross might signify nothing more than a crossroads. To a black person a cross—especially a burning cross—might represent hated intimidation by the Ku Klux Klan. We can see from these examples that a cross is not a religious datum *per se* but *may* be a religious datum for us, depending on the significance or human value that we attach to it.

If we apply our definition of religion to the example of the cross, we see that the cross as a crucifix is one symbolic expression of what Roman Catholics ideally regard as being of unrestricted value for them. It signifies a divine sacrifice that offers the believer a restored relationship with God. Consequently in this case the cross as a crucifix is a religious datum.

The same cannot be said of a cross functioning as a road sign because there it does not signify "a symbolic expression of, and appropriate response to, that which people deliberately affirm as being of unrestricted value for them." In the second instance, then, the cross does not qualify as a religious datum.

Now let us carry our example of the cross one step further. Can the act of burning a cross on the lawn of a black person be considered a religious datum? Consider your answer carefully before you continue reading. Is it yes or no?

1. "No, because it represents an evil and ignorant act." (See section A.)
2. "Yes, because the cross is a religious datum, and it is being used in this action." (See section B.)
3. "Perhaps, if the act of burning the cross expresses the unrestricted value of the person who burns it." (See section C.)

A. You said, "No, because it represents an evil and ignorant act," but this is not correct. Remember that our definition of religion does not require that a religious datum be either helpful to humanity or a wise action. An act can be both ignorant and evil from one perspective and still be considered a religious datum. History provides us with an illustration: wars of religious persecution—the so-called holy crusades—which a humanist would not consider beneficial to humanity.

To determine whether an action is a religious datum, you must decide whether or not it expresses the unrestricted value of its agent, and you cannot state flatly that any act—including burning a cross on the lawn of a black person—cannot be considered a religious datum because it is evil or ignorant. For the correct answer turn to section C.

B. You said, "Yes, because the cross is a religious datum, and it is being used in this action." This answer is incorrect because it assumes that the cross is in itself a religious datum. Remember, however, that there are no religious data in and of themselves, that is, totally apart from some human perspective that regards them as religious. If you had been told in the example that the KKK cross burner regarded the cross as an expression of what he or she valued unrestrictedly, then your answer would have been correct. For an analysis of the correct answer, turn to section C.

C. You said, "Perhaps, if the act of burning the cross expresses the unrestricted value of the person who burns it." Your answer is correct according to the terms of our discussion.

In our example we do not have enough information to decide whether or not the cross burner regards that act as a "symbolic expression of" or an "appropriate response to" what he or she values unrestrictedly. It may or may not be a religious datum. Some data may be permanently ambiguous, even after thorough investigation and interpretation.

Now let us consider *humanism* (i.e., an interpretation of human existence that dispenses with belief in the supernatural, that considers the good of humanity on earth as the supreme ethical goal, and that applies the methods of reason and science to solve human problems). Let us try to decide whether or not the humanism exemplified by the two individuals described in the following passage can be considered a religious datum.

Joe and Barbara, college students majoring in political science, do not regard themselves as religious. They refer to themselves as humanists. Joe considers himself a humanist because he feels that humanism is of practical value at this stage of history; he values it because he believes that societies under its influence are induced to increase their standard of living. Barbara on the other hand, thinks that humanism best expresses the highest possibilities for humanity's final destiny. She constantly criticizes the "other-worldly" emphasis of religion and tries to make clear in her own actions that the final hope for humanity and for the world rests in people's reasonable and just dealings with other people.

Read all three of the following statements and then determine which one is most accurate for our example in terms of our definition of religious data:

1. "Humanism is not a religious datum because both Joe and Barbara are humanists and they reject religion." (See section A.)
2. "Humanism cannot be considered a religious datum because Joe consciously affirms it for practical reasons at this particular point in history." (See section B.)
3. "Humanism, in Barbara's case, may be considered a religious datum because she states that it best expresses the highest value that humanity can attain, and attempts to respond to it appropriately in her own life." (See section C.)

Consider your answer carefully and then turn to the sections indicated to see if you judged correctly.

A. If you said that the statement "Humanism is not a religious datum because Joe and Barbara are humanists and they reject religion" is inaccurate, you judged correctly.

In terms of our definition a humanistic interpretation of life can be considered a religious datum when the individual holding such ideas deliberately affirms them as being of "unrestricted value for him or her." It makes no difference at all whether or not a person labels his or her affirmation religious, or even whether he or she recognizes it as such. So even though Joe and Barbara do not regard themselves as religious (they do in fact deny it) and humanism in itself cannot be considered religious, we will argue that, in Barbara's case at least, humanism is a legitimate religious datum.

If you were not able to recognize the first statement as an inaccurate conclusion, you should reread the definition of religious data presented earlier in this chapter.

B. If you said that the statement "Humanism cannot be considered a religious datum because Joe consciously affirms it for practical reasons at this particular point in history" is an inaccurate conclusion from the example given, you are right.

You may have been misled by the reference to Joe alone, since, in this case, a humanistic interpretation of life cannot be considered a religious datum because he does not deliberately affirm the ideas as being of "unrestricted value for him." On the contrary, Joe regards humanism as useful at this time to increase the standard of living, and we are given no indication that he regards the standard of living as being of unrestricted value.

However, in Barbara's case we can conclude that a humanistic interpretation of life is affirmed as being of "unrestricted value for her," which permits us to categorize her humanism as a religious datum. Since the statements are to be judged in terms of the total example, we cannot accept the second as an accurate conclusion; it is only half correct.

Identification of a datum as either religious or nonreligious requires careful and thorough investigation of all the circumstances in each individual case.

C. In terms of our functional definition of religion, (3) is the best answer for us. Humanism, in Barbara's case, may be considered a religious datum because she states that it best expresses the highest values that humanity can attain, and so forth. In this case humanism is a religious datum because it is an expression of what Barbara affirms to be of "unrestricted value for her." Although Joe values humanism, he does not value it unrestrictedly. Remember, our definition does not say that all people will be religious, or that they will share the same object of religious value. Something may be regarded as of supreme importance to the life of one person while it is considered trivial by another.

What do we make of Barbara's assertion that she is not religious? Our definition does not say that either a person or a community has to be aware of being religious when assigning unrestricted value to something. So from our perspective it is legitimate to designate Barbara's humanistically expressed, unrestricted value as religious, even if her own understanding of religion does not lead her to the same conclusion.

By using our functional definition of religion and from the circumstances surrounding each datum, we can determine religious data and avoid two common pitfalls. First, we can avoid the situation in which data are determined by or limited to what has been studied in the past, and thus we can overcome traditionalism. It is not necessary for a belief or ritual to be associated with any of the great religions in order for us to consider it a religious datum. The weekly act of watching the Sunday afternoon football game may, under certain circumstances, be as much a religious ritual as the celebration of the Mass.

Second, we can avoid leaving the determination of data to an instinctive or intuitional feeling that may be unconsciously biased or dogmatic. For example, a statement such as "I feel strongly that the drug experience has nothing to do with religion and therefore will not give it any consideration in the study of religion" would prevent us from considering the relationship between drugs and religion.

In the procedure that follows we do not assume a fixed number of re- ligious data. Our scope of data may include ideas, ideals, individuals, feel- ings, man-made objects, and natural and social phenomena. Data may refer to a group of people, the act of voting, an extreme emotion, a star, a cross, or an idea of God. In determining the particular data— that is, what is being studied—for the field of religion, we arrive at our conclusion only as a result of our own study; we do not assume from the start that there are a fixed number of particular data for us to consider.

In summary, we may say that the data—the "what" of the field of re- ligion—can be identified only by applying our definition to an individual datum and then investigating the particular case to determine whether the aspect of unrestricted valuation is present.

WHO IS STUDYING IT?

The second question we must address ourselves to in determining the field of study of religion is, Who is studying it? In other words, who are the students of religion? Is there any particular kind of student best qualified to participate in the study of religion? Does the student of religion need some special kind of insight, knowledge, attitude, or belief that is different from that required of students in other fields?

Let us see if you can answer these questions yourself, using the knowl- edge that you have gained thus far. Carefully consider the following an- swers to the question, Is the student of religion required to possess some special characteristics that a student entering some other academic field would not be expected to exhibit? Using our functional definition of re- ligion and our procedure for identifying religious data, determine which of the answers is appropriate.

  1. "Yes, the student in the field of religion should be either religious or
     a participant in some religion, so that he or she can recognize re-
     ligious data and treat them fairly." (See section A.)
  2. "No, the student of religion is not required to exhibit any special atti-
     tude, insight, or belief different from that of a student entering some
     other academic field." (See section B.)

A. Answer (1) is incorrect because it is not necessary for an individual to be religious in order to either recognize religious data or treat it appropri- ately. Remember, we said that we identify a religious datum by applying our functional definition and carefully considering the specific circum- stances surrounding the datum. Any field of academic study will require that a student learn its functioning definitions and that he or she treat the data without bias and with accuracy, honesty, and completeness. No other characteristics are required of a student in the field of religion.

Please read section B carefully.

B. Answer (2) is most certainly correct; a student in the field of religion does not need any special kind of insight, knowledge, attitude, or belief different from that required of students beginning a study of philosophy or anthropology or any other academic discipline. It does not matter whether the student is religious or not because being religious does not provide him or her with our functional definition of religion, nor does it ensure that he or she will be unbiased in the treatment of data. It only matters that the student be careful in applying our functional definition so that he or she will be able to recognize data and treat them accurately and honestly.

This requirement, of course, applies to any academic field of study and to any method of study used. While the object of interest of a student of religion will perhaps be different from, say, that of a biology student, each may value his or her field of study equally.

The answer to the second basic question, Who is studying it? is that all kinds of students pursue the study of religion. No special qualifications are required.

HOW IS IT BEING STUDIED?

The third basic question we must address ourselves to in defining the field of study of religion is, How is it being studied? We want to know what method or methods we will use to study religion. By *method* we mean "a systematic mode of procedure to achieve a goal or goals."

Since the range of religious data is broad and the interests of students are various, we will use many different methods to study religion. There is no one method identified with the study of religion. Several methods commonly used include the philosophical, psychological, historical, sociological, and comparative/structural approaches. Let us examine what we mean by these methods.

When we consider selecting a method for our study, we must take two factors into account: (1) the particular interests of the student and (2) the appropriateness of the method as a means of studying religious data.

Let us consider the first factor. If you are interested in the truth or falsity of a religious proposition, you will select a philosophical method for studying the data. If you are interested in the documented origin of a system of belief, you will use a historical approach. You may be interested in the historical development of a belief system as well as the truth or falsity of its tenets. In this case you would use both historical and philosophical methods. If you are interested in discovering how the form of one religious community compares with that of another, you may employ a comparative/structural method. If you want to know the effect of religious myth on individuals, you will use the psychological method; if you are interested in studying the nature of a religious community, you will employ the sociological method. It is important to remember that the kind of question you ask will influence your choice of method.

The second factor to consider in choosing a method for our study—its appropriateness—is also very important. It is essential to select a procedure that suits the nature of the data we are considering. Just as we would not use a telescope to examine the structure of a cell, so we would not apply the rules of critical historical study to analyze a religious myth. Nor would we investigate the religious datum "God" using empirical categories appropriate to size, shape, and weight. Such procedures would be unsuitable because they fail to consider the sense and form in which the religious datum is regarded as meaningful. If the form of religious myth is not that of modern historical writing, and if the concept of God is not that of a physical object, then methods of analysis that attempt to treat them as such are inappropriate. The selection of a method for the study of religion must take into account the method's capacity to respect the integrity of the religious data.

In summarizing our answer to the question, How is it being studied? we must conclude that there is no one method that is adequate for all purposes. We must select from available methods those that are appropriate to the questions being asked, to the particular interests of those engaged in the study, and to the nature of the religious data under consideration. Only then can we be sure that our method will be appropriate to the wide range of data we will consider, as well as to the wide variety of student interests.

WHY IS IT BEING STUDIED?

The fourth and final question we will address ourselves to in determining the field of study of religion is the "why."

There are at least three legitimate reasons why a person might study religion. They are

1. emancipation from ignorance
2. information and skill
3. appreciation

Let us consider each of these expectations.

EMANCIPATION FROM IGNORANCE

If a liberal education in general aims at emancipating a human being from ignorance and parochial dogmatism, then a student can legitimately expect religion as a field of study to also exhibit this aim. Therefore any course in the study of religion should help the student achieve this goal by furnishing various data that express people's religious values and by providing methods for discriminating critically among them.

INFORMATION AND SKILL

Any course in the area of religion will try to identify the field of study, introduce examples of religious data, and provide a method or methods for studying the field. Thus if you expect to gain information about the field, its data, and its methods so that you can understand and then interpret for yourself, you will not be disappointed.

APPRECIATION

In terms of our definition the field of religion involves critical study of the expression of people's unrestricted valuation. A study of this field is not intended to make students religious; rather, the goal is to develop students' interpretive skills, which they can then use to discriminate the crucial elements in their own, or other people's, quest for ultimate value. Thus students may legitimately expect that this book will help them develop their critical skills in order to increase their appreciation and understanding of people's expression of unrestricted or unconditional valuation.

Now let us see if you can analyze some expectations for yourself. Following are several statements concerning what people expect from religion as a field of study. Keeping in mind our three legitimate expectations, read each statement carefully and determine which one or ones seem to agree with those expectations. (You may want to refer again to the material just presented.)

1. "In my high school psychology course we touched on religion. I would like to be better informed about the nature of religious expression and the ways of looking at it so that I can check for myself some of my teacher's conclusions."

2. "I'm not religious myself, or at least I don't think I am, but a lot of my friends say our generation has been deeply influenced by religion. I would like to be able to distinguish a religious influence from others so that I can appreciate the sense in which religion has been important or unimportant to my generation and to me."

3. "For years I've been instructed in religion by an old Irish priest who was, by his own admission, not interested primarily in teaching. It's time I had some religious instruction from a teacher who is a trained scholar. I would like to make sure that what I believe is what I should believe."

4. "I'm going to major in chemistry and I've never taken a course in religion. As long as I have to take some courses in liberal arts, I think

religion might be interesting. I would like to know how to study something like religion and how to test my ideas about it."

When you have completed your analysis, check your answers against the following paragraph.

Statements 1, 2, and 4 are legitimate expectations of religion as a field of study because they are based on a desire for emancipation from ignorance, for information and skill, or for appreciation. Statement 3 is not legitimate because, although the study of religion may address many of a student's private concerns, such a goal is not its deliberate intent. Religion as an academic discipline is not intended to provide the student with ready-made religious decisions that will either confirm previous commitments or convert him or her to a religious faith. The aim is instruction in the study of religion, not religious instruction.

In conclusion, let us repeat: Religion as a field of study clearly intends to educate by making people self-conscious about the nature of the field, its data, and its methods. It aims to provide the learner with information about its data and to develop his or her skills for appreciating or discriminating that data.

Part II

VARIETIES OF
RELIGIOUS EXPRESSION

The Varieties of Religious Experience, by William James, written in 1901–1902, remains one of the major documents in the field of religious studies. It is the word *varieties* that concerns us in the following pages. Like James, we assert that there are many different types of religious experiences and a multiplicity of forms in which these experiences can be expressed. The chapters in this section are devoted to an exploration of five significant forms of religious expression: myth, belief, ritual, scripture, and art. In addition, one chapter examines different "accents" that the world's religions place on various religious expressions.

MYTH

"It would not be too much to say," writes Joseph Campbell in *The Hero with a Thousand Faces*, "that myth is the sacred opening through which the inexhaustible energies of the cosmos pour into human cultural manifestation." Certainly the mythic stories of the gods and the creation of the world were once deeply religious, providing a basis for the conviction that all existence was holy. The profound question raised by Michael Sexson in the opening chapter of Part II is whether myth has retained or lost its religious significance in the modern world. Is myth an inescapable fact of human nature, as Campbell suggests, or is it merely an outmoded expression of the way we once were, a faded memory of a world lost forever?

BELIEF

Expressions of religion are also found in basic beliefs concerning the human predicament and in the ideal that people seek to reach. Belief—the intellectual assent to certain cognitive propositions—is part of humanity's varied response to what it believes to be of unrestricted value. Ronald R. Cavanagh examines the nature of belief in Chapter 4 and offers a mode for interpreting beliefs in various religions.

RITUAL

A visit to a mass in St. Patrick's Cathedral in New York City, a Sabbath service in Temple Society of Concord in Syracuse, a Baptist service in Moscow, a Hindu Temple festival in Calcutta, Muslim prayers in Karachi, or a Shinto wedding in Kyoto, Japan—all reveal unmistakable performances of patterned action. The ritual may include praying, bowing, eating, chanting, washing, lying prostrate on the ground, or clapping one's hands. Whatever is done in those settings is a type of religious expression. Richard B. Pilgrim provides a way of understanding ritual and interpreting various kinds of ritual in Chapter 5.

SCRIPTURE

The sacred texts of every religion are still another type of religious expression. James G. Williams offers a clear definition of scripture; he suggests major ways to approach scripture; and he provides a sketch of various methods for interpretation of scripture. Scriptures, he tell us, may include myth; they may prescribe rituals and give particular beliefs that the faithful hold with complete conviction. Yet the scriptures themselves are in a category not covered by other types of expression.

ART

James Karman, the author of Chapter 7, writes that art is one of the important expressions of religion. Whether it takes the form of painting, sculpture, music, or architecture, art reveals the spirit and inner life of people. In fact it is through the cultural style evident in the arts that we can discover the meaning of human life in any culture. In addition, art serves as a teacher of the religious tradition to each succeeding generation.

ACCENTS

Occasionally the student of religion, wishing to take a telescopic view of the religions of the world, asks, How are the world's religions the same and in what ways are they different? While Huston Smith assumes that there is a pervading philosophy underlying all major religions, he presents a convincing argument that there are differing "accents" in the religions belonging to each of three cultural traditions. Chapter 8 provides a comprehensive perspective on religious diversity as a conclusion to our exploration of varieties of religious expression.

CHAPTER 3

Myth: The Way We Were or the Way We Are?

MICHAEL W. SEXSON

The word *myth* belongs with the terms that Humpty Dumpty says deserve extra pay for doing so much work. To its detractors, such as David Bidney, the word suggests that which is unreal and untrue. Bidney admits that as a cultural force myth must be taken seriously, but "only in order that it may be gradually superseded in the interests of the advancement of truth and the growth of human intelligence."[1] To Bidney, myth is an outdated and inauthentic form of religious expression. But to defenders, such as Mircea Eliade, myth is the source of reality and truth inasmuch as it provides human beings with models and patterns of behavior thought to be divinely established. Myth, then, is not simply another *form* of religious expression—it *is* religion—complete, authentic, and ineradicable.

Which of these two views is correct? The one that understands myth as a primitive form of religious thought destined to be outgrown as civilization advances? Or the one that sees myth as a necessary factor in our relationship to reality? In order to decide this question it is necessary to give equal time to both views. First, the case against myth will demonstrate how the history of the Western world is, in effect, a history of demythologization—humanity's gradual revolt against myth and eventual adoption of an enlightened consciousness no longer burdened by primitive and superstitious elements. This case does not so much condemn myth as relegate it to the status of a harmless, naive conception of the world that reminds us of the way we once were.

This case will be followed and significantly qualified by a full-scale defense showing that myth is an important symbolic form that orients us to all dimensions of reality. Myth is, in addition, a reflection of the deepest aspects of the human mind, a powerful religious expression not of the way we were but of the way we are.

THE WAY WE WERE

Unlike a lie, which is a conscious and deliberate attempt to mask the truth, a myth is not malicious but simply naive. It concerns something we formerly believed but have since outgrown. It is about the way we were "once upon a time." It spoke of marvelous encounters between gods and mortals, told of wondrous supernatural creatures, and explained how things and people came to be the way they were. Myth answered all questions and, because of its comprehensiveness, permitted people (to paraphrase Tevye in "Fiddler on the Roof") to know exactly who they were and what God expected them to do.

Today, however, we have put away such childish things. We know that "once upon a time" is a time that never was, a time unmeasurable by historical methods, a time existing only in the fancy of storytellers. We know too that the remarkable dealings between gods and mortals were merely the encounters of our own lively imaginations with nature. We have discovered that the question of origins, both of things and of people, is far more complicated than the mythical mind supposed. To answer the question of human limitations by referring to the story of a forbidden fruit is, we must all admit, a bit childish, rather like telling the tale of how the leopard got its spots. Simple *aetiology*, or explanation in the manner of Kipling's "just so" stories, will not do for sophisticated moderns. The question of origins is, as we say today, problematic.

The present world is inhabited by sadder but wiser people, men and women who are no longer naive but realistic. The realist of today casts a cold eye on the world and knows that God never was, except as a fiction; that spirits do not dwell in trees; that windmills are not giants; that stars do not tell stories of heroes but testify instead to the cold, inhuman immensity of limitless space.

The story of the Western world is, in effect, a story of demythologization. If it is true, as Freud believed, that "ontogeny recapitulates phylogeny"— that is, that the life of a culture, like the life of an individual, passes through definite stages of growth—then it becomes possible to "read" the history of Western culture as the poignant and painful story of children, who, in their progress toward maturity, cast off all their illusions.

A brief history of demythologization might begin with Xenophanes, a Greek thinker who lived six centuries before the Common Era. Surrounded by people who believed in the literal reality of Zeus, Hera, Apollo, and the rest of the Homeric gods, Xenophanes struck a surprisingly modern note when he insisted that the gods were projections of the human mind, mere anthropomorphic inventions. If horses and cattle could draw, he said, they would draw gods who looked like horses and cattle.

On the stage of Athens Plato's uncle Critias exposed the traditional gods as a deliberate deception. Plato himself, born in a time when myths were crumbling everywhere, contrasted *logos* (truth) with *mythos* (fiction). While he acknowledged the functional value of myth (for certain crude minds, he thought, myths will always be necessary), Plato clearly believed that centaurs and the chimera and "countless other remarkable monsters of legends" could never be considered literal realities. Socrates, after all, was not a spinner of tall tales like Uncle Remus but a critical, inquiring thinker.

If, in the service of demythologization, Xenophanes was the first to propound a theory of projection, Euhemerus, a third-century Greek writer, is given credit for generating the view that mythology has its origins in history. Euhemerus proposed that the gods were actual, historical individuals, most often kings, whose lives and deeds became wildly exaggerated by the popular mythological imagination. As proof of his theory Euhemerus cited the extraordinary career of Alexander the Great, a historical figure who in his own lifetime was worshiped as a god. Euhemerism was well received in the Greco-Roman world, and at the beginning of the Christian era it provided religious polemicists with a method of denouncing pagans. Clement of Alexandria, an early Church father, quoted Euhemerus when he attempted to convince pagans that their gods were, after all, only men.

Another popular method of demythologizing involved treating the stories of myth as allegories, profound moral truths put forth in poetic form for easier digestion. The allegorical method was fashionable not only among the early Greek sophists but with later Greco-Roman Stoics, Neoplatonic philosophers, and various seekers after hidden messages right up to the present. Although less hostile to myth than the euhemerists, the allegorists too are demythologizers, for they seek to rigidly translate the terms of myth into other, more abstract terms. Perhaps the most famous example of all allegorical method is the Christian interpretation of an Old Testament book, The Song of Solomon (or "the song of songs"). The book, an elaborate erotic myth describing in vivid sensual detail the preparation of a bride for her beloved, was said by later Christian apologists to be an allegory of Christ's love for the church.

The voyages of Columbus and Magellan marked the beginning of the end for the old mythological empire that since ancient times had housed the illusions of most people throughout the world. Shortly thereafter, in 1543, Copernicus put forth the heliocentric view of the universe and shattered forever the anthropocentric, or man-centered, aspect of myth. Enlightenment philosophers continued to hammer away at the collapsing structure by proclaiming that Western civilization had passed through two great periods of myth and superstition—the ancient world and the Middle

Ages—and was now, after the "rebirth" of the Renaissance, ready to assume the hard-won mantle of "reason" appropriate to a mature adult.

It was in the nineteenth century, however, that the fatal blow was struck. Although this age witnessed a tremendous resurgence of interest in myth, primarily through the works of poets and philosophers, the spirit of the age was, in a word, science, and science held the field against all rivals. What could not be empirically verified by the scientific method was relegated to the category of superstition.

The views of the classical scholar Sir James G. Frazer are representative of an age that was heir to the enormous expansion of awareness initiated by the Renaissance. Frazer's classic work *The Golden Bough,* a thirteen-volume study of magic and superstition, brought into the full light of critical scrutiny the extraordinary naiveté of the mythical mind. Frazer established once and for all that mythical behavior, the basis of all religion, was a crude attempt to explain the natural world, an attempt destined to be replaced by the empirically sound methods of science.

Very few would have disagreed with Frazer's elegantly phrased conclusion to his exhaustive survey of myth and magic:

Here at last, after groping about in the dark for countless ages, man has hit upon a clue to the labyrinth, a golden key that opens many locks in the treasury of nature. It is probably not too much to say that the hope of progress—moral and intellectual as well as material—in the future is bound up with the fortunes of science, and that every obstacle placed in the way of scientific discovery is a wrong to humanity.[2]

The twentieth century was ushered in with the death of Friedrich Nietzsche, the great German iconoclast whose famous phrase "God is dead" heralded the final and irrevocable collapse of the great mythological empire of the past. The death of God was, it appears, the death of myth. And the death of myth was the victory of science, of history.

Religion is rooted in myth, and myth is rooted in illusion. This proposition seemed self-evident to two of the present century's most influential thinkers. Karl Marx asserted that the mythical, other-worldly dimensions of religion blinded people to their true task: converting this planet into paradise. Religion, he said, is the "opiate" of the masses. And to Sigmund Freud religion was "the obsessional neurosis of children," destined to be outgrown as humanity evolved. Freud believed that in the process of growth humanity was bound to turn away from religion, and that the beginning of the twentieth century marked the transition from childhood to maturity.

If ontogeny does indeed recapitulate phylogeny, we stand now as a culture on the other side of the lost world of childhood with its unfounded dreams and fears. We have, at long last, grown up, emancipated ourselves from myth and magic, overthrown religion as a debilitating illusion. Naturally there is a wistfulness, a nostagia for the past, a longing to return to a world where the gods were meaningful realities. Such feelings, however, will pass as we become accustomed to our new-found freedom. "To see the gods dispelled in mid-air," wrote the great American poet Wallace Stevens, "is one of the great human experiences. It is not as if they had gone over the horizon to disappear for a time; nor as if they had been overcome by other gods of greater power and profounder knowledge. It is simply that they came to nothing."[3] This, however, is cause not for despair but for joy, the joy of a consciousness liberated from bondage to superstition and myth.

We now regard as self-evident the validity of the methods of the past that began the process of demythologization. Mythical stories are quite obviously allegories, for they simply cannot stand the test of historical/critical scrutiny; the truth of euhemerism can be tested today simply by observing how popular historical figures—politicians and film stars—rapidly become shrouded in myth and legend. And a popular film, "The Planet of the Apes," puts forth the idea that in a world governed by apes the object of religious devotion would naturally be the projection of a giant, idealized ape. This idea, novel and revolutionary when proposed by Xenophanes 2500 years ago, now seems so obvious as to be bland.

It is no longer necessary to discredit myth by linking it to lies and deception. It is not important any more to measure the stories in Genesis against scientific discoveries. The mythological empire of the past that enslaved the religious sensibilities of countless millions no longer has any truth claim on a significant portion of the present population. In our maturity we do not reject the old stories but recollect them in tranquillity, as we recall the fancies of childhood. The mythical empire remains with us, a lost glory of the earth, always reminding us of the way we were "once upon a time."

THE WAY WE ARE

Does history tell a tale of humanity's incessant attempts to rid itself of myth? Or does it testify to the utter impossibility of such a task? Myth cannot be "outgrown" because it is one of the ways in which the human mind seeks to apprehend reality. It is the most significant form of religious expression. Myth reminds us not of what we were but of what we are. Life without myth would be life without a sanction, without meaning. "What," asks the depth psychologist C. G. Jung, "is the use of a religion without a mythos, since religion means, if anything at all, precisely that function which links us back to the eternal myth?"[4]

This linkage, furthermore, is not an evasion but a direct contact with truth. The "once upon a time" world of which myth speaks is not an insipid pipe dream of children and savages but a reality more real than the passing forms of history. Eliade points out that the events in myth—the creation of the world and mankind, the origins of mortality, the discovery of food plants, the adventures of the gods and goddesses, and so forth—took place in *illo tempore,* the "great time," a time outside of time that existed before the current time-haunted "profane" world. The mythical events, then, being without precedent and occurring outside of time in a "sacred" dimension, are original, "primordial" happenings that become exemplary models for all behavior in the profane world. In short, whatever happens on earth, in history, is unreal, illusory, while what happens in myth is real and substantial. Furthermore, humanity's task is to coordinate its earthly activities with the activities spoken about in myth so as to participate fully in reality. Eliade, like Jung, believes that the desire of humanity has always been to enter, through myth and ritual, the "great time" or beginnings, in order to get in touch with the primordial or "archetypal" events that alone deserve to be called real.

Eliade's conclusion is that myths are sacred, exemplary, and significant. Instead of leading humanity away from reality, myths provide safe passage into reality; instead of promoting social delusion, myths, by encouraging imitation of preexistent models, promote social cohesion; instead of alienating people, myths put them in touch not only with themselves but with the entire cosmos.

Support of Eliade's contentions may be found by looking briefly at the Akitu or New Year's festival of the ancient Babylonians. This ceremony, which took place over a twelve-day period, centered on the recitation of the myth of creation, which told how Marduk, the warrior hero of the gods, defeated Tiamat, the terrible mother-monster.

After shooting an arrow into the foul cavern of Tiamat's mouth, Marduk sliced her massive corpse in two and from her body created the heavens and the earth. He mixed together the repugnant blood and bone of one of Tiamat's henchmen and created human beings. Since these creatures were made from the body substance of a traitor, their duties on earth would be to serve, revere, and worship the gods all the days of their lives. Marduk then appointed the gods to their various positions in the universe and established for all time the immutable laws of the cosmos.

Such events, obviously, did not take place in history but occurred in *illo tempore,* before human history began. Since they were unique, original, and exemplary, they were more important than any mere historical occurrences. The events of time, after all, were concerned only with humanity's brief historical existence. The events of myth were concerned with being itself; that is, they were ontological rather than historical.

During the twelve-day ceremony the celebrants sought to remember what happened in the beginnings and, to the best of their ability, imitate that crucial event that established order out of chaos—the killing of Tiamat. By reciting the creation myth the people recalled what was real and true and, easily suspending their disbelief, entered into those primary events. They actually became Marduk, and as they listened to the words recounting the god's victory over the monster they experienced a profound transformation—they became purged, cleansed, reborn. The chaos in their souls was replaced by a cosmos—a sense of order, purpose, and direction. Dramatic rituals surrounded the recitation: The king was ceremonially deposed and reinstated; a condemned criminal was led through the streets and mercilessly beaten by the people; and two groups of actors dramatized the victory of the forces of good over the forces of evil. In each of these rituals the primary mythical event—Tiamat's defeat by Marduk—was imitated, and therefore actualized. Chaos (formlessness, disorder, evil) was replaced by cosmos (form, order, goodness) not only in myth but in reality. Or, to be more accurate, in the Akitu festival myth *was* reality. By reciting the creation myth and participating in related rituals, each member of the community put himself or herself in direct contact with the supersensible realities of myth, which were, at the same time, the mundane realities of everyday experience. With myth, all people knew exactly who they were and what they were expected to do in the temporal sphere. With myth, life was rich, meaningful, and good, for it involved participation in being.

Myths serve an aetiological function. This cannot be denied. They tell, surely, how the leopard got its spots, why man must work by the sweat of his brow, why women must bring forth children in pain, and so forth; but in light of the foregoing discussion, this explanatory function must be understood ontologically, as an attempt to answer the question of how all things came, fundamentally, to be the way they are. "To be or not to be," Hamlet said, reducing the world's most profound question to six exact monosyllables. The answer, Hamlet discovered, lay not in history but in myth, not in the temporal realm devoid of being but in the realm where "there is special providence in the fall of a sparrow." Hamlet is interested not in the way things seem but in the way they are.

The comparative mythologist Joseph Campbell agrees that myth may best be thought of as a comprehensive symbolic form that orients people to all dimensions of reality. In his four-volume study of world mythology, *The Masks of God,* comparable in its own way to *The Golden Bough,* Campbell compellingly demonstrates how shortsighted, perhaps even naive, Frazer was in his estimation of the significance of myth, magic, and the primitive mind.

Myth, Campbell argues, serves four primary functions—the mystical, the cosmological, the sociological, and the psychological. First, by opening back into the mystery of things, into the "eternal myth," it helps reconcile our own consciousness with the preconditions of its own existence; second, it provides an image of the cosmos acceptable to the science of the time; third, it tells us who we are in the social scheme; and fourth, it helps us through various crises in life, from birth to death This fourth function, Campbell says, is the most important, since it supports the other three. Borrowing heavily from the research of Jung, Campbell shows that myth, while enabling us to pass meaningfully from one stage to another in the drama of our individual existence, also allows us to participate as collective beings in the greater drama concerning the journey of humankind. The contents of myths are archetypes, images and patterns that, though changing according to time and place, remain structurally constant. Campbell showed in his first book, *The Hero with a Thousand Faces*, that the adventures of all the great heroes of myth from Marduk to Superman are remarkably similar. They are governed by the same enduring formula—"separation–initiation–return." Behind all the bewildering disguises, the thousand faces of the hero, is the single, unchanging face, the true hero of myth and legend. Understood psychologically, the hero story is the depiction, in symbolic terms, of the quest of the human soul for complete realization. Campbell and Jung imply that through contact with myth, we become sensitive to the drama of the human spirit; suspending willingly our disbelief, we share the precious secret discovered by the ancient Babylonians and many others throughout history: The hero is not Marduk or Hercules or Sir Galahad or Superman—these are the local, transitory faces, mere temporary manifestations, destined always to change and die—the true hero, by contrast, is the self, that is, me. I am the hero.

The fourth function of myth, then, is to understand the Sanskrit phrase *tat tvam asi*. Formally, the term means "That thou art"; more colloquially, it means "You're it!" This short phrase, properly understood, yields up the central meaning, the key message, of myth. The Western world, at least since Aristotle, has insisted that something cannot be itself and something else at the same time. This is the law of noncontradiction, and it cannot be broken. "*A tat tvam asi*," "you are *not* it," has been the message of the West ever since Xenophanes drove a wedge between the self and the self's imaginings. What you fancy is not real. What you believe is illusion. This dualistic habit of thinking has led us not to our sophisticated adulthood, free at last from the gods and demons in our heads, but to despair, for to be divested of myth is to be devoid of self. The truth is, however, that we can never be divested of myth, for the human being is basically the *animal symbolicum*, the symbolizing animal, and myth is a significant form of symbolic activity. To speak about Western history as a story of demythologization is, in effect, to create another myth, the myth of demythologization. Once we realize that we have created the myth of mythless humanity, we begin to hear, once again, a whispering from the depths, the call of our primordial self insisting that we are not simply a local, historical, and transient creature named John Smith but a collective, universal, and immortal being whose name is legion. "You're it!" myth proclaims, urging us to heal the split between mind and world, between ourselves and our possibilities.

Our task now is threefold. First, we must realize that myth is not just a past but a present glory of the earth. It is all about us, and always has been, even when we thought ourselves rid of it. The historical events that are called movements toward demythologization, when rightly seen, are themselves mythical movements. The voyages of Columbus and Magellan were themselves mythical in character, quests for the perfect world of the beginnings. Even the historical stages of Enlightenment thinkers are echoes of earlier, mythical accounts of the "four ages of man." Marxism, the most professedly antimythical philosophy, reconfirms the importance of the myth of the golden age, except that Marx locates the perfect world not before but after history.

The mythical impulses of old have not only survived into these "myth-less" modern times but are doing an active, if not thriving, business. The "cosmological" function of myth is still operating in the world picture put together by scientists and historians, a picture as "mythical" as anything concocted by the mythmakers of primitive societies. Indeed, the so-called "big bang" theory of the origin of the universe popular with most scientists today has striking similarities to a vast number of creation stories collected by folklorists; and descriptions of such things as "quasars," "quarks," "antimatter," and "black holes" among astronomers are more curious than anything the mad mind of the mythmaker ever invented.

Myth has survived in myriad other ways—in the continuance of new year celebrations, in festivities following childbirth and weddings, in activities surrounding the building of houses and moving into new homes, in the exemplary models created by characters in novels or the cinema.

In short, we must recognize the valid role played by myth and imagination in our relationship with reality. Humans, it must be admitted, are symbol-making animals, and all their modes of relating to reality are symbolic in form, including the ones they insist are not symbolic. Our goal is not to "remythologize," for this presupposes that myth has been eradicated from our lives; rather, it is to awaken ourselves and others to the discovery that myth is, radically and unalterably, the way we are.

The second task is to annihilate the notion that ontogeny recapitulates phylogeny. This utterly fallacious proposition suggests that the mind of the primitive is somehow "inferior" to our own and that archaic societies are less "enlightened" than ours. Claude Lévi-Strauss brilliantly demonstrates in *The Savage Mind* that archaic thinking is not less, but perhaps more, sophisticated than our own. Mythical thought is not extraordinarily naive, as Frazer believed, but comprises a well-articulated system—precise, orderly, and poetic. As poetry, it often makes connections between things that to the desensitized, rationalistic mind seem unwarranted. There is a belief among certain archaic peoples, for example, that the touch of a woodpecker's beak cures a toothache. "The real question," Lévi-Strauss says, "is not whether the touch of a woodpecker's beak does in fact cure a toothache. It is rather whether there is a point of view from which a woodpecker's beak and a man's tooth can be seen as 'going together' . . . and whether some initial order can be introduced into the universe by means of these groupings."[5]

A final task is to understand euhemerism, allegory, and projection, not as methods of demythologization but as perspectives on myth. Theorists from Xenophanes to Freud were right when they asserted that myth involves the projection of the mind onto the outer world. However, it took the "Copernican revolution" in philosophy and the researches of depth psychology to show that myth projects not the surface but the depth contents of the mind. Through myth, the deep structures of the mind are revealed.

Euhemerus was right when he saw myth as related to history. There is no doubt a historical aspect to most myths, for without a "local habitation and a name" they would become, as Shakespeare says, "airy nothing." Myth, however, cannot be reduced to history. To prove that Zeus was really a historical figure, a king, is reductionistic; it manages to kill not only myth but also history, for we are left, finally, with dull, dead facts. The critical/historical method may be a dubious gift, like that of King Midas. Everything the historian touches turns immediately to fact, a much-revered but deadly treasure.

The allegorist understood correctly that myth cannot be taken literally. Today very few people argue that Jonah was actually swallowed and then spewed out by a large fish, or that the garden of Eden can be located in time and space. The allegorist, however, like the euhemerist, is reductionistic. When the Roman historian Sallust changed the marvelous myth of the Judgment of Paris to a dull drama involving the universe, beauty, and sense perception he reduced the myth to an abstract, conceptual analogue. He did not understand that myth reveals more things in heaven and earth than can be dreamed of in anyone's philosophy.

The pre-Socratic philosopher Heraclitus noted long ago that the mind can never be exhausted, so profound are its depths. Myths—the gateway to the depths of the mind—can never be summed up in univocal, abstract explanations. Like dreams and like art, they leave us with the feeling that there is much more to be seen, learned, experienced. In myth there is no end, no bottom, no limit. The quest for the impossible dream goes on and on, and that, one may suppose, is the way it should be.

In sum, the task of humanity today is not to regain myth but to recover the poetic power of mind capable of unveiling, at the very center of being, the ancient, eternal, ineradicable myth that gives life purpose, value, and meaning.

CONCLUSION

What, then, is the truth of myth? Which of these two divergent views is correct? Is myth the way we were or the way we are? Is it false or true, illusion or reality? Or is there a third option that claims that myth is both true and false, both illusion and reality? Is this third option the way out of the dilemma, or is it simply yielding to an easy synthesis that will collapse when examined critically?

This chapter has not attempted to provide easy answers to such difficult questions. It is satisfied merely to have brought the questions into focus so as to let the reader make his or her own judgments and decisions. It is content to have shown conclusively that the word *myth* richly deserves whatever extra pay it receives.

NOTES

1. David Bidney, "Myth, Symbolism and Truth," in Thomas A. Sebeok, ed., *Myth: A Symposium* (Bloomington: Indiana University Press, a Midland Book, 1965), p. 23.
2. Sir James G. Frazer, *The Golden Bough*, edited and abridged by Theodor H. Gaster (New York: S. G. Phillips, 1959), p. 649.
3. Wallace Stevens, "Two or Three Ideas," in *Opus Posthumous* (New York: Alfred A. Knopf, 1957), p. 206.
4. C. G. Jung, "Answer to Job," translated by R. F. C. Hull, in *The Portable Jung*, edited by Joseph Campbell (New York: Viking Press, 1973), p. 544.
5. Claude Lévi-Strass, *The Savage Mind* (Chicago: University of Chicago Press, 1960), p. 9.

QUESTIONS FOR THOUGHT, REFLECTION, AND DISCUSSION

1. The critic Philip Rahv, in *The Myth and the Powerhouse*, says that the current interest in myth represents fear of history. History, to Rahv, is the current of powerful change that destroys custom and tradition and therefore liberates humanity from the past. Myth, with its emphasis on stability, repetition, and tradition, resists change and therefore is an enemy of human freedom. Discuss.
2. Mircea Eliade insists that mythical behavior is primarily an imitation or copy of a preexistent model or pattern. Can this contention be validated by observing the behavior of modern people? In what sense can their actions be called imitative? What models or preestablished patterns determine the way they act?
3. Both of the viewpoints presented in this chapter seem to agree on at least one point—that myths cannot be taken literally. What exactly does it mean to take something literally as opposed to symbolically?

PROJECTS

1. Which of the two viewpoints on myth seems most convincing to you? Analyze your reasons for making the choice you did (or for not choosing

at all). Then organize a discussion or debate on the issue, making use of evidence from the chapter and other available sources. It might be interesting to argue for the validity of the perspective other than the one you chose.

2. One way to test the thesis that myth remains powerfully active in the modern world is to invent one. Compose a working mythology that (a) accounts for the origin of the world and human beings, (b) tells of a perfect world that existed *in illo tempore*, (c) explains how, through some blunder, humanity lost this world, and (d) speaks of how, through specific rituals, this perfect world can be regained.

   Be precise in working out the ritual activity relating to the mythology. Act out the appropriate rites. Determine whether an invented mythology is a "true" mythology.

3. After observing the first photographs sent back from Mars by the Viking I spacecraft, the science fiction writer Ray Bradbury remarked, "There is life on Mars—and it's us." Discuss this comment in light of the theory of projection from Xenophanes to Jung.

4. Apply the methods of projection, euhemerism, and allegory to the stories found in the opening chapters of the Bible.

SELECTED BIBLIOGRAPHY

Bidney, David. "Myth, Symbolism and Truth." In Sebeok, Thomas A., ed., *Myth: A Symposium*. Bloomington: Indiana University Press, a Midland Book, 1965.

Campbell, Joseph. *The Hero With a Thousand Faces*. Princeton, N.J.: Princeton University Press, Bollingen Series, vol. 17, 1968.

————. *The Masks of God: Creative Mythology*. New York: Viking Press, 1968.

————. *The Masks of God: Occidental Mythology*. New York: Viking Press, 1964.

————. *The Masks of God: Oriental Mythology*. New York: Viking Press, 1962.

————. *The Masks of God: Primitive Mythology*. New York: Viking Press, 1959.

————. *Myths to Live By*. New York: Viking Press, 1973.

Cassirer, Ernst. *Language and Myth*, translated by Susanne K. Langer. New York: Dover, 1946.

Eliade, Mircea. *Images and Symbols*, translated by Philip Mairet. New York: Sheed and Ward Search Books, 1969.

————. *Myth and Reality*, translated by Willard R. Trask. New York: Harper & Row, Harper Torchbooks, 1968.

————. *The Myth of the Eternal Return*, translated by Willard R. Trask. Princeton, N.J.: Princeton University Press, Bollingen Series, vol. 46, 1971.

————. *Myths, Dreams and Mysteries: The Encounter Between Contemporary Faiths and Archaic Realities*. New York: Harper & Row, Harper Torchbooks, 1967.

————. *Rites and Symbols of Initiation: The Mysteries of Birth and Rebirth*. New York: Harper & Row, Harper Torchbooks, 1965.

————. *The Sacred and the Profane: The Nature of Religion,* translated by Willard R. Trask. New York: Harcourt Brace Jovanovich, 1968.

————. *The Two and the One.* New York: Harper & Row, Harper Torchbooks, 1969.

Frazer, Sir James. *The New Golden Bough,* revised and abridged by Theodor H. Gaster. New York: Mentor, 1975.

Jung, C. G. *Man and His Symbols.* New York: Dell, 1968.

————. *Memories, Dreams and Reflections,* edited by Aniela Jaffe. New York: Pantheon Books, 1973.

————. *The Portable Jung,* edited by Joseph Campbell. New York: Viking Press, 1971.

Lévi-Strauss, Claude. *The Savage Mind.* Chicago: University of Chicago Press, 1960. Paperback.

Ohmann, Richard M., ed. *The Making of Myth,* vol. I. New York: G. P. Putnam, 1962.

Rahv, Philip. *The Myth and the Powerhouse.* New York: Farrar, Strauss & Giroux, a Noonday Book, 1966.

Rose, Herbert J. *A Handbook of Greek Mythology.* New York: E. P. Dutton, 1959.

Zimmer, Heinrich. *The King and the Corpse: Tales of the Soul's Conquest of Evil.* Princeton, N.J.: Princeton University Press, Bollingen Series, vol. 11, 1971.

CHAPTER 4

Belief

RONALD R. CAVANAGH

INTRODUCTION

Wherever religion is found, one form in which it is expressed is in beliefs about a God or gods, human beings, the nature of the cosmos, and the purpose of life. An inquiry into religious belief, then, is surely an important aspect of the study of religion. Religion is a complex field that includes very different sorts of data, issues and methods. For instance, there is probably no living religious tradition that does not involve some set of myths, rituals, doctrines, ethical teachings, and writings that record and interpret the history of the tradition's social and cultural interaction. Within the context of these religious expressions we will try to establish the meaning of religious belief. The focus will be on the indentification and analysis of the basic beliefs of some of the major religions of humanity. These beliefs, objectified in the myths, rituals, and so forth of the various traditions, give expression to distinctive "visions of life," or religious interpretations.

TWO FUNDAMENTAL DEFINITIONS

The ambiguous term *belief* must first be carefully defined. Your previous reading of "The Term *Religion*" (Chapter 1) makes clear that our definition of belief will not be the only possible one. Others might define the term differently, since definitions are simply rules of usage. However, when it meets our predefinitional priorities our definition should not only clarify and stabilize what we mean by the term *belief* but also prove to be a useful tool in our attempt to identify basic beliefs in the world's religions.

Second, since we wish to analyze religious beliefs insofar as they constitute differing "visions of life," we must also carefully define the rather vague phrase "vision of life." In so doing we will propose a "conceptual model," that is, one made of concepts or thought rather than clay or plastic, etc. This model will function like a "recipe" to indicate exactly what elements go into making a "vision of life." The religious expression of all traditions appears in some way to represent the style or pattern of interpretation indicated by our model. Thus when the expressions of a particular tradition illustrate the elements identified by our model we will cite these expressions as evidence of one tradition's "vision of life." We do not claim that this model is the only one that might function in this way. However, we do claim that it does not abuse, distort, misrepresent, or prejudice the analysis of any of the beliefs that we will consider.

SOME NECESSARY LIMITS

Let us clarify two very important points. First, it is not the function of our definition or the function of our model to determine the contents of beliefs or visions of life. Our definition of belief will tell us what the term *belief* means formally or abstractly; it will not give us the specific content of the belief. For example, specific beliefs such as the Muslim belief in Allah the Creator will not be indicated by a general definition. Our definitions will indicate the formal structure of religious belief and vision. They give us no a priori (i.e., before actual investigation) indications as to what is actually believed or what actual differences exist among religious visions. To get at the particular contents of belief we must move beyond the realm of definition to a critical investigation of the religious traditions themselves.

Second, the phenomenon of religious belief may itself be approached from a number of different perspectives. For example, a very important question that a philosopher of religion may ask about a religious belief is, Is religious belief X true? While this is certainly an important question, it is not the major question of this chapter. We are not concerned with claims about the truth or falsity of specific religious beliefs or with arguments that one religious vision is superior to another. The sole purpose of comparing and contrasting religious beliefs is to appreciate the relative differences among religious beliefs and visions. Our intention is not to recommend, judge, or defend any particular set of religious beliefs.

Similarly, the historian may ask the important question, What is the origin and particular historical development of religious belief X?" This will not be a central question for us. Rather, we will concentrate on identifying the meaning or the significance that differing religious visions have held and now hold for human life. Our questions will take the following pattern: How does this vision of life lead a person to understand the basic problem or obstacles to complete and satisfying living? How does this vision determine one's goals? If one can achieve the desired end contained in one's vision, how and under what conditions may one do so? Since there are numerous religious beliefs and visions, we must be selective. The criteria for selecting beliefs include such issues as the number of people influenced, the contemporary religious expression or relevance of religious expression for the modern mind, and the conceptual or universal expression of the belief rather than more particular expression in localized settings and practices.

AN EXPECTATION

Let us remind ourselves that it is not the intention of the academic study of religion either to make people religious or to attack their religiosity. Instead, we will affirm the principle that ignorance is never a virtue and attempt to break down the barriers of parochial prejudice. We will try to achieve this by critically informing you of the phenomenon of religious belief so that you can appreciate the role it has played in the evolution of human experience.

Finally, it is important to note that, because of the technologies of communication and transportation, humankind's religions now belong to a single world. In our age it becomes possible for members of various religions, as well as those who profess no particular religion, to speak to one another in an informed and sympathetic manner. If this chapter succeeds in expanding your vision and your capacity to understand a pervasive dimension of human experience, then it will have justified its place in this volume as well as in the human effort that you will expend in gaining a more global citizenship.

THE TERM *BELIEF*

THE AMBIGUITY OF THE TERM

It is not difficult to show that the term *belief* is ambiguous or that its usage differs in various contexts. As an example, consider some of the different emphases found in a few familiar usages: "I believe so; I don't know for sure, but . . ." (suggesting that belief is a tentative attitude or opinion to be contrasted with knowledge); "You had better believe it; it is as plain as the nose on your face" (suggesting that belief entails a perception or a recognition that something is the case); "I believe in you, Mark, and therefore I'm giving you responsibility for . . ." (suggesting that belief is a personal disposition to trust or have confidence in); "You are making a believer out of me, Jane" (suggesting that belief is characteristic of a person who has been persuaded or led to a conviction); "The Nicene Creed expresses the Christian belief" (suggesting that belief is a credal or doctrinal statement).

These examples are not intended to be exhaustive. I believe (i.e., implying probability rather than certainty) that you could add to them if you were asked to. However, they should illustrate enough diversity of usage to establish the need for a functional definition.

Our first step should be to ask just how we wish to study the phenomenon of religious belief. In this way we can construct some predefinitional priorities, that is, some criteria or standards for judgment, for evaluating definitions.

PREDEFINITIONAL PRIORITIES

Our purpose is to study the phenomenon of religious belief in a way that aids in identifying, comparing, and contrasting the beliefs that comprise the respective visions of life of some of the world's religions. Our main concern will be the significant effect that an individual's belief has on his or her understanding of the human condition, on his or her ideal goals within this condition, and on the means of realizing those goals within this condition.

We further affirm the definition of religion as follows: "Religion is the varied symbolic expression of, and appropriate response to, that which people deliberately affirm as being of unrestricted value for them." For this reason we must understand belief as one aspect of religious expression and response. Further, it must be an expression of that which is deliberately affirmed as being of intensive and inclusive importance for human life.

Given our specific goals and definition of religion, any satisfactory definition of belief must be inclusive, specific, and without prejudice. Since we wish to study the religious beliefs and aspirations of many peoples, we must avoid a definition that a priori excludes actual contents of known religious traditions. In addition, our definition should enable us to distinguish a religious belief from a general belief that is without religious significance. Finally, our definition should avoid the determination that all religious beliefs are either true or false, helpful or harmful to human beings. These judgments should not precede critical study but should follow it.

In conclusion, the specific definition of religious belief must show it to be one aspect of the general function of a religious person's "deliberate affirmation" of that which expresses unrestricted value. In so doing, religious belief will generally be characterized as the assertion of an alleged fact of such unrestricted importance that the believer orients his or her whole life around it. For example, the assertion of the "fact" that God acted in the Exodus to free a people for a specific mission may, if one makes it the focus of one's personal life, be considered an expression of religious belief. We must now become more specific about the nature of assertion, belief, and their further qualification, defined within a religious context.

BELIEF AND RELIGIOUS BELIEF

Assertion

All belief, religious and nonreligious, involves assertion. Thus it is important for us to consider the nature of an assertion. An assertion is a symbolic expression that declares, avows, or claims that something is in fact the case. We will define assertion as "a symbolic expression of an alleged fact."

Fact: Alleged / Demonstrated   In this definition the term *fact* denotes an accurate statement (i.e., one that is true, needs no correction, and has avoided error) signifying a real, objective state of affairs. An alleged fact is a statement that claims to be an accurate or true representation of an objective state of affairs but has not yet had its claim demonstrated or proved. This is not to say that its claim is false, only that its truth or falsity has not yet been demonstrated by an appropriate method. An alleged fact may be contrasted with a demonstrated fact. A demonstrated fact is a statement whose claim to represent accurately an objective state of affairs has been proved or sufficiently established by appropriate procedure. What these methods might be, or who decides when a demonstration is sufficient, or what is to be done when different methods appear to produce different demonstrations, are questions that will not concern us in this chapter. We are not concerned here with the question of the truth of specific beliefs.

Objective State of Affairs   A fact (alleged or demonstrated) may or may not be regarded by someone as personally important. Thus the demonstrated fact that "Jim has a wart on his nose" expresses what is actually the case, regardless of what Mary wants or likes. A fact representing a "real" or "objective" state of affairs signifies conditions that are not exclusively private or simply a matter of subjective expression. A factual statement claims that some experience has public consequence. It is effective beyond the idiosyncratic experience of one subject. A demonstrated fact reveals such a state of affairs to anyone who adequately uses an appropriate method of demonstration.

Symbolic Expression   In our definition the phrase "symbolic expression" indicates that every act of assertion implies the explicit or implicit use of human language in the interpretation of a situation. Humans use symbol systems (i.e., languages) to give order, theme, or meaning to the contents of their experience. At this point we will be concerned only with explicit, written symbolic expression as opposed to behavior resulting from the spoken word. The latter, however, is a legitimate expression of belief. For example, if a highway patrol officer asks me, "Do you have a license?" I may either orally assert "Yes, I do" or, without benefit of spoken word, simply take out my license and display it. In the latter case I am making an assertion without speaking. Nevertheless, my specific action implies that I have understood the question and am making a specific, intentional response to it. If we were to study religious belief by observing religious rituals, we would make use of this distinction.

Summary   In conclusion, we have said that all belief involves assertion and that an assertion is a symbolic expression of alleged or demonstrated fact.

The Belief Relationship

In saying that belief always involves assertion, we are saying that belief is always a relationship consisting of at least two poles. The first pole represents the subject for whom the relation is internal; the subject intends, holds, and affirms the relationship. The subject is characterized by a positive psychological state, attitude, or disposition in which there is enough confidence and trust to make an assertion. The subject of the relationship is the believer or one who does the believing. The second pole represents the object of belief, what is believed, or the assertion of an alleged fact. In the belief relationship the subject perceives, understands, or "sees" the object to be an accurate expression of an objective state of affairs.

Let us consider an example of the belief relationship: "Siddhartha Gautama the Buddha believed that all life is suffering." In this example Siddhartha is properly designated as the historical subject or believer because it was he who was confident enough in his perception of experience to affirm the assertion "all life is suffering" as true. The belief relationship involves a positively disposed subject in a deliberate act of affirming the truth of a symbolic assertion.

Belief May Be Mistaken

Let us consider the following example: "John believed that Mary loved him." Is this in fact the case? John has alleged that it is. Has he demonstrated this fact? As far as our example goes, he has not brought forth a conclusive demonstration. Does this mean that John should not have said that he "believed" that Mary loved him? In answering this question we will make an important point concerning the nature of belief: Belief may be mistaken and still be belief.

As long as the subject (John) is in a positive psychological state with regard to its object (Mary loves John), he may legitimately be said to believe that the assertion is true. It is the condition of intentionality, awareness, that is the essential characteristic of belief. The issue is not whether this assertion has been or could be demonstrated. Even if John has deluded himself about Mary or Mary has deceived John, it still may be said that John believes that Mary loves him. In sum, belief may be mistaken. Belief that involves error is nonetheless belief.

Belief and Knowledge

Any definition of belief would be vague if it did not clearly distinguish between the belief relationship and the knowledge relationship. The primary difference between the logical relationships of belief and knowledge is that while belief may be mistaken, knowledge may not be mistaken. The knowledge relationship is understood to include what we have already described as belief. It thus involves a subject in a positive psychological state toward an assertion of an alleged fact. Thus knowing is belief *plus* an additional factor. The knowledge relationship includes belief plus the ability to demonstrate the truth of an alleged fact. For example, NASA once *believed* that it was possible to place people on the moon. We now *know* that it was correct.

Religious Belief

According to our definition of religion, an assertion expresses a subject's religious belief only on the condition that the subject positively regard it as expressing something of unrestricted personal value. The feature that distinguishes religious belief from any other belief is that the subject of religious belief "perceives" the object of belief as being of unrestricted importance for his or her life. In the preceding statement *perceiving* does not mean that the eyes of the religious believer see some state of affairs that the eyes of a nonreligious believer do not see. This is not the case because they may both agree on the expression of an alleged fact. Rather, it refers to the "discovery" of a pattern of pivotal importance within an experience. For example, on looking at many colored tiles on a wall I suddenly realize that it is a mosaic showing the pattern of a man's face that conveys a central insight into the fundamental human condition.

The perception of a person's religious belief requires that the person discover a meaningful pattern in his or her experience of life that becomes all-important. Such a perception organizes that person's attitude, his or her understanding of life, and the pattern of behavior within his or her life. Thus Gautama the Buddha, upon empirically observing the sights of an old man, a sick man, a corpse, and a monk, "perceived" (i.e., had the insight of interpretation) that finally all life was suffering and that the essential meaning of life is found in the escape from this suffering. Similarly, the prophets of Israel looked upon the economic and civil corruption of their community and "perceived" in this the inevitability of judgment by a righteous God who demanded that human life reflect justice in all its aspects. Through the "perception" of an order or pattern of meaning in the facts of life, the religious believer understands and evaluates life differently from those who are not religious believers.

The phrase "unrestricted personal importance" indicates how religious belief directly affects the believer. It emphasizes both the "intensity" and the "comprehensiveness" of the effect the object of belief has on its subject. For example, Gautama the prince must give up his kingdom and devote himself completely in body and mind to the quest for Nirvana (i.e., the state of complete release from suffering). Similarly, the prophets must endure painful rejection by their community without the possibility of compromise in word or deed. The subject of religious belief positively affirms this object in the quest to realize a full, meaningful life.

A Functional Definition

We will define religious belief as "the varied symbolic assertion of alleged fact, the unrestricted value of which is so perceived and positively affirmed as to shape the attitude, understanding, and intentional behavior of a subject's life."

Religious Belief in Ideal Form   Understood against the background of our discussion, it is our claim that this definition is specific, inclusive, and without narrowness, compartmentalization, or prejudice. However, it is important for you to note that our definition represents what we consider to be our ideal standard for religious belief. It may be that we will find no people whose beliefs actually inform and direct with constancy their whole disposition, understanding, and activities. Yet if people hold beliefs that they think should be functioning in this way, then we are dealing with religious belief. Nothing is more typical of the religious life than the tension between ideal expression and actual realization. In this chapter we will concentrate on the ideal conceptual expression of belief and not on the effectiveness of the application of such belief.

The Place of Fact in Religious Belief   Finally, our definition stresses the notion of "fact regarded as being of unrestricted importance" because we seek to avoid interpreting expressions of belief as simply emotional language or as simply language expressing a policy of behavior, a commitment to a way of life. Important as emotion and volition are in religious belief, they do not exclude the intellectual element. When a person makes a valuation about the world as creation (i.e., the outcome of an intentional act) or the world as illusion, it makes a significant difference to that person whether or not the world is a creation or an illusion. If one believes that the world is in fact an illusion, it makes no sense to orient one's whole life toward a proper relationship to its creator (since it is not a creation). Rather, it would make sense to seek to liberate oneself from the ignorance of this world by turning inward to the depths of one's own being, which view, in fact, is of genuine import to the believer.

However, we must now note that religious belief is open to a wide variety of "interpretations" of fact. For example, the Christian view of the world as creation was held by those who regarded the earth as the center of the universe (e.g., the sun revolves around the earth); it is still held today by those who espouse a heliocentric view (e.g., the earth and other planets revolve around the sun). The idea of creation is held by those who interpret life through evolutionary theory as well as those who affirm nonevolutionary theories. While fact is genuinely important to religious belief, specific interpretations of facts often show a range of differences. What does not vary is the believer's perception of the unrestricted value of his or her belief.

Classification of Religious Beliefs

Our functional definition of religious belief indicates precisely what we mean by this notion. However, no definition reveals what particular believers in the past or present have believed or do believe. In order to obtain this information it is necessary to conduct a careful study of the data of religious expression (e.g., myths, creeds, etc.). It is often helpful in initial

investigations to attempt to locate and describe the beliefs that come under
such common but important classifications as the following:

1. *Anthropological beliefs.* Beliefs that belong in this classification include assertions about the nature of humanity. The following questions will give you a sense of direction. (You can add to this list.) Is
   the human being the body, soul, spirit, or some relationship? What is
   the origin and nature of the body? Is humanity a product of evolution? Is the human being mortal, immortal, or both in different re-
   spects? Does a person normally experience more than one life on
   earth, in Heaven or Hell, and so forth?

2. *Cosmological beliefs.* Beliefs that belong in this category indicate the
   nature, order, or patterns of significance constituting the world or
   worlds known to humanity. Was the world intentionally created or an
   accident? Is it real or illusory? Is it temporal or eternal? Is there more
   than one level or dimension to the world (e.g., the underworld, Hell,
   Heaven, Paradise, etc.)? Is the world regarded as good, bad, ambiguous, etc.?

3. *Numinological beliefs.* Beliefs that belong in this category indicate the
   specific nature of the sacred, the holy, or the divine. For example, is
   the divine asserted to be personal or impersonal, one or many, eternal or temporal, loving or indifferent? Is the divine understood to be
   an aspect of or separate from nature, individuals, groups, history, or
   some combination of these?

VISION OF LIFE

Purpose

While some studies are concerned with the truth or historical development of belief, we are concerned here with the difference various beliefs
make for the life of the believer. We wish to appreciate what difference it
makes for the life of a subject whether he or she believes that an object is
true and of unrestricted importance.

Our concern is reflected in such questions as the following: How does a
set of religious beliefs inform a person's understanding of the world and his
or her own possibilities within it? What aspirations, ideals, or goals is a person admonished to realize if he or she affirms a set of religious beliefs? How
does a set of religious beliefs suggest that a person might realize his or her
ideal?

When we have asked and answered these questions with respect to
various religious traditions, then we will seek to appreciate the differences
that arise when their answers are compared and contrasted. We seek a
sympathetic and informed understanding of other human beings to the extent that religious belief is an expressed aspect of their lives.

BASIS OF COMPARISON

How can you compare apples with oranges or the beliefs of Islam with those of Hinduism? Few people would confuse an apple with an orange, or the Islamic belief in Allah as the supreme creator of the universe with the Hindu belief in Brahman as the void of being. The question is how such different beliefs can be compared.

We certainly can compare apples and oranges with regard to their respective prices, weights, colors, shapes, and the like. Comparison is possible if there are common categories (e.g., price, weight, etc.) that apply equally to the items considered. This is as true for apples and oranges as it is for the beliefs of Islam and Hinduism. Our task is to indicate a common category that applies equally throughout the specific traditions of religious belief. The common category used will be called "vision of life."

Our definition stipulates that any religious belief will shape the thinking and intentional response of the believer to the situations that make up his or her life. It provides the subject with an overall orientation to life, or an interpretation of "what it's all about."

For this reason we will call the general category of religious belief "vision of life." This designation indicates that religious belief functions to give the believer a whole-life interpretation of the meaning of life itself.

VISION OF LIFE: THE TRANSFORMATIONAL MODEL

If you were to examine a precisely scaled plastic model of the SST (supersonic transport), you could, by using the scale of the model, calculate the corresponding measurements of the actual aircraft. A conceptual model uses words or concepts which, when taken together, comprise our common category "vision of life."

The three essential elements that comprise our transformational model for a vision of life are as follows: (1) the essential problem confronting the life of a person, (2) the essential ideal to which a person ought to aspire in life, and (3) the essential mode for the realization of the ideal for personal life.

We have called our model "transformational" because it indicates how a person understands the essential problem confronting life to be overcome through some mode of activity that realizes the ideal goal of personal life. In this sense the essential problem of life is changed, resolved, overcome (i.e., transformed) for some person who attains his or her ideal goal in the process.

In our outline the term *essential* indicates that which is most basic or fundamental. An essential aspect of life is one that is so pervasive that it touches every aspect of life. No situation of life is free from its presence, involvement, or effect. It is an inclusive quality that limits or conditions any life situation.

Essential Problem

The first element of our model contends that religious belief reveals an "essential problem" for the life of a person. It is one that cannot be avoided and in some respect seeps into every experience of life. Life is understood to be different from what it ideally ought to be. Humankind is understood to be confronted with a problem to the extent that the ideal it aspires to is not fully actualized in its present situation.

To locate this first element of our model in the religious belief of a particular religious vision, you will ask such questions as, What is the basic roadblock to life's genuine satisfactions? What obstacle is it that prevents a person from achieving his or her highest aspirations? What principal defect must be removed before life can realize its essential goal?

You will find in your study that when you ask these questions about the Hindu and Buddhist visions of life you receive answers quite different from those you would receive if Judaism, Christianity, and Islam were under consideration. For example, in the Indian religions the essential problem of life revolves around the experience of suffering and the particular, distinct, finite nature of an individual's existence that makes him or her vulnerable to suffering. In Judaism, Christianity, and Islam the essential problem is not the individuality of the self but the injustice and the insensitivity in the way one's self relates to the "other" (i.e., God, nature, society as distinct from, yet related to, the individual person). The centrality of the ethical dimensions of these traditions becomes clear when we ask of them, What is the chief obstacle that blocks the hopes and expectations of humanity?

Essential Ideal

Our model indicates, as its second element, that a vision of life contains an interpretation of the "ideal" that humanity ought to seek in order to overcome its essential problem and realize its hope for a most meaningful and valuable life. The single term *ideal* has three very important emphases. First, the expression of the ideal indicates the believer's understanding that there is in fact a genuine possibility open for his or her life. The subject can experience a new and ideal life. The ideal is a real possibility. Second, the ideal within a "vision of life" is experienced as a normative (i.e., ideal standard) possibility (one required of the believer). The believer experiences the ideal as something he or she is obligated to realize in order to realize the essential ideal for personal life. Thus the ideal represents both what is a possibility for personal life and what ought to be realized as the highest goal of life. In a religious vision the ideal set for personal life is as essential as the problem indicated earlier. It contends that when a person truly, or without deception, considers what his or her potential "really" is, then that person will recognize what "ought" to be realized as his or her true identity. Third, to live contrary to this ideal is to be an unauthentic, incomplete person. One would be missing the mark, failing to experience the highest value open to one.

To locate this element in the religious belief of a particular religious vision you will ask such questions as, What would result if the chief obstacle to the fullest personal realization were removed, bringing about the highest personal satisfaction? What would the most valuable experience open to humanity consist of? Toward what end should a person aspire if he or she would find the most fruitful culmination of personal life?

Hinduism and Buddhism answer these questions in terms of the individual's search for a true self that has disengaged itself from the portion of the self that is vulnerable to suffering and is therefore free from pain, death, and the frustrations of the world. Judaism, Christianity, and Islam, on the other hand, respond with terms like "Day of the Lord," "The Messianic Age," "The Kingdom of God," and "Paradise," giving emphasis to the historical, ethical, communal, and eschatological (i.e., death, resurrection, a new kingdom, etc.) dimensions of experience.

Essential Realization

The third element of our model indicates that religious belief claims there is an effective means or power that transforms persons from the essential problem of life in such a way as to bring about an ideal resolution for personal life. The means to accomplish this transformation may be understood as the "vehicle" or "procedure" involved in the fulfillment of the ideal.

In order to locate this element in the religious belief of a particular religious vision, you will ask such questions as, What is the nature and location of the power or the resources necessary to realize the ideal solution of a person's essential problem? Do people possess such power within themselves, or must it come from beyond them? What are the chances of the ideal solution being realized by an individual or a community in the world or beyond it? Is such a realization inevitable, not likely, or singly dependent on what humanity itself does or does not do?

Your study will show that while a Christian may contend that a person cannot simply "save" himself or herself, the Theravada Buddhist would argue that a person can and must "save" himself or herself. Similarly, where Judaism, Christianity, and Islam emphasize the medium of history as crucially important to the mode of realization, history does not receive such emphasis in the Indian religious experience.

Limitations

It is important that you note the limits of our model. We do not claim that it is the only one that could function in this manner. More important, we do not claim that the focus it gives to questions about religious belief is the only legitimate focus or the most interesting point of view on religious belief. We do claim that it does not distort or misrepresent the religious beliefs of any tradition. However, if in your studies you think that you have found that it does, this should be pointed out. A model is created to do a specific job, and if it fails to do this job it must be altered or disposed of.

This model tells you what is meant by an essential problem, an essential ideal, and so forth, but it does not tell you what specific content is to be given to these categories by Hinduism, Buddhism, and other religions. Your reading and study of the materials will provide the data on which you must exercise judgment. The model is intended as an aid; only you can perform the study. Similarly, while our model provides a basis for comparison, only your study and judgment can lead you to appreciate the similarities and differences that appear among the religious beliefs of humanity. You are the most important element in this study.

CONCLUSION

We have functionally defined religious belief as "the varied symbolic assertion of alleged fact, the unrestricted value of which is so perceived and positively affirmed as to shape the attitude, understanding, and intentional behavior of a subject's life." We have further stated that because religious beliefs function to provide a whole-life interpretation they will be called a vision of life. A model, called the transformational model, was developed to indicate the specific aspects of a vision of life. They were shown to be (1) the essential problem confronting the life of a person, (2) the essential ideal to which a person ought to aspire in life, and (3) the essential mode for the realization of the ideal for personal life. Sample questions indicating how to locate each of these elements within a particular religious vision were given in the discussion of each element.

At the outset of this chapter we affirmed the principle that ignorance is never a virtue and that students in the field of study of religion must attempt to break down the barriers of parochial prejudice. Toward this end we have developed means for identifying and focusing discussion on the phenomenon of religious belief, which has played and continues to play a crucial role in the evaluation of human experience. Through this discussion you can encounter the assertions of human hope and expectation that confess the nature of life's meaning amidst its many challenges and threats. While this study does not intend to produce religious believers, the understanding that can result affords you insights into human tears and laughter, fears and confident action. Since religious belief symbolically represents, orients, and transforms the life of the believer, your appreciation of this pervasive human dynamic both enhances your self-understanding and contributes to the quest for a more global citizenship.

QUESTIONS FOR STUDY, REFLECTION, AND DISCUSSION *

Hinduism

1. How is the "self" on the path of Desire different from the "self" on the path of Renunciation?
2. What does humanity really desire, according to Hinduism?
3. In what ways is the self different from the Self?
4. How may a person's temperament affect his or her choice of Yogas in Hinduism?
5. How does Hinduism regard a person as a layered being?
6. What is meant by the terms *jiva, samsara, karma,* and *Atman-Brahman?*
7. Why is the notion of "maya" so important to the Hindu view of the world and humanity's place within it?

Buddhism

1. In what sense is it correct to say that Siddhartha Gautama the Buddha was a "rebel saint?"
2. What types of questions was Buddha willing to answer, and to what types did he refuse to respond?"
3. In what sense may it be said that Buddha was a pragmatist?
4. What is meant by the terms *dukkha, tanha, nirvana, anatta,* and *skandas?*
5. Do any of the teachings of the Eightfold Path sound familiar/strange to you?
6. What are the major differences between Mahayana Buddhism (The Big Raft) and Theravada Buddhism (The Little Raft)?
7. What is the significance of the "image of the crossing" for all aspects of Buddhism?

Islam

1. What were the prevailing social, moral, and religious conditions at the time when Muhammed began to preach his message of ethical monotheism?
2. How does the Islamic doctrine of creation in its view of the world and of human individuality differ from the corresponding views in Hinduism and Buddhism?
3. How do the Five Pillars of Islam compare with the Eightfold Path of Buddhism?

---

* To prepare for these questions, it is suggested that you read *The Religions of Man,* by Huston Smith.

4. What appears to be one of the important reasons for the speedy growth of Islam today?
5. How would you compare the Muslim attitude toward Muhammed with that of the Buddhist to Siddhartha Gautama and that of the Christian to Jesus of Nazareth?

Judaism

1. How does the early Jewish idea of God compare with the notions of the sacred held by contemporary peoples?
2. How does the Jewish understanding of history influence the Jews' beliefs of creation and creaturehood?
3. How do the Hindu ideas of maya and Atman-Brahman contrast with the central tenets of Judaism?
4. What are the primary characteristics of the prophecy of the Writing Prophets of Israel?
5. What do the terms *revelation, exodus,* and *covenant* mean?

Christianity

1. How does the life of Jesus compare with that of Siddhartha and that of Muhammed?
2. In what sense did the teaching of Jesus differ from the Jewish thought of his time?
3. How are the following terms related: *incarnation, crucifixion, resurrection, atonement,* and *trinity?*
4. What are the defining characteristics of the Christian Ekklesia?
5. How does the Christian notion of incarnation differ from that found in Hinduism and Mahayana Buddhism?

PROJECTS

1. Read the first chapter of Huston Smith's *The Religions of Man* and make notes on Hindu beliefs in regard to

   a. the essential problem in human existence.
   b. the goal, or what the Hindus really want.
   c. the various means or modes they have for achieving their aspirations.

   After you have done this you should have an outline of the basic beliefs in Hinduism.
2. Read carefully all of the chapters in *The Religions of Man.* As you read, make notes on

a. the problem in the human condition confronting all people.

b. the essential ideal to which a person ought to aspire in life.

c. the essential mode or way for the realization of the ideal.

3. After you have completed your study of *The Religions of Man* and outlined the key beliefs in each major religion, select another text such as *Man's Religions*, by John Noss. Add to your list of major beliefs of the world's religions in each of the three areas. Then make a list of all major assertions that are not included in the three categories of problem, goal, and mode of achieving the goal.

4. Select a novel or play that reflects the belief system of one of the major religions of the world. The book might be Chaim Potok's *The Promise* (Jewish); T. S. Eliot's *The Cocktail Party* (Christian); Tanizaki Junichiro's *The Makioka Sisters* (Japanese Buddhist–Shinto); or *Nectar in a Sieve*, by Kamala Taylor (Hindu). After reading the book, write an interpretive essay demonstrating how it expresses

a. the problem.

b. the ideal.

c. the mode of achieving the ideal.

SELECTED BIBLIOGRAPHY

Comstock, W. Richard, et al. *Religion and Man: An Introduction.* New York: Harper & Row, 1971.

Dye, James W., and William H. Forthman, eds. *Religions of the World.* New York: Meredith, 1967.

Frost, S. E., Jr., ed. *The Sacred Writings of the World's Great Religions.* New York: McGraw-Hill, 1972.

Hutchison, John A. *Paths of Faith.* New York: McGraw-Hill, 1975.

Noss, John B. *Man's Religions.* New York: Macmillan, 1974.

Smart, Ninian. *The Religious Experience of Mankind*, ed. New York: Scribners, 1976.

Smith, Huston. *The Religions of Man.* New York: Harper & Row, 1965.

Spiegelberg, Frederic. *Living Religions of the World.* Englewood Cliffs, N.J.: Prentice-Hall, 1956.

Steng, Frederick J., Charles L. Lloyd, and Jay T. Allen, eds. *Ways of Being Religious: Readings for a New Approach to Religion.* Englewood Cliffs, N.J.: Prentice-Hall, 1973.

CHAPTER 5

Ritual

RICHARD B. PILGRIM

THE IMPORTANCE OF RITUAL

It has been suggested that the Western religious traditions have celebrated the Word and the Eastern traditions the Silence. Whatever grain of
truth may exist in such an inflated generalization, no religious tradition is
without the Act. Indeed, it might even be argued that the ritual act not
only is universal to religion but is the single most important characteristic
of any living religiousness! This claim, too, may seem inflated—especially
given the popular notion of ritual as "meaningless repetitive action." However, a look at the religions of humankind—both historically and structurally—reveals at least the possibility, if not the truth, of the bold assertion of the importance of ritual. Not only have all religions included ritual,
but the concrete act of doing religion—especially in the heightened sense
of doing that ritual represents—both completes and creates the very core
of religion as a lived experience of what is real and sacred for someone. A
ritual of marriage, for example, when religiously done, brings to experiential completion the unity of two people. In their eyes they are now as one
and exist in a sacred wholeness with a new or renewed sense of who they
are and what is real for them. In short, if one looks at ritual with an empathy and sympathy for the religious meaning it may hold for its participants, one is struck by its power.

Of course, like any other religious phenomenon, ritual may lose its
power for someone, degenerate into mechanical repetition, and become
meaningless. When this happens, however, either new and different rituals
take their place or living religiousness dies. Our own contemporary society
reflects the process of the death of religious meaning and/or the creation of
new rituals. While religious forms like ritual are some of the most conservative of all cultural forms, they do change, and in our own culture these

changes are very evident and rather rapid. Nonetheless, the importance and power of ritual for being human makes it difficult to envision a world without some kind of religion, and religion without some kind of ritual.

TYPES OF RELIGIOUS RITUALS

It is to the advantage of any study to clarify exactly what is being studied. Since the word *ritual* may denote a variety of things, it is necessary to give some indication of just what kind of phenomena fall under the heading "ritual" in this chapter.

Unless one is to consider all ritual as religious, or religious ritual as the only kind of ritual properly speaking (both alternatives being possible but arbitrary and unhelpful), the key to delimiting ritual resides in understanding just what distinguishes a religious ritual from a nonreligious one. If we understand ritual to be specifically patterned and usually repeated behavior that is not merely the daily routine of living, it does not necessarily involve religious value and meaning. A social or cultural event such as a party or a concert might, for example, be considered a ritual but not necessarily religious.

For the purposes of this chapter, a ritual is religious if it carries an ultimate value, meaning, sacrality, and significance for someone, that is, if it somehow functions for someone at the foundation of what is considered real and sacred. To quote a recent study of religious ritual, "When repetitive actions refer to essential structures of the universe, and paradigmatic modes of being, then we have genuine ritual."[1] Ritual, thus delimited, may fall within one (or more) of the following types:

1. Rituals associated with ecological cycles, that is, rituals whose time, nature, and intent are closely associated with the cycles of the natural universe. For example, rituals of planting and harvesting, of hunting and animal cycles, of spring or fall, of movements of stars and planets fall within this type.
2. Nonecological liturgical calendars, that is, rituals of a given religion or culture that follow a regular, cyclic pattern of repetition but are not primarily associated with the cycles of the natural universe. The Jewish and Christian year of special holy days is a good example of this, although one can find such yearly calendars in other religions too.
3. Rituals of the human cycle, that is, rituals that focus on the individual process of birth, growing up, and death. Often referred to as "rites of passage," human-cycle rituals include the rituals of every culture that are associated with birth, naming, initiation, marriage, death, and so forth.
4. Noncyclic "crisis" rituals, that is, rituals that, while often repeated, do not necessarily follow any regular cycle of repetition but are done "on

demand" whenever necessary. Good examples of such rituals would be divination techniques, curative rituals, and certain kinds of fertility rituals.

This typology is not exhaustive, and one may find rituals that fall into two or more of these categories. However, it is important to suggest descriptively the kind of phenomena we include under the rubric "ritual." This, together with a notion of what constitutes a religious ritual, delimits in a general fashion the subject of this chapter.

ISSUES IN THE DEFINITION AND UNDERSTANDING OF RITUAL

In spite of the universality and importance of ritual in the religions of humankind, the study of ritual emerged late within the general study of religion. While the reasons for this late development of ritual studies may be varied, one important reason is that the immediacy of the living act (verbal or nonverbal) is more difficult to investigate than the word, symbols, and institutions that make up religion. Until recently, and outside more narrowly conceived theological studies of ritual within any given religious tradition, ritual studies have been a sporadic affair at best—both in the social sciences and in comparative religion. Recently, however, increasingly sophisticated work has appeared in both anthropology and the history of religions that has resulted in a deeper understanding of the nature and function of religious ritual. Let us look at some types of definitions and/or understandings of ritual in general.

One view of ritual focuses on ritual and history. While it is not precisely a definition of ritual, this historical interest in ritual manifests itself in several ways. The first leads to an inquiry into the function that ritual plays in the transmission of cultural and religious symbols, values, and self-understandings—the transmission of a culture's "history." Another interest is expressed in the study of the historical relation between myth and ritual, that is, the question of whether ritual precedes or comes out of myth. While such "origin" questions now tend to be answered in "both/and" rather than "either/or" terms, they have enlivened religious studies for some time.[2] A third historical concern has surrounded the relationship between ritual and the arts. Many scholars have pointed to the close affinity between ritual and drama, for example, while others have focused on literature. In any case the general thrust of these concerns is to indicate the importance of ritual as a point of origin for many of the arts.[3]

Another view of ritual, while not historical, is related rather closely to the relation of ritual and the arts. Ritual is here understood as play. Largely stimulated by the work of one man,[4] this sophisticated notion of the function of play in human culture includes ritual as one primary type. Under-

standing genuine play as finally "serious," and using such interpretive categories as make-believe, ordered activity, and play space/sacred space, this
view draws parallels between play and ritual that are both interesting and
suggestive. While it is helpful in understanding the part of ritual that is
play and/or entertainment, perhaps this view is finally not sufficient, if for
no other reason than the fact that important aspects of ritual separate it
from play.

Some of the most dominant theories of ritual, however, have come from
the social sciences—particularly psychology and anthropology. In general,
these approaches have explained ritual in terms of its psychological and/or
sociological-cultural functions. Thus, in a kind of heavy-handed earlier version of this approach, Sigmund Freud saw religious ritual as analogous to
private, pathological, obsessional neuroses but serving egoistic rather than
sexual needs. Similarly, but sociologically, Emile Durkheim saw in ritual a
means for the expression of the "collective consciousness" of any social
group and for the discipline, integration, and vitalization of group order
and solidarity.

Freud and Durkheim are exemplary models of the social-scientific approach, particularly as it has existed in anthropology until recently. The attempt is less to explain or understand religion on its own grounds than it is
to explain religion in terms of the "reality" of the psychic and social life. In
fact, as a more recent anthropologist has said, "the functional explanation of
religion does not explain religion; rather it explains a dimension of society
. . . by reference to religion."[5] In short, the focus of these approaches is
on the nature of psyche and society rather than directly on religion (or ritual) itself. Such approaches are sometimes referred to as "reductionistic,"
since they reduce (change or transform) what is first and foremost a religious phenomenon to a social or psychological one and are not so much
wrong as simply inadequate for those who are interested in the religious
character of religious phenomena.

Generaly speaking, these limiting viewpoints have informed anthropology up to the present, as the following paragraphs indicate:

Myth and ritual have a common psychological basis. Ritual is an obsessive repetitive activity—often a symbolic dramatization of fundamental "needs" of a society,
whether "economic," "biological," "social," or "sexual." Mythology is the rationalization of those same needs.[6]

Ritual actions do not produce a practical result on the external world—that is one
reason why we call them ritual. But to make this statement is not to say that ritual
has no function. Its function is not related to the world external to the society. It
gives the members of the society confidence; it dispells their anxieties; it disciplines
the social organization.[7]

There is, however, within the social-scientific understanding generally
and within anthropology specifically, an approach that is more sophisticated

and more sympathetic both to the multivalent symbolic character of ritual and to religious meaning and value. The exemplary models are Clifford Geertz and Victor Turner.

Geertz's view might best be summed up by his own statement: "The anthropological study of religion is . . . a two-staged operation: first, an analysis of the system of meanings embodied in the symbols which make up the religion [or ritual] proper, and second, the relating of these systems to social-structural and psychological processes."[8] For Geertz, religion is a complex symbol system reflecting, creating, and integrating a culture's sense of reality, meaning, values, social ordering, and so forth. It is a powerful mediating and ordering force operating to bridge the gap between the ethos of a culture (the actual state of affairs) and its mythos (or its ideals and "imagined world"). Within this system ritual is crucial to the fusing of these worlds and to the establishing of religious conviction. Geertz says of ritual, for example,

In a ritual, the world as lived and the world as imagined, fused under the agency of a single set of symbolic forms, turn out to be the same world, producing thus that idiosyncratic transformation in one's sense of reality. . . . It is, primarily at least, out of the context of concrete acts of religious observance that religious conviction emerges on the human plane.[9]

While Geertz is thus sensitive to the power of religion and ritual to create worlds of religious meaning, he still reflects the social-scientific understanding by maintaining as his chief concern the self and society—albeit by reference to religion. His approach, in turn, has to do with the very concrete and practical issue of living a life both individually and as a group. Thus he says,

The tracing of the social and psychological role of religion is thus not so much a matter of finding correlations between specific ritual acts and specific secular social ties. . . . More, it is a matter of understanding how it is that men's notions, however implicit, of the "really real" and the dispositions these notions induce in them, color their sense of the reasonable, the practical, the humane, and the moral.[10]

Victor Turner, who has perhaps done more for ritual studies from within anthropology than any other single person, shares some of Geertz's general approach in his more concentrated study on the nature of ritual. Building his generalizations about ritual from very specific studies of particular rituals (in this case the Ndembu tribe in Africa), Turner has made insightful interpretations of the nature and value of ritual for human culture and society. Central to this interpretation is probably the notion of ritual as a kind of dramatic process whereby normal social structure is broken out of; a temporary unity is attained in which dichotomies of social hierarchy, as well as ideal/real, general/particular, and the like, are overcome; and the central values and structures of society are reinforced and/or charged with creative power. This dynamic process is one in which, as Turner says, "ritual adapts and periodically readapts the biopsychical individual to the basic conditions and axiomatic values of human social life."[11] More specifically, and using his central categories of "liminality" and "communitas," he says that in ritual

communitas breaks in through the interstices of structure, in liminality; at the edges of structure, in marginality; and from beneath structure, in inferiority. It is almost everywhere held to be sacred or "holy," possibly because it transgresses or dissolves the norms that govern structured and institutionalized relationships and is accompanied by experience of unprecedented potency. . . . There is a dialectic here, for the immediacy of communitas gives way to the mediacy of structure . . . [for] men are released from structure into communitas only to return to structure revitalized by this experience of communitas.[12]

Turner's understanding of communitas and liminality will be explained further later. Here it is important to recognize his view of the power that ritual has as a breaking out of the normal and as a creative revitalization of that "normal." Like Geertz, then, Turner believes that ritual does not simply reflect social ordering but is a powerful tool for both reflecting and creating the deepest cultural values and for revitalizing and even changing social structure itself. Nevertheless, the identity of Geertz and Turner is that of anthropologists concerned with ritual, which is finally a concern for social (and psychological) dynamics, as indicated in the quotation from Turner.

The social-scientific view in general and anthropological perspectives in particular provide an important and plentiful source of ritual studies. The preceding pages only suggest key examples of representative views—both old and new.

A final kind of understanding—one that this chapter will follow in a later section—might be called, for lack of a better term, *phenomenological*. This approach, founded in the Western branch of philosophy called phenomenology and adapted to religious studies by such people as Gerardus van der Leeuw, Joachim Wach, and Mircea Eliade, suggests a mode of analysis and interpretation that seeks to uncover the fundamental intentions of any given phenomenon on its own plane of reference. Translating this approach into our concern for ritual, we set aside any preconceptions about what is "real" or "true" and "let the phenomenon speak for itself" of its intentions and meanings as a religious phenomenon. While these meanings and intentions may, at points, overlap with certain social-psychological ones discussed earlier, the emphasis of the phenomenological approach is on the religious structure and meaning, and not primarily the social or psychological structure and meaning, of ritual. What this means in a more particular way will become clearer in the interpretation of ritual that follows.

In order to proceed with a phenomenological approach to the study of religious ritual, and so that there may be guidelines setting forth both the scope and the limits of this study, we now propose a definition of ritual:

> Ritual is a specific and usually repeated complex "language" of paradigmatic word and gesture.

In this definition the phrase "specific and usually repeated . . . word and gesture" describes or helps distinguish a ritual from other kinds of action. The phrase "complex language" points to the multivalent and complex meanings that ritual embodies as a kind of system of symbols. Finally, the word *paradigmatic* seeks to capture the central religious intention of ritual as something that reflects and establishes *norms, archetypes, or paradigms;* that sanctifies or makes sacred; that has power, efficaciousness, and creativity; and is understood as true, meaningful, necessary, and real in an ultimate kind of way.

Reminder: This mode of understanding ritual is a generalization based on ideal conditions, that is, conditions in which ritual is done in a genuinely religious way. Similarly, this kind of understanding makes no ontological truth claims but tries to view ritual as it functions for religious people who participate in it, that is, its implicit and explicit religious meanings for them.

TOWARD AN INTERPRETATION OF RITUAL

The religious and/or paradigmatic character of ritual includes three primary elements: (1) the sacred context within which ritual normally takes place; (2) the transcendent power that marks the core of its meaning; and (3) the transformative power that gives it its efficacious character. Within these elements one can also see something of the complexity of ritual as a symbolic language and reasons for its repetitious nature.

RITUAL IN A SACRED CONTEXT

In the proper (sacred) context the central words of the Latin mass, *hoc est corpus meum* ("this is my body"), are filled with power and meaning for believing Catholics. Outside of that context the same words become mere "hocus-pocus." This rather dramatic example succinctly points to the importance of a sacred context for contributing to the religious meaning and power of ritual. This sacred context includes sacred times, sacred places, sacred traditions, and sacred participants. In short, ritual does not usually take place in a vacuum but is performed in particular places at particular times, within particular traditions, and involving certain kinds of participants.

Sacred time suggests that the nature of time is not experienced by religious traditions or religious people as homogeneous or all of a kind throughout. Rather, certain times are more auspicious and sacred than others—more correct and right as times for rituals to take place. Perhaps the clearest example of sacred time is the sabbath in the Judaeo-Christian traditions. Such times are sacred not only by traditional usage but because God, or the gods, have established them as such. However, certain times are also sacred and proper for ritual because whatever is considered real and/or divine makes or has made its presence known then. Thus holy days in any traditions, or even particular times of any given day (e.g., sunrise or sunset), are sacred times because the Holy ordained it as such or the presence of the Holy is felt then. In other cases, such as the birth and maturation of a human being, certain times are seen as crucial and "sacred" because they mark important turning points in that life.

The time of a ritual, therefore, may lend to its power, meaning, and sacrality, and thus to its paradigmatic character. An Easter sunrise service, for example, is perhaps more powerful and meaningful because it is performed at dawn, for not only is Easter time the time of Christ's resurrection but dawn is the time of the resurrection of light and life. Examples abound, of course, but the suggestion here is simply that the time of a ritual—as a sacred time—contributes to its sacred context and to its paradigmatic and religious meaning.

Sacred place serves a similar function. Certain places carry sacred value and significance. For example, in noting the parallels between play and ritual one author says,

We found that one of the most important characteristics of play was its spatial separation from ordinary life. A closed space is marked out for it, either materially or ideally, hedged off from everyday surroundings. Inside this space the play proceeds, inside it the rules obtain. Now, the marking out of some sacred spot is also the primary characteristic of every sacred act. . . . Whenever it is a question of taking a vow or being received into an Order or confraternity, or of oaths and secret societies, in one way or another there is always such a delimitation of room for play. The magician, the augur, the sacrificer begins his work by circumscribing his sacred spot. Sacrament and mystery presuppose a hallowed spot. [13]

Ritual space thus implies a break in normal space, just as ritual time implies a break in normal time. Whether it is designated as such by the gods or simply by being a place where sacrality is felt, this space is the right space for the ritual. Sacred space, whether a church, a mountain top, a grove in the jungle, a city, or even a home, then becomes a crucial part of the general sacred context.

For the most part, the complex language of symbolic word and gesture that makes up a ritual takes place in a context of tradition and history. While on the one hand ritual may transform and create symbols and traditions, on the other hand it also makes use of that which has come out of a past. For example, not only does the *hoc est corpus meum* of the Latin mass point to some particular ritual words that are a part of a tradition of doctrine, institution, and practice within Roman Catholicism, but the Latin language itself has been—at least until recently—a part of that *sacred tradition*. Similarly, Coke and potato chips cannot be substituted for bread and wine in the Christian communion because they are not a part of the sacred tradition. Sacred tradition thus points to any part of, or the whole of, that which has gone before and yet still informs the ritual. Whether it consists of mythology, history, particular symbols and practices, people, gestures, community, or a set of institutions, the ritual usually takes place within, and makes significant use of, the sacred tradition. The sacrality of that tradition—whether part or whole—then lends to the sacrality, meaning, and power of the ritual.

Finally, a sacred context includes people who are involved in the ritual—with particular reference to the participants who are most central to the actual doing of it. Most often these "specialists in the sacred" are the priest or shaman, the rabbi or minister, the diviner or sorcerer. By virtue of the special sacred power and authority of such people, they become a part of the sacred context. Whatever the nature of such power within any given religion, or however it has been attained, the *sacred participants* not only are important to the sacred context but in some instances are absolutely crucial to the efficaciousness of the ritual itself! The exemplary model in almost every culture is the priest or his or her equivalent. The priest is the one who, almost by definition, "handles the sacred" or is the "ritual doer." This does not mean that all rituals must have priests or even that all rituals must have some religious authority in charge, but it does suggest the general importance of such figures and the role they play in the sacred context and religious meaning of ritual.

Together, the four elements or aspects of the sacred context that we have described briefly contribute to the general sacrality, meaning, and power of the ritual. While some of the sacrality present in the sacred context is closely related to matters that follow, it seems useful to distinguish sacred context as one part of the religious meaning and paradigmatic character of ritual.

TRANSCENDENT POWER

The core of the religious meaning and power of ritual is its ability (1) to re-present and/or be present with that which is considered most sacred, real, holy, and powerful, and (2) to suspend and transcend the normal mundane world of time and space and thus create a world that is whole, true, ordered, sanctified, and celebrated. Separately, these aspects may conveniently be referred to as the "transcendent Presence" and the "transcending Present," respectively. Together, these factors may be considered the "transcendent power" of ritual, for both localize the meaning and power in a mode of transcendence.

The transcendent Presence of ritual is perhaps best expressed by the historian of religions Mircea Eliade. The emphasis in Eliade's work is on ritual as a reversal of time in which the primordial creative acts of the gods—as related primarily in myth—are reenacted and made present. In this view myth (i.e., the acts of the gods) represents a divine and paradigmatic model for ritual, and it is in the repetition of such models that the sacred (i.e., the gods or whatever is considered as transcendent reality) is made present and the ritual has power. Eliade says, for example, that "every ritual has a divine model, an archetype." Quoting Hindu scripture, he says, " 'We must do what the gods did in the beginning. Thus the gods did; thus men do.' This Indian adage summarizes all the theory underlying rituals in all countries. We find the theory among so-called primitive peoples no less than we do in developed countries." [14] For Eliade, myth reveals the primary locus of ritual power, for it is in the creative acts of the gods, particularly "in the beginning" or in the primordial time, that true power, reality, being, and creativity lie.

To illustrate his thesis Eliade focuses on the tendency to repeat the cosmogonic myth, or the myth of the original creation of the world. The original creation is the creative act *par excellence,* and ritual, as a means both for entering into that primordial time (*illo tempore*) and for repeating or reenacting the myth, participates in the power of the original acts of creation. As Eliade says,

Thus the cosmogonic myth serves . . . as the archetypal model for all creations, on whatever plane—biological, psychological, spiritual. But since ritual recitation of the cosmogonic myth implies reactualization of that primordial event, it follows that he for whom it is recited is magically projected in *illo tempore,* into the "beginning of the world"; he becomes contemporary with the cosmogony. What is involved is, in short, a return to the original time, the therapeutic purpose of which is to begin life once again, a symbolic rebirth. [15]

While it is possible that Eliade's view overemphasizes the importance of the cosmogonic myth in all ritual and even of myth itself in ritual, nonetheless where myths do function in ritual they suggest the transcendent power of the "acts of the gods" and the importance of the relationship of myth to ritual. This relationship is especially true when one interprets myth and "acts of the gods" to include the "mythic" and creative events of legend, sacred history, or history itself. In this broader sense of myth as archetype and paradigmatic model, any number of acts and events—from Moses to Mao Tse-Tung—may take on mythic character and be repeated and reenacted in ritual. In fact for most rituals one might say that the ultimate locus of transcendent power is in the "acts of the gods" if we understand this to mean any creative events or acts that establish something that is real for someone. If we use the word *myth* to refer to all these paradigmatic models, then myth is indeed crucial to ritual and to its transcendent power, and it is through myth that the transcendent is a Presence in the ritual.

In rituals in which mythic models and archetypes are not found, however, one must look elsewhere for symbols of the presence of that which is most real, sacred, and powerful. In Tibetan Buddhist rituals, for example, the various buddhas and bodhisattvas are symbols of Buddhahood itself. Here, mythic archetypes in the sense of "acts of the gods" are not as important as the transcendent power of a particular mode of being or ideal called Buddhahood or enlightened Being. However, whether in mythic form or not, the "presence" of the sacred (however conceived) remains a crucial part of the transcendent power of ritual. Evan Zuesse puts it this way:

Ritual obtains its special effect through its adherence to models. What is repeated in ritual is the creative constitution of the real . . . [with] a sacred antiquity and a primordial quality. . . . To do the rite again is to join with the ancestors and regenerate the ideality of their lives. . . . The particular is made paradigmatic, and the archetypal is made concrete and bodily present. Time is broken through.[16]

While Zuesse's language sounds like that of Eliade, the former avoids limiting these models to myth and the "acts of the gods." He may well include such transcendent and sacred ideals as love or Buddhahood as importantly present in the ritual. In any event the point of our first element in "transcendent power" is the Presence (however conceived) in ritual of the sacred, or whatever creatively constitutes the real. Thus in most Jewish and Christian ritual, for example, not only are mythic archetypes and stories repeated but, more simply, God's presence is invoked.

The second element in transcendent power, the transcending Present, while certainly related to the first, is a distinct way of talking about transcendence in ritual. Here the focus is less on the sacred, or whatever creatively constitutes the real, than on the particular quality of religious experience in the ritual, which in this case is a sense of transcending the normal and mundane character of life, time, space, social order, and so forth and making all things new and whole. This shift in focus allows us to understand better the experiential and existential character of ritual and the contribution of that character to the meaning and power of ritual as religious and paradigmatic. The following analysis of an African ritual suggests both meanings of transcendence:

The ritual sphere is the sphere *par excellence* where the world as lived and the world as imaged become fused together, transformed into one reality. Through ritual man transcends himself and communicates directly with the divine. The coming of divinities to man and of man to divinity happens repeatedly with equal validity on almost every ritual occasion. The experience of salvation is thus a present reality, not a future event. In short, almost every African ritual is a salvation event in which human experience is recreated and renewed in the all-important ritual Present.[17]

This interpretation of African ritual is precisely our point about the transcendent power of ritual in both its elements. On the one hand, there is the sacred or transcendent Presence, the coming of divinity to humanity and of humanity to divinity. On the other hand, there is the ritual or transcending Present as a moment in and out of time that is a "salvation experience" of transcending self and world and of existentially realizing the unity of all worlds—whether "actual" or "ideal." (This comment on ritual as a "salvation event" recreating and renewing human experience also suggests what we will discuss later as "transformative power.")

More specifically, however, the transcending of normal time and space refers to the sense of being lifted out of normal time and normal space. This experience is also what Turner refers to as *liminality,* for to be liminal one must have broken out of—or not belong to—the normal social order and hierarchy of social authority, and ritual is one key place where this experience of transcendence takes place. To be liminal in ritual, at least for Turner, is thus to have transcended the normal social order. The peyote pilgrimage of the Huichol Indians of Mexico is a good example of such transcendence. In the ritual Present not only are normal time and space transcended as the Indian worshipers walk in the time and place of the gods (Wirikuta), but social roles are reversed and, for example, the old person is called "the baby."

Another aspect of this transcending Present is the experience of unity and wholeness—or the fusion of worlds as expressed in the previously cited analysis of African ritual. The experience of transcending is not merely a going *beyond* but also a *coming to* something—in this case the experience of wholeness, unity, order, sanctity, and celebration. In expressing this aspect of ritual Zuesse emphasizes the concrete, bodily, and experiential immediacy of ritual and the bringing together of the prereflective world of sensation and feeling with the reflective world of self and cultural consciousness. Zuesse suggests, for example, that "since ritual is a paradigmatic way of the body knowing itself to be in the world, ritual acts have a crucial importance for consciousness and existence, binding together things and awareness into a unity." [18] Such unity can be manifested not only in the bringing together of prereflective and reflective worlds but also in a joining of the microcosmic world of our immediate experience and the macrocosmic world of universe or cosmos, as well as the worlds of self and others.

Zuesse thus echoes Turner's understanding of communitas, or the sense of communal oneness. In Turner's view the transcendence of social order in liminality gives way (in ritual) to the sense of true community, shared world and shared equality—which, as Turner suggests, might best be described through Buber's understanding of I–Thou relationships. The Huichol pilgrimage again provides a good example. During the time of the pilgrimage a special group unity is attained—literally done and undone before and after the pilgrimage by a ceremonial binding and unbinding. More generally, such notions as the Christian "communion of the saints" or the Jewish sense of "peoplehood" and family are experienced in Christian and Jewish rituals and expressed there.

The experience of unity and wholeness may thus appear in different ways in rituals, but that vivid sense of unity carries with it a transcending quality that seems to establish a world, an order, a meaningful orientation in reality, and to sanctify and celebrate that world. In Eliade's terms, this is the process of coming to live at the center of the world—in cosmos and not in chaos. More specifically, another author says, "Thus cult is not just any order re-enacted but the true order, the order under which man lives and which shapes his image of reality." [19] Such an order is not merely an intellectual understanding of things, although this may be closely related to it. Rather, it is a deep and all-encompassing sense of the meaning and truth of things. As Zuesse suggests,

Ritual gestures forth the world as meaningful and ordered. It establishes a deep primary order which precedes the world that can be spoken, and out of which the word proceeds, to which it returns. . . . Every gesture . . . is a revelation of a way of being located in the universe; each gesture points out a universe too, and makes spaces in it for human life. [20]

It is at this point, then, that rite is truly right, for in a very fundamental way ritual sets things right and makes them meaningful.

Finally, the transcending Present of ritual sanctifies and celebrates the world thus constituted. In ritual the world is not only whole but holy, sacred, and good. The festive character of many rituals points especially to this sanctification and celebration.

Together, these two factors—transcendent Presence and transcending Present—constitute the "transcendent power" of ritual and mark the core of its religious meaning and power. The transcendent power might also be referred to as the *sine qua non* of genuine ritual, for without it or some modified version of it ritual would indeed be "merely ritual"—that is, empty gesture and relatively meaningless form.

TRANSFORMATIVE POWER

One distinct mode of the general power that obtains in ritual, yet one that is closely related to the transcendent power, is the power to change and transform people and their world. While, of course, the transcendent power itself is transformative in its ability to transcend and transform experience and the constitution of reality, the transformative power we now speak of is the effect that ritual has once the transcendent power is present and presumed. Whether it is put in terms of social/cultural transformation, as Turner and others do, or in terms of the potential for making many things, as Eliade does, ritual can be understood to have the power to change—especially if seen from the point of view of the participants. For

Eliade, for example, in copying the creative acts of the gods, and especially the cosmogony, ritual can both create (e.g., a child) and regenerate (e.g., the world and time itself).[21]

While what we are speaking of here should not be construed simply as magic, ritual is "magic" in the sense that distinct effects are seen to issue from it. At the risk of important exclusion and oversimplification, the possible effects of ritual might be discussed under four broad categories: (1) the personal or individual; (2) the collective or group; (3) the natural ecosystem; and (4) the cosmic totality. As with the types of rituals mentioned earlier, these categories are neither exhaustive nor mutually exclusive. Any single ritual may involve all of them, or other rituals may involve effects that do not exactly fit any of them. However, these categories are suggestive of the kinds of transformative power rituals may have.

The Individual

First, ritual clearly affects the individual, and these effects may go all the way from "I feel better" to "I'm born again!" However construed, and for whatever society, ritual inevitably has some kind of effect on the individual, even when that is not its primary intent. The kind of individual effects we point to here, however, are less those of the general emotions than of deep transformations in identity and social/religious role—effects that are often expressed in terms of rebirth, renewal, healing, or wholeness.

Perhaps the clearest examples of rituals that thus transform individuals are the rites of passage or "rituals of the human cycle." Rituals of birth, naming, initiation, marriage, and death, to mention only the most obvious, are processes by which the individual passes through life in a series of transformations; these rituals are indeed a Way through life. In many cultures these rituals signal not only the process of growing up but also that of moving "upward" toward a more spiritually fulfilling existence. Thus the Way is not only psychological and social role transformation but religious as well. Eliade suggests this interpretation when he focuses on initiation rituals as exemplary models for individual transformation. Singling out the symbols of death and rebirth in such rituals, Eliade discusses initiation as a process of death and rebirth whereby the child dies to an old mode of being and is reborn to a new and more sacred one—adulthood. He says, for example, "Initiatory death provides the clean slate on which will be written the successive revelations whose end is the formulation of a new man. . . . This new life is conceived as the true human existence, for it is open to the values of spirit."[22]

In a less dramatic yet nonetheless important understanding of this characteristic of the effect of ritual, Zuesse focuses on self-definition as one of the primary intentions of ritual, suggesting, on the one hand, the importance of connections, relationships, and links with others in the process of self-identification and, on the other, the crucial character of ritual as being a primary place where these links happen. Zuess concludes that "ritual is therefore part of an elemental process of self-definition and self-maintenance."[23] In short, we come to know who we are in relation to others, and ritual is a crucial place for establishing "true relationship" and, thus, true selfhood.

Other important understandings of transformative power in ritual reside in images of healing and wholeness as heard in the Catholic mass: "Lord, I am not worthy to receive you, but only say the word and I shall be healed." Taking their cue from the unity and wholeness represented in the transcendent power, these images suggest the power of ritual to heal at various levels: physically, psychologically, or spiritually. Unlike his teacher Sigmund Freud, the great psychoanalyst Carl Jung would understand the power of ritual to heal and not simply reflect obsessions of various sorts. Thus one writer, reflecting the Jungian point of view generally and drawing analogies between certain rituals and therapy, says, "Healing means leading the patient to understand the meaning of his life, of his suffering, of his being what he is. With this insight would surely come a well-established religious attitude, and the result would be not merely a remission but a real cure, which could also be called a transformation."[24] Such a comment could well be made for ritual, too, for it is precisely in ritual that the participant comes in contact with the deepest meaning of things and is made whole again. The language of healing and health can thus be understood religiously as well as physically and psychologically, and it is one way of understanding the transformative power of ritual as it affects the individual.

The Group

While much of the anthropological research on ritual has been concerned with its social function, much of that research has been insensitive to both the creative, transformative character of ritual and to what we are calling here its religious meaning. The two primary exceptions, as previously noted, are Geertz and Turner, for both are appreciative of the power of ritual to establish and transform social order and cultural values.

However this may be, it is not the relationship between something called ritual and religion, on the one hand, and something else called social order, on the other, that demands our attention. Rather, it is the religious character of human collectivity that ritual helps restore and/or create that is of key interest. For this we must look to other interpretations and other categories—such categories, again, as renewal and wholeness.

Taking a cue from the unity discussed under transcendent power and from Turner's view of communities in ritual, certainly one thing that can be said about ritual is that it creates a sense of true and shared community among its participants and perhaps between them and others as well—living and/or dead. Be it two people in a marriage, a tribe in a tribal ritual, or a larger notion such as the "communion of the saints" in Christianity, ritual helps restore, create, and bind the sense of "comm(on)-unity" that is, for the participants, true and sacred.

More specifically, and as mentioned earlier, both Turner and Zuesse describe the particular character of individual relationships within ritual as "I–Thou," that is, a relationship of shared mutual humanity and integrated relatedness. While this factor may be discussed under the sense of unity in the transcendent power, it is relevant here insofar as it continues after the ritual and affects the whole sense of community and social cohesiveness.

It is also important, as Zuesse interestingly points out, that the sense of community may also result in ethical beliefs and actions. To take a Christian example, if ritual helps establish not only the sense of a communion of saints but a more general sense of our total common humanity bound ideally in love, then one effect of the ritual might well be whatever "good works" issue from it for the good of all. Thus words near the end of the mass say, "We have heard God's Word and eaten the body of Christ. Now it is time for us to leave, to do good works, to praise and bless the Lord in our daily lives." Similarly, Confucian ritual was designed to issue in an ethical stance of filial piety, and Buddhist ritual to result in compassion for all beings. In short, whether it expresses the particularistic ethic of a given tribe or culture or a more universal ethic such as those found in the "world religions," ritual could well be considered as affecting the group by inspiring ethical sensibilities and patterns of behavior. Ritual can thus affect, change, and even transform the group. These changes become important parts of the potential of ritual as transformative power.

The Ecosystem

Certainly in the eyes of its participants, but perhaps also in some sense of "reality," ritual may work its "magic" on the nonhuman order too—on the fertility and growth of plants and animals, and the workings of sun, moon, and stars. Perhaps most obviously exemplified in fertility rituals of various sorts (including here, perhaps, human fertility too), the power of ritual is seen as restoring and/or recreating the growth and flow of all natural life. The rain and sun dances of the Native American, the rice-transplanting ritual of Japan, the hunting rituals of tribal Africa, the spring rituals of many cultures, and countless other examples suggest the pervasive character of this interest in ritual's transformative power. Whether they are considered "magic" or not, such rituals are religious because transcendent power is present—and particularly the power of the sacred Presence. In speaking of the Dogon tribe of Africa, Ben Ray shows the importance of the creation mythology, and the creator god Amma, for all aspects of Dogon life, and especially of the major rituals that call upon or somehow "repeat" these creative acts. In one particular example the ritual representing of Amma's "signs" (i.e., important gifts of Amma at the time of creation) brings plenitude and order to the whole natural (and other) world. Ray summarizes thus:

The placement of these Signs on sacred objects is an efficacious act that "produces" the things to which the Signs refer. . . . The painting of these Signs upon the alter helps to maintain the world in existence. . . . Signs are also painted upon the major totemic sanctuaries in order to perpetuate the totemic animals and natural species associated with them. . . . During the spring agricultural rites, the head of the family inscribes at the center of his fields a pattern representing the 266 Signs and cosmic Seeds. This, together with Amma's blessing, will fructify the newly sown fields. In this way, the Signs revealed in the myth function as the archetypal forms enabling the Dogon to both comprehend and control this universe.[25]

In this way the transformative power may both relate to the transcendent power and work its effects on, for example, the particular reproduction of plants and animals and the general maintenance of natural life. However it is expressed in any given ritual, the importance of transformative power cannot be overlooked. While our "modern" sensitivities might be slighted by such matters, we overlook a crucial intent of ritual throughout all cultures if we avoid them.

Cosmic Totality Itself

Many rituals express an intent to renew, change, or transform the cosmos in general. This intent includes all the others described previously, but goes beyond them in trying to get at the very core of time and life itself. For Eliade, the exemplary model for such ritual is the new-year ritual, for it is in new-year rituals that the sense of time itself as winding down and being recreated is most present. In this view "the New Year is a reactualization of the cosmogony, it implies starting time over again at its beginning, that is, restoration of the primordial time, the "pure" time, that existed at the moment of Creation. . . . It is also a matter of abolishing the past year and past time."[26] In short, new year's time is the ritual time *par excellence* when a new creation follows on the degeneration and demise of the year and of time itself and the totality of existence is made new, whole, fresh, and sacred again.

A functional equivalent to the new-year ritual, however, is the fire altar sacrifice of ancient Hinduism. Here the cosmos itself, represented by the god Prajāpati, is rebuilt and renewed annually in the building of the fire altar and the creative sacrifice of Prajāpati. These and similar rituals have been among the most important in primitive and traditional cultures. It is often in these major rituals that the cosmogonic myth is repeated, for at stake is the very character and flow of life and time in general. Our own greatly weakened version of this ritual can be seen in our new year's celebrations, revealing as they do the chaotic New Year's Eve party (symbolic of the demise of time and year) and the New Year's resolution (symbolic of renewal and order). More appropriately, however, our equivalent rituals probably reside in our dominant religious traditions and are exemplified in Easter and Rosh Hashanah.

However they are manifested, however, these rituals become paradigmatic models of ritual as transformative power and paradigmatic gesture—life and time itself are seen as restored and renewed.

CONCLUDING REMARKS

The definition of ritual as paradigmatic gesture follows from the preceding interpretation. The sacrality, power, and importance of ritual for the religious life suggest that it is precisely that which it is "meet and right so to do." Being "paradigmatic," it reflects and establishes paradigms of powerful experience, belief, and behavior; is perceived as truly real and meaningful; and is creative and efficacious. In short, being paradigmatic it is right and worthy—even necessary—to repeat. As Zuesse says, "repetitive actions are the clearest expression of the will to be and to be human. The random behavior of the general organism is adjusted and articulated in a specific, emphatic fashion. It is because this fashion is true, and necessary, that it must be repeated." [27] Ritual thus reveals not only a "thirst for [pure] being" or a "need to plunge periodically into this sacred and indestructible time," as Eliade emphasizes, but also a means by which humanity controls, constructs, orders, fashions, or creates a Way to be fully human; indeed, it makes a world that has meaning and power. In this sense perhaps every genuine religious ritual is also a "salvation event," as suggested by Ray for African ritual, for ritual renews and makes things right—it "saves," heals, and makes whole again.

Anything defined as paradigmatic would seem to operate at these levels and be crucial to the living religious life. As contemporary humankind struggles to find a Way (or Ways) to fulfill its humanity, it is no wonder that the increasing absence of meaningful ritual—inside or outside of established religious traditions—poses a problem. Perhaps the wholeness, health, and salvation of our individual, collective, ecological, and cosmic life depend, in part, on rediscovering the power of ritual.

NOTES

1. Evan Zuesse, "Meditation on Ritual, *Journal of the American Academy of Religion* 43, no. 3 (September 1975): 529.
2. See a rehearsal of this discussion in Clyde Kluckhohn, "Myths and Rituals: A General Theory," in William Lessa and Evan Vogt, eds. *Reader in Comparative Religion*, 2d ed. (New York: Harper & Row, 1965), pp. 144–158.

3. See, e.g., the following works: Theodor Gaster, *Thespis* (Garden City, N.Y.: Doubleday, 1961); Gerardus van der Leeuw, *Sacred and Profane Beauty: The Holy in Art* (New York: Holt, Rinehart and Winston, 1963); and Andreas Lommel, *The World of the Early Hunters* (London: Evelyn, Adams & Mackey, 1967).

4. See J. Huizinga, *Homo Ludens* (Boston: Beacon Press, 1955).

5. Melford Spiro, *Burmese Supernaturalism* (Englewood Cliffs, N.J.: Prentice-Hall, 1967), p. 66.

6. Kluckhohn, p. 158.

7. George Homans, "Anxiety and Ritual: The Theories of Malinowski and Radcliffe-Brown," in Lessa and Vogt, p. 128.

8. Clifford Geertz, "Religion as a Cultural System," in Michael Banton, ed., *Anthropological Approaches to the Study of Religion* (London: Tavistock, 1966), p. 42.

9. Ibid., p. 28.

10. Ibid., p. 41.

11. Victor Turner, *The Forest of Symbols* (Ithaca, N.Y.: Cornell University Press, 1967), p. 43.

12. Victor Turner, *The Ritual Process* (Chicago: Aldine, 1969), pp. 128f.

13. Huizinga, pp. 19f.

14. Mircea Eliade, *Cosmos and History* (New York: Harper & Row, 1959), p. 21.

15. Mircea Eliade, *The Sacred and the Profane* (New York: Harper & Row, 1961), p. 82.

16. Zuesse, p. 529.

17. Ben Ray, *African Religions* (Englewood Cliffs, N.J.: Prentice-Hall, 1976), p. 17.

18. Zuesse, p. 519.

19. Adolf Jensen, *Myth and Cult Among Primitive Peoples* (Chicago: University of Chicago Press, 1963), p. 53.

20. Zuesse, pp. 518f.

21. Mircea Eliade, *Rites and Symbols of Initiation* (New York: Harper & Row, 1965), p. xii.

22. Ibid., p. xiv.

23. Zuesse, pp. 524ff.

24. C. A. Meier, *Ancient Incubation and Modern Psychotherapy* (Evanston, Ill.: Northwestern University Press, 1967), p. 128.

25. Ray, pp. 31f.

26. Eliade, *The Sacred and the Profane*, p. 78.

27. Zuesse, p. 528.

QUESTIONS FOR STUDY, REFLECTION, AND DISCUSSION

This chapter may be difficult to understand without consistent application to particular examples of ritual that are easily accessible to the reader. The following points for discussion should also include reference to such examples.

1. Discuss the issue of what would distinguish a religious ritual from some other ritual and consider the variety of possible examples.

2. With any given example of ritual, consider its place within the typology for rituals given in the chapter.

3. Discuss the methodological and interpretive differences one might find among theological, historical, social-scientific, and phenomenological approaches to ritual.

4. Discuss in detail the meaning of sacred context, transcendent power, and transformative power in ritual—with application of these categories to specific examples of rituals.
5. Discuss ritual as important and paradigmatic both for religious people to date and for the future of humanity.

PROJECTS

In general, projects associated with ritual should seek out specific rituals and analyze them according to all or part of the material in the chapter—both to understand that particular ritual better and to confirm and/or criticize the chapter's interpretation. Here are some examples:

1. With any given ritual you have read about, viewed on film, or observed in person, look closely for expressions of any one (or all) of the following:

    a. How important is the ritual to the participant?
    b. Is it a religious ritual? If so, what kind is it?
    c. How might the anthropologists represented in the chapter find ammunition here for their point of view?
    d. How does the idea of sacred context apply here?
    e. What is the nature of the transcendent Presence operating here, and does mythology seem to play a part?
    f. In what ways is the experience of a transcending Present—including the sense of unity, order, sanctity, and celebration —expressed here?
    g. What is the efficacious character of this ritual; what does it do or transform?
    h. Is this ritual paradigmatic for anyone?

2. Construct a ritual of your own, keeping in mind the chapter as a guide to why you would do it, how you would do it, and whether you could do it.
3. Write a "history" of your own ritual life, including a reflection on the importance (or lack of it) of that life for your own sense of what is real, true, and meaningful.

SELECTED BIBLIOGRAPHY

Ritual Studies (see additional references in notes)

Eliade, Mircea. *The Myth of the Eternal Return: or Cosmos and History*. Princeton, N.J.: Princeton University Press, Bollingen Series, vol. 46, 1971.

————. *Rites and Symbols of Initiation: The Mysteries of Birth and Rebirth.* New York: Harper & Row, Harper Torchbooks, 1965.

————. *The Sacred and the Profane: The Nature of Religion,* translated by Willard R. Trask. New York: Harcourt Brace Jovanovich, 1968.

Grimes, Ronald L. "Ritual Studies: A Comparative Review of Theodor Gaster and Victor Turner." *Religious Studies Review* 2, no. 4 (October 1976).

Kluckhohn, Clyde. "Myths and Rituals: A General Theory," in W. Lessa and E. Vogt, *Reader in Comparative Religion: An Anthropological Approach.* New York: Harper & Row, 1972.

Turner, Victor W. *The Ritual Process: Structure and Anti-Structure.* Chicago: Aldine Press, 1969.

Van Gennep, Arnold. *The Rites of Passage,* translated by Monika B. Vizedon and Gabrielle L. Caffee, Chicago: University of Chicago Press, 1960.

Zuesse, Evan M. "Meditation on Ritual." *Journal of the American Academy of Religion* 43, no. 3 (September, 1975).

Ritual Descriptions (examples only)

Brown, Joseph Epes, ed. *The Sacred Pipe: Black Elk's Account of the Seven Rites of the Oglala Sioux.* Baltimore: Penguin Books, 1971.

Myerhoff, Barbara G. *Peyote Hunt: The Sacred Journey of the Huichol Indians.* Ithaca, N.Y.: Cornell University Press, 1974.

"To Find Our Life: The Peyote Hunt of the Huichol Indians," a 65-minute film distributed by Audio Visual Services of the University of California at Los Angeles and by the Film Library of Syracuse University.

"Image India: The Hindu Way," a series of films on Hindu rituals distributed by the Film Library of Syracuse University.

CHAPTER 6

Scripture

JAMES G. WILLIAMS

WHAT IS SCRIPTURE? A COMPARATIVE APPROACH

Every religious community has its scriptures, and these writings are an important expression of religiousness. Such a simple assertion, however, seems to prompt immediate questions. What is scripture? How does scripture develop in a religious community? How can we interpret the various scriptures? This chapter seeks to answer these three fundamental questions with special regard to the scriptures of Islam, Judaism, and Christianity.

Response to the first question, What is scripture? can be made in a straightforward manner by affirming that scripture is the sacred literature of a religious community. Yet this answer is too simple and needs further exploration.

Scripture is part of a community's myth and ritual and validates that myth and ritual. It is a writing or collection of writings that a community reads as divinely inspired. It is the set of texts that is authoritative in the life of the religious community as the community asks its most pressing questions and seeks to form its conduct. Scripture provides "mirrors for identity" for those in the tradition it represents.[1]

Scripture is the source of mythical models that serve a twofold function: (1) as images to be repeated or re-presented and (2) as constructs of meaning that shape the future as the believers project themselves onto the moving margins of history.

From the broader perspective of philosophy of religion, scripture is a certain *genre* or kind of religious expression: any writing that shapes and validates the unrestricted valuations of an individual or group. In this sense there are many "scriptures," ancient and modern, ranging from the *Rig-Veda* to the *Thoughts of Chairman Mao*. In this chapter, however, we are concerned with the scriptures that have become canon for three religions of great influence in the Middle East and the West: Judaism, Christianity, and Islam.

Canon is derived from a Greek word that means "rule of measure" and "carpenter's rod." For the Christian Church it came to mean "norm," specifically scriptures that were fixed and normative for the life of the church. As used here, it refers to the scripture that a community deliberately affirms as normative for evaluating all other writings and life in general. So it is that canon is fixed and unalterable scripture, whereas noncanonical scripture is subject to change. Canon is always scripture; scripture is not always canon.

The process of scripture formation is rooted in the interplay between crises in history and the answers of the tradition. New insights or answers emerge from a kind of religious dialogue with the past and future; this dialogue, when written down, is scripture. In this discussion we will be concerned with what went into this dialogue.

All of the highly developed and enduring religious traditions have possessed and transmitted scriptures whose efficacy is founded on the idea of the creative word, the word that is charged with religio-magical power. Not all traditions, however, center on this sacred literature. Hinduism, for example, has sacred writings, but those writings are not the primary integrating symbol of Hindu religious life. Islam, on the other hand, is the supreme "religion of the book;" the Holy Qur'an of Islam is the word of Allah (God). Judaism is also a religion of scripture, and scripture contains *Torah*, which is the divine teaching and divine law disclosed in the story of God and Israel.

Christianity is a somewhat different case. It is certainly a scriptural religion. In fact Muslims count Christians among the "people of the Book." Yet Christianity's symbol center is not the Bible; it is Jesus Christ, the Word become flesh. Islam and Judaism have sacred languages because scripture is expressive of unrestricted value in their myth and ritual. If scripture is important in Christianity, still the Christ is the Word. Thus Christianity has no sacred language like its sister traditions.

To understand this matter of sacred language we need to observe that there are two distinct types of religious traditions. In one type of tradition the founder is of divine descent, a god or a manifestation of the sacred. This type of tradition may be called the *avatar* tradition, after the Hindu term for divine manifestation. The second tradition is one in which the founder is not God but the messenger of God.

Within the daily life of most of its devotees, Hinduism is predominantly an avatar tradition. The Buddha, in Mahayana Buddhism, is the avatar or incarnation of sacred reality. In this type of tradition the divine word appears in the flesh. The center of this tradition, then, is not scripture or sacred text but the divine being or the divine word in human form. Scriptures, though extensively employed in ritual and meditation, are secondary to the incarnate god. Historically, Christianity has been much closer to the avatar type of religion. We may need to qualify this assertion somewhat for two reasons: (1) Sacred text has been important in the Christian tradition; (2) "God became man" in Christian symbolism has meant not simply the appearance of God in flesh but also that God is man in one aspect of the divine being. Nevertheless the power of Christian religiousness has been rooted in its affirmation of the incarnation, the appearance in history of the Word as the way, the truth, and the life. Christianity has no sacred language based on its scripture, for its sacred language is the Christ.

In the second type of tradition the founder is not himself God or the word of God; he is, rather, the purely human messenger from God. This messenger comes with a proclamation of God's will for his people. This type of tradition has a sacred language, the language of its scripture, which preserves the messages of the messenger or prophet of God. The scripture in this case relates stories of origin, norms for community life, and ritual activity. The very reading of the sacred text of scripture confers a blessing, making the believer a recipient of divine power. Islam is just such a tradition—the type of tradition originating in the coming of a messenger of the god. His messenger is Muhammad, the Apostle of God. The scripture is the Holy Qur'an. Muslims may speak, study, and write in any language, but they may hear or read the Qur'an only in Arabic.

Judaism is somewhat like Islam in this regard: Orthodox Jews may speak, study, and write in any language, but they may pray or study Torah only in Hebrew. This fact of orthodox Judaism shows to what extent it is a scriptural religion. Yet it is also a fact that to be a Jew has meant to belong to a people and a culture, a "community of the God of Israel," which differentiates Judaism from all other traditions. Israel is the people in whom "God's history" is told as well as written. So it is that we find two important types of religious figures at the origins of Israel: the ancestors and the prophets. The ancestors embody peoplehood; the prophets are commissioned to bring the divine word to Israel.

Scripture, then, is the religious literature of a people, sometimes conveyed in a languge believed to be sacred, originating in times of community crisis and forming and supporting the convictions of the people.

THE SCRIPTURE RELIGIONS: THEIR STORY

The basic stories of a religious tradition make up a mythical or sacred history. In studying any religious tradition it is necessary somehow to enter into its fundamental stories and to see from their point of view. One's story is one's identity; to know someone is to know that person's story "from the inside." So it is in studying religion. Religion does not exist in the abstract; it is always concretely disclosed in some tradition that has many stories and usually one grand story of origins. Imagine this author as a guide who believes in the truth of the Hebrew Bible, the New Testament, and the Qur'an. Let him lead you into these scriptural stories, beginning the journey with the stories of Islam.

THE STORY OF MUHAMMAD

Muhammad, the messenger of God, was born after his father's death. Orphaned at the age of six by his mother's death, he was cared for by Allah's grace through an uncle. When this sweet and gentle person, "the highly praised one," was 40 years old he received the first revelation of God on Mt. Hira. It was his custom to spend a vigil on Mt. Hira during the month of Ramadan. The angel Gabriel, who appeared to him, ordered him to "proclaim in the name of thy Lord." Muhammad was afraid and said that he could not. Gabriel struggled with him and tried to smother him until Muhammad finally relented and agreed to recite.

Muhammad returned home to his faithful wife, Khadijah. He was in great doubt and perplexity after his experience on Mt. Hira—afraid that his vision was of Satan; he even contemplated suicide. But Khadijah believed in the revelation and encouraged him, as did a few other relatives.

Muhammad began proclaiming God's judgment and the necessity of repentance. In the first few years of his prophetic ministry he attracted very few believers in Mecca. Then, when he began to attract a following of considerable size, his followers were harrassed in various ways, mainly through economic boycotts. Eventually Muhammad and the Muslims migrated to Medina; the Muslim calendar dates from this emigration in 622 AD. In Medina Muhammad continued to receive revelations, most of which had to do with social and political life. He was at first an arbiter between feuding tribes, but soon he was the ruler of Medina. He was responsible for the Constitution of Medina, which was a model of ideal government.

The Qur'an was revealed to Muhammad over a period of twenty-two years, sometimes in very short units and sometimes in longer speeches. These revelations guided him through various vicissitudes and were sometimes abrogated or changed to take into account new conditions. Completed by the end of Muhammad's life, the Qur'an is the Word of Allah, perfect spiritually and aesthetically. It is like an infinitely variable kaleidoscope of the divine power and reason, revolving around one fixed center:

There is no god but God.	(He alone, the One, is the Source and the End of all life, the One whose reality is disclosed in all true or nonidolatrous religion.)
And Muhammad is the Messenger of God.	(The One who revealed His will to previous messengers has confirmed previous revelations through the perfect prophet.)

THE STORY OF JESUS

As the Sacred Word was delivered by Muhammad as God's vessel, it came also centuries earlier in the form of a Jewish man, Yeshua ben Yoseph (Jesus, son of Joseph). As Muhammad was mature, around 40 years old, when revelation came to him, Jesus was approximately 30 when he began proclaiming the good tidings that God's full and complete rule was near at hand. He had various arguments with Pharisees (scribes or rabbis) about the interpretation of scripture (Old Testament), but finally it was the ruling classes' (Sadducees and Herodians) fear that led to his execution; they were apprehensive lest he lead a popular, messianic uprising against Roman rule and thus threaten their security and wealth.

Yeshua ben Yoseph viewed himself as a sign of the new age of God, as a prophet reinterpreting the scripture, indeed as the one anointed by God (Messiah) to usher in the consummation of God's Kingdom. Others understood him to be an eschatological prophet and secret Son of Man. Still others believed him to be the Son of David, the Son of Adam, and the New Moses, and even the very embodied divine Word addressing humankind. For St. Paul, he was the final disclosure of God's "righteousness" for those who believe in him as the fulfillment of the sacred story (Romans 10:4).

Our sacred story of Jesus is actually a "divine journey" that began when God triumphed over chaos, made Adam, and called Abraham and blessed Sarah. This God is the One who did not refrain from bowing down to enter the lowly, filthy huts and hovels of those who were enslaved in Egypt. He guided these disenfranchised people through the water and across the wild to the land of promise; this is the God who took David to be shepherd over Israel. This God is the Very One who is "born of a woman," who has bent down to let himself be raised from a cradle in Bethlehem. And all of the events of this long odyssey of God are of the same order, except that now the event of Jesus is complete—a fulfillment.

THE STORY OF ISRAEL

Israel, like all other nations and peoples, originated in Human Kind (Adam and Eve). The father of Israel was Abraham, the mother was Sarah. Abraham and Sarah and their descendants were resident aliens among other people and in other kingdoms until the possession of the promised land. There were continual threats from foreigners. The greatest threat, however, came from God, who, desiring to test Abraham, commanded him to offer his son Isaac as a sacrifice (Genesis 22). Israel was not safe even from God. But on the other hand, God was also not safe from Israel (see Genesis 32:24–32).

The story of Torah begins with the choosing of the patriarchs and matriarchs, moves on to the liberating of Hebrew slaves from Egypt under Moses as the Lord's commissioned one; it includes guiding these Hebrews through the wilderness and across the Jordan river into Canaan. There they built a civilization and a great temple. When the temple was destroyed by the Babylonians in 587 B.C., certain Judaean elders in Babylonia came to the prophet Ezekiel and asked him, "How shall we live?" (Ezekiel 33:10). Indeed, how shall we live? How can we sing the song of the Lord in a foreign land? The temple destroyed, Jerusalem's walls in ruins, many Judaeans taken into exile—yes, how shall we live? The answer came from the great prophets and the very form of the Pentateuch: We shall live by the knowledge of the Torah, which tells us that even though we were promised the land of Canaan, God's Israel can and will survive outside the land. Did not the ancestors wander among foreign people? Is not Mount Sinai outside of the holy land? Did Moses, even Moses, enter the land of promise? We will return; God will restore us; but in the land or out we will still survive as Israel.

God permitted the people to return to Judah; a second temple was built; and the people of Israel continued to survive. When the second temple was destroyed by the Romans (70 A.D.), the Jewish scriptures became even more important; they included the Torah (teaching), the Nevi'im (prophets), and Ketuvim (writings).

HISTORICAL-CRITICAL PERSPECTIVE

While telling the stories is one way to begin an understanding of scripture, it is only one way. A second way is that of the critical scholar—specifically the historian. The student following the historical method may or may not be a believer. His or her perspective will be different but not necessarily in opposition to that of a person who is uncritically on the "inside" of the tradition whose scripture is being studied. It may be that the historian will provide new insights about scripture that are otherwise unavailable.

Only two religious traditions and their scriptures—Judaism and Christianity—are discussed on the following pages. A similar historical-critical perspective could be developed for the Islamic Qur'an if space permitted.

THE HEBREW BIBLE

The Literature Prior to Canonization

The ancient Israelites possessed a literature long before the idea of a canonical scripture or book emerged in their history. This literature included many of the myths and legends in the Book of Genesis; the stories of Saul and David; accounts of the Kings of Judah and Israel; early collections of the oracles of prophets like Moses, Hosea, Isaiah, and Micah; and other writings. Much of this literature was transmitted orally for generations before being written and worked into larger blocks of material. The history of Biblical literature covers over 1500 years if we date from sometime in the middle of the second millenium B.C., in the case of some of the tribal stories and sagas, to the last Biblical books, Daniel and Esther, in the second century B.C. The history of written literature would be about 1000 years from the work of the original authors through the collecting, editing, and arranging of these writings to their final canonization.

Inspiration and Revelation

There were undoubtedly many literary works in ancient Israel that are completely lost to us now. Other writings survived to form what we know as "Scripture" because they were valued in the temple and later in the synagogues; others because of their literary beauty and patriotic interest. Within their traditions their merit was viewed as that of prophetic inspiration. According to Jewish tradition, the prophets, filled with the divine spirit and speaking God's words, were able to transcend normal waking consciousness and receive divine inspiration.

First there was the Revelation, that is, the Exodus and the establishment of the covenant at Mt. Sinai, where Moses was the messenger of God and ruler-arbiter of the Hebrews. This formative event, which was decisive in the configuration of Judaism as it started taking shape in 621 B.C., transformed the Hebrews into Israel, the People of the Lord.

The prophets appeared later, after Israel had become a nation-state under David. Theirs were words of curse and blessing, tearing down and building (see Jeremiah 1:9–10), but they never became as important as Moses in the Jewish tradition. In fact in traditional Judaism the prophets are understood as inspired men who confirmed the Law of Moses and proclaimed reform of their socioreligious order on the basis of this law.

Canonization of the Law

Law (Torah) consists of Genesis, Exodus, Leviticus, Numbers, and Deuteronomy. The religious symbol of the divine book, the celestial scroll, is known from the earliest recorded period of ancient Near Eastern civilization. It was in Israel, however, that the conviction first appeared that the deity had given a book to guide, educate, and sanctify a whole people. But the "revelation of the book" occurred over a long period of Israel's history and represented the entrance of divine speech into the vicissitudes of history in response to various social, political, and military problems.

The prophets were originally the only class in ancient Israel whose utterances would have the authority to become Scripture or who could authenticate a writing as Scripture. Jeremiah (who prophesied ca. 626–585 B.C.) was probably the first prophet to "write" his book; he dictated a collection of his oracles to his disciple/scribe Baruch. However, the oracles reported by earlier prophets had been collected and were in circulation by the time of Jeremiah.

So the idea of inspired writings had become established by the reign of King Josiah (639–609 B.C.). It was in the eighteenth year of Josiah, 621 B.C., that a book was found in the Jerusalem temple. It is generally agreed by critical Biblical scholars that this book contained the nucleus of the Book of Deuteronomy (Chapters 12–26; perhaps also 4:44–48:20, 10:12–11:25, et al.). The reforms of Josiah (II Kings 23:4–24) were based on Deuteronomy 5, 12, 16–18, and 23.

Josiah and his contemporaries attributed the book to Moses, in accordance with explicit statements of its author (Deuteronomy 4:44–45, 5:1, 29:1). From a modern historical point of view Moses could not have been the author; yet this does not mean that the author was a "forger" in the modern sense. Ancient literary conventions were different from ours. The ideals of the author were sound in his own context: He sought to present the final proclamation of Moses on the basis of what was otherwise known about Israel's origins. Only the authority of the great founder of the religion of the people of Israel could have induced king and people to reform their faith and practice.

Deuteronomy, which was found in the temple and to which additions were made until about 550 B.C., had a lasting influence. It marked the beginning of Judaism's becoming a scriptural religion. The acceptance of Deuteronomy as divine Word tended to make revelation through the prophets superfluous. The priests henceforth became primarily interpreters or supplementers of the written law, and the prophets either did the same or disappeared as God's messengers (see Psalms 74:9, I Macc. 4:46, etc.).

Gradually Deuteronomy grew to the size of the whole Pentateuch. About 550 B.C. a Deuteronomic editor combined Deuteronomy with two important epics of Israel's origins, the Yahwist and the Elohist. The Yahwist source is so called because the earliest critics noted that the divine name *YHWH* occurs in some passages of the Pentateuch. (YHWH, probably pronounced "Yahweh" in preexilic Israel, is rendered *Lord* in most modern translations). The Elohist source is so named because the generic noun *Elohim* ("God") occurs in other passages. Source analysis is a complicated matter. In fact the "sources" are so intertwined at some points that the whole field of source analysis has been called into question. We should recognize the different traditions of Israel's origin and their different theological tendencies, but we should also be suspicious of minute source criticism.

Nevertheless, according to this approach, we have three of the main sources that modern critical scholars have distinguished: Yahwist (J, for Jahwist in German; ca. 950 B.C.), Elohist (E, ca. 850 B.C.), and Deuteronomy (D, 621–550 B.C.). The fourth is the Priestly Code (P).

With full genealogies, little narrative, and its own sacred chronology, the Priestly Code spans the period from the creation of the world to the occupation of Canaan under Joshua. It includes the first creation story (Genesis 1) and other parts of Genesis; parts of Exodus, including whole blocks in Chapters 25–31 and 35–40; all of Leviticus; and much of Numbers. It reflects the ritual practices of the second temple (finished in 515 B.C.) from about 515–450 B.C. as these were furthered and perhaps reformed by Ezra (ca. 405 B.C.). The full Pentateuch as we know it must have been completed and accepted by about 400 B.C., as the reading from the Law in Nehemiah 8 would seem to indicate.

The Torah as Pentateuch is a "mirror for exiles." Ending as it does before the book of Joshua, which narrates the conquest of the land of Canaan, the Pentateuch in its final form reflects the Babylonian exile and is a message to exiles. The identity of Judaism is authenticated not by possession of the land (although the land has always been important in Judaism) but by being possessed by the Torah.

Canonization of the Prophets

The Prophets (Nevi'im) in the Hebrew Bible consist of

1. The Former Prophets: Joshua, Judges, I–II Samuel, I–II Kings.
2. The Latter Prophets: Isaiah, Jeremiah, Ezekiel, Book of the Twelve (Amos, Hosea, Micah, Nahum, Habukkuk, Zephaniah, Haggai, Zechariah, Jonah, Joel, Obadiah, Malachi).

By 400 B.C. the Jews possessed a number of ancient books besides the Pentateuch that were popular but not yet considered divinely revealed. These were the books later to be known as the "Former Prophets" and the "Latter Prophets."

About 550 B.C. the Deuteronomists edited the history found in Joshua through II Kings to teach the lesson that obedience to the Law of Moses, as expressed in Deuteronomy, is divinely blessed and that violations of the Law are punished by YHWH. After the canonization of the Pentateuch (400 B.C.), various priestly notations as well as glosses were made to these books that expressed national pride and popular religious feeling (e.g., the exaltation of David, the magnificence of the first temple).

As for the Latter Prophets, the earlier prophetic denunciations of a wayward, self-satisfied Israel were supplemented in the exilic and postexilic periods mainly with oracles showing hostility toward foreign nations and prophecies of the future triumph of Israel led by YHWH and his Messiah.

By 300 B.C., when prophecy had all but died, certain redactors prepared the present edition of the Prophets in four volumes: Isaiah, Jeremiah, Ezekiel, and the Book of the Twelve.

The section of the Hebrew Bible called the Prophets must have been accepted as divinely inspired by 200 B.C. In Ben-Sirah (Latin *Ecclesiasticus*), a book in the Aprocrypha written about 180 B.C., the Prophets are given the status of sacred writings along with the Law.

The Law guided the Jews' present life; the Former Prophets gave them a sense of Israel's national heritage and the Latter Prophets evoked hope for a new age. Sometime between 200 B.C. and 30 A.D. a reading from the Prophets (*haftara*) became part of synagogue worship, although it has never been as important in traditional Jewish liturgy as Torah.

Canonization of the Writings

The Writings (*Ketuvim*) in the Hebrew Bible consist of Psalms, Proverbs, Job, Song of Solomon, Ruth, Lamentations, Ecclesiastes, Esther, Daniel, Ezra, Nehemiah, and Chronicles.

For a book to become Scripture it has to survive and gain wide acceptance in ritual or popular patriotic or religious feeling and to be attributed to a great personage of the past or be anonymous. Some of the writings are attributed to a great figure of mythic proportions (David, Solomon, Daniel) or are of anonymous authorship (Job, Lamentations). Anonymity helped in that the writing could be viewed as a kind of "ageless wisdom" and not the expression of one timebound individual. Otherwise, authorship would have to be prophetic, because an inspired book could be written only by a prophet. In addition to those who were prophets in a strict sense, by 200 B.C. David and Solomon were also considered *Nevi'im*, prophets.

Two books, Ecclesiastes and Job, stand as literary monuments of ancient Israel. This is true of Job, composed in its present form by a poet who embodied Israel and humanity in a non-Israelite, the righteous sufferer Job.

We do not know exactly when the Writings became Scripture, but our present collection was considered divinely inspired by the first century A.D. if not earlier. The time line in Figure 6-1 shows the scripturizing process leading to canonization, with a time line of Israel's history to place it in perspective.

Jamnia and Alexandria

The destruction of Jerusalem and the temple by the Romans in 70 A.D. further enhanced the importance of Scripture for the Jewish people: The sacred center no longer included the House of the Lord, so the Jews became fully and completely a "people of the Book," a people with a sacred text that could be carried, recited, and studied wherever they might live, a sacred text symbolizing in verbal form the omnipresence of the one creator God.

The destruction of the temple made it even more important to fix the canon. This, plus the evangelizing activities of the Christians, led the Palestinian rabbis to close the canon at the Councils of Jamnia in 90 A.D. and 118 A.D. They decided that only the twenty-four books in the Hebrew Bible were sacred text and that "the gospel and the books of the heretics do not make the hands unclean" (i.e., are not holy).

In Alexandria, however, where there was a large Jewish community,

FIGURE 6-1. Time line of Israel's history and scripture canonization.

Periods	Important Figures and Events	Process of Scripture Formation
Patriarchs ca. 2000–1500 B.C.	Abraham, Isaac, Jacob, Joseph	*SACRED HISTORY TRADITIONS*
Hebrews in Egypt, Exodus ca. 1500–1200	Moses Exodus (ca. 1250) Joshua	
Judges 1200–1000	Deborah Gideon Samuel Saul	
United Kingdom 1000–922	David Nathan Solomon	Yahwist (J) ca. 950 — Deuteronomic Reformers
Judah 922–586 Israel 922–721	Great Prophets Deuteronomic Reform (621)	Elohist (E) ca. 850 — Deuteronomy (D) ca. 621–550 — JE ca. 700
Exile 586–539	Destruction of Temple (586)	Priestly Traditions — JED ca. 550
Postexile Persian Rule 539–332	Second Temple (515) Nehemiah Ezra	Priestly Collection (P) ca. 500–450 — Pentateuch* ca. 400
Hellenistic Rule 332–167		The Prophets* ca. 200 — Prophetic Traditions
Hasmoneans (Maccabeans) 167–64	Maccabean Revolt (167–164) Second Commonwealth	Psalms, Various Writings, etc. — The Writings* ca. 100
Roman Rule 64 B.C.–395 A.D.	Councils of Jamnia (90 A.D., 118 A.D.)	Official Canonization at Jamnia, 90 A.D., 118 A.D. K'tav (Scripture) Fixed: Torah (Law) Nevi'im (Prophets) Ketuvim (Writings) = Tanak

(Bracket at left spanning United Kingdom through Judah/Israel: *United Monarchy*)

NOTE: * = completion of one of three major segments of the Hebrew Bible: Law (Pentateuch), Prophets, and Writings.

Jews tended to accept as Scripture any work in Hebrew or Aramaic that
had originated in Palestine. Jews in the Diaspora (the "scattering" throughout the Graeco-Roman world) spoke Greek. After the translation of the
Pentateuch into Greek (ca. 250 B.C.), they tended to regard all books
translated from Hebrew into Greek as divinely inspired. Furthermore,
they did not believe, like the Palestinian Jews, that prophecy had ceased
with Ezra and Nehemiah.

The result was that many of the writings in the Jewish Apocrypha
(Greek, "hidden") were evidently regarded as sacred text by the Alex-
andrian Jews. These probably included the Prayer of Manasseh, the Prayer
of Azariah, the Song of the Three Children, the Wisdom of Solomon, Ben-
Sirah (Ecclesiasticus), Judith, Tobit, the Epistle of Jeremiah, and I and II
Maccabees. The Apocrypha is regarded as canonical by the Roman Catholic
and Greek Orthodox Churches, whereas Protestant denominations accept
only the Hebrew canon as fixed by the Councils of Jamnia.

The canon as fixed by the Palestinian rabbis at Jamnia eventually was
fully accepted in Judaism, except for a few Gnostic movements.

The Jewish Understanding of Scripture

In the Jewish understanding of Scripture as it evolved in the "Talmudic"
period (ca. 200 B.C.–500 A.D.), two features stand out: (1) the distinction
and interrelation of law and prophecy, and (2) identification of preexistent
wisdom with Torah.

The Jews firmly believed that the books of the Scripture had been inspired by God, and this meant that the books of the Bible had been revealed to prophets. All Biblical authors were seen as prophets in a broad
sense. After Ezra and Nehemiah, however, the Holy Spirit had departed
from Israel; no inspired Scriptures could be written; prophecy had ceased.

Yet neither the prophets themselves nor their oracles were the center of
meaning of the Scripture: At the center was Torah, the teaching as story
and law. And this teaching has its authoritative basis in the first five books
(Pentateuch). The rabbis emphasized law (or ethos), although not to the
exclusion of story (or mythos).

As for wisdom and Law, the identification of the two is already stressed
in Ben-Sirah 24:8–23 (180 B.C.). One of the favorite texts of the rabbis was
Proverbs 8:22:

> The Lord acquired me [wisdom] at the beginning of His way, The first of His an-
> cient deeds.

From this proof text the rabbis could maintain that all the supremely important creations of God, such as the Law, paradise, the throne of glory,
the temple, and so forth, were created before the world. They could maintain this because they viewed these as expressions of divine wisdom.

The Torah, said the rabbis, existed before creation. When Moses as-
cended to heaven, he found God with the Torah in His hand and reading

the passage about the red heifer (Numbers 19:1–10). In fact Torah, as the preexistent wisdom of God, even includes the world: The whole world is but a thirty-two-hundredth part of the Torah.

Judaism thus fully integrated into its own distinctive religious tradition the ancient Near Eastern tradition of the Heavenly Book, the celestial archetype of the revealed Scripture and the entire cosmos. This symbol of the Heavenly Book would later be of great importance in the Manichean and Elchesaite movements and above all in Islam.

THE NEW TESTAMENT

The Literature and Canonization

The story of Jesus, his teachings, death, and resurrection, was circulated orally at first among his disciples. It may be that by 40–45 A.D. there was a written collection of his sayings. The earliest writings in the New Testament were those of Paul (ca. 48–64 A.D.). We see in his letters that the authority of Jesus as Lord was beginning to open up and supplement the authority of the Hebrew Bible. But the idea of a Christian scripture as distinct from the Jewish scriptures did not fully emerge until 100 A.D. or later.

The Gospels originated in the context of local congregations, and it was some time before they were brought together. Perhaps by about 120 A.D. the Four Gospels were widely known and used. The Book of Revelation was composed about 90–100 A.D. The pastoral and general epistles would be dated 100–150 A.D., perhaps one or two of them later.

In the meantime many other pieces of Christian literature were written and circulated. The problem of Christian writings—that is, which should be authoritative for the Christian in his or her faith and life style—became acute in the second century A.D. For example, a certain Marcion made a list of Christian writings that included the Gospel of Luke and ten letters of Paul. This was the first example of a "canon," a normative list of books for the churches. This induced other church leaders in the late second century to begin to frame their own lists of official scriptures, which included the Hebrew Bible as the Old Testament.

There were various lists of canonical New Testament books until the canon of the New Testament was established in the fourth century A.D. Athanasius, Bishop of Alexandria, sent an Easter letter to his churches in 367 A.D. This list corresponds to the present books of the New Testament. At the Council of Carthage in 397 A.D. the same books were listed for use in African churches. This set of books was confirmed in a letter of Pope Innocent I in 405 A.D., including the 27 books from Matthew to The Revelation of John.

Inspiration and Revelation

Christianity has traditionally not been as definite about the cessation of prophecy, or the possibility of inspired utterances and writings, as Judaism and Islam. In fact many writings of the early church fathers were regarded as scripture, inspired by the Holy Spirit. It seems, however, that prophecy and scripture were not usually lively possibilities after about 200 A.D.

The reason Christianity has been somewhat looser than Judaism and Islam with respect to the fixing of scripture is that its center of revelation is Jesus as the Christ. The "revelation" is basically what happens to the believer in encountering the act of God in Jesus. Christ as the "righteousness of God" has a twofold aspect: (1) passion and resurrection and (2) the teachings of Jesus. (Note how the Christian revelation, like the Jewish, distinguishes itself into mythos and ethos.) The former, passion and resurrection, were given paramount attention in primitive Christianity. Later, as the church became an institution, the teachings of the Lord were of greater concern than at first. So Jesus as God's event was the center of revelation. The inspired writings were those that were authored by people who had been associated with Jesus, or by those who claimed to have had such an association. In other words, the question of inspiration, as it always does, extended into the question of the authoritative tradition of interpretation. By the early third century A.D. it had become a question of apostolic authority: A given book claiming authority had to be written by an original apostle or by someone closely associated with an apostle.

Some Critical Problems in the Study of the Gospels

The Synoptic Problem.   The first three Gospels, Matthew, Mark, and Luke, are called the "synoptics" by modern New Testament interpreters because they can be "seen together," that is, read together as similar. In actuality, in the synoptic Gospels we have three varied accounts of Jesus that present us with a complex pattern of agreements and disagreements. They agree on the outline of Jesus's life and ministry, the order of most of the material presented, and much of the wording of the sayings of Jesus. Often two Gospels agree against the third one. Disagreements include minor variations in wording, difference in structure, material used, and changes in accounts. Luke, for example, has accounts of Jesus's teaching that are not found in the other two Evangels. In order to see changes in narratives, one need only compare the resurrection stories (Mark 16:1–8; Matthew 28:1–10; Luke 24:1–11).

The way in which the synoptic problem is usually treated by modern critical scholars stems from the documentary hypothesis formed in the nineteenth century. According to this method of research, Matthew and Luke used Mark as a literary source. This perspective solves certain problems. Yet Matthew and Luke contain a great many teachings attributed to Jesus that are not in Mark. These latter passages are accounted for by a hypothetical collection Q (Q = German *Quelle*, "source"). When material peculiar to each of the three Gospels is taken into account, the basic source hypothesis may be diagramed as shown in Figure 6-2.

This critical hypothesis, like the source hypothesis in Old Testament studies, must be taken with a grain of salt. But it does have the virtue of indicating, in a sensible manner, the long and interwoven process of oral and literary tradition behind the present Gospels.

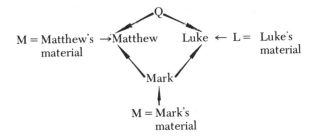

FIGURE 6-2. Source hypothesis for the Synoptic Gospels.

The Messianic Question.   Did Jesus think of himself as the Messiah? This is a difficult question owing to the problems in the early sources. The Gospels are documents of faith and, in their final form, are two generations removed from the lifetime of Jesus. The Gospel writers believed that Jesus was the Messiah and that he had proclaimed himself as such. But the Gospels are not biographies, and in no sense do they trace the inner development of Jesus's thinking.

The title most frequently on Jesus's own lips in the Gospels is "Son of Man" (see Daniel 7:13). In nineteen passages in the synoptics Jesus speaks of the Son of Man as a future figure, an eschatological figure (i.e., a figure of the "end"). In all these cases the Son of Man is referred to in the third person (see Mark 8:38; 13:26; 14:62; Luke 11:30; 17:24, etc.). Is Jesus referring to someone other than himself? Then there are many units about the suffering Son of Man (Mark 9:31; 10:33; 14:21; et al.). Again these references are given in the third person, even though many of the sayings refer to Jesus's imminent crucifixion.

The majority of critical interpretations, especially those most influenced by the German schools of thought, have concluded that Jesus identified himself neither as Son of Man nor as Messiah. The evidence suggests that Jesus was ambiguous about this identity. Other Biblical critics, however, who have been trained within the context of Judaism and Judaic studies, tend to view the question differently. According to this view, Jesus did not consider himself as Messiah per se, but he did appropriate the title "Son of Man" for himself as a sign that he embodied, so to speak, the people of Israel in their suffering and eschatological triumph.

There are many other critical problems; two of the most important are the variances in the accounts of the resurrection and the meaning and function of the stories of the virgin birth in Matthew and Luke. Two consider-ations stand out: (1) Neither the virgin birth nor the resurrection of Jesus is a historical statement (though they may make references to history and historical conditions). They are, rather, affirmations of faith that arise out of the story of God's odyssey. (2) As such, they express themselves in their "natural" language, that of sacred history or myth.

The Message of Jesus

Jesus taught the arrival of God's rule in a manner that was paradoxical; that is, he often turned his audience on its head as he presented, in the most striking manner, sayings and parables that were either enigmatic or contrary to what his hearers expected. Often there is humor in his sayings ("straining at a gnat and swallowing a camel"), the humor that sees the pos-sibility of the world's transformation so that the "last" will end up "first" and vice-versa (Mark 10:31 and parallels). Or there is the well-known story of the tiny mustard seed, which is a parable of the Kingdom of God. Though tiny, when grown it is "the greatest of shrubs and becomes a tree, so that the birds of the air come and make nests in its branches" (Matthew 13:32). The mustard "tree" is actually a fairly small bush! But the Kingdom of God turns everything topsy-turvy; trees will be plants, plants will be trees.

Jesus's teachings and use of images are suggested in the variety of para-bles and proverbs. The Kingdom of God is like the joy of someone who finds a hidden treasure; the Kingdom of God is like the power of leaven in dough; the Kingdom of God is like a shepherd searching for a lost sheep; the Kingdom of God is like a great feast, to which the original invitees would not come, so that finally the poor were *compelled* to come in; the Kingdom of God is like the Jewish traveler who was shown unexpected compassion by a detested Samaritan.

The Christian Understanding of Scripture

The classical Christian understanding of the divine Word is based pri-marily on the prologue of the Gospel of John:

> And the Word (ho logos) *became flesh and pitched its tent among us, and we viewed his glory, glory as of the only son of the father, full of grace and truth.*

This translation of the Greek text shows the web of allusions to the Hebrew Bible. The Word is clearly God's utterance in creating (Genesis 1). It is simultaneously the wisdom by which God created (Proverbs 8). But the symbol of the Word had undoubtedly taken on a Hellenistic coloring, that of cosmic reason. "Pitched its tent" is reminiscent of God's presence coming to Israel in the tent; this divine presence cannot be controlled, but comes and goes. "Only son" is an allusion to the testing of Abraham, in which he was commanded to sacrifice his only son as an offering to God

(Genesis 22). Now God has given his Beloved as an offering to humanity.

Now, how does this verse in the Gospel of John help us see more clearly the dominant Christian understanding of scripture? In two ways. (1) Christian scripture is fundamentally an ongoing reinterpretation of Jewish scripture. (2) Christian scripture has its source and end in the "Word became flesh." Scripture, in principle, is the expression of the "we" of John 1:14: "We have beheld his glory." Scripture originates in the "witnesses of the presence." It became a principle in the church that canonical scripture was based historically on the apostolic witness. It is an important theological question for Christians whether scripture, as witness to the Word, can and should remain open because the Word may still "pitch its tent" here and there in human existence, making the witnesses also part of the Word.

METHODS OF INTERPRETATION

It is impossible here to present a complete essay on methods of interpretation fully illustrating Jewish, Christian, and Muslim methods of interpreting scripture. Thus selected examples of methods of interpretation will be presented under two headings: (1) traditional Christian interpretation of the Bible and (2) modern critical methods, which originated primarily among Protestant Christian scholars but now are widely accepted among Roman Catholics and Jews, and provide an *entree* for nonbelievers into Biblical studies. In both subdivisions of this discussion the Parable of the Good Samaritan, Luke 10:25–37, will be used as the illustrative text.

TRADITIONAL CHRISTIAN EXEGESIS

Traditional Christian *exegesis*—exposition or "leading out" of meaning from the text—shared much with Jewish and Muslim interpretive methods and concerns. In order to see themselves in the scriptures as a mirror for their identity, the church fathers developed methods to adapt the language of the past to the language of their own situations and concerns; the Word, after all, was never *passé*. These methods came to be known as literal, allegorical, moral, and anagogical. A bit of verse circulated as late as the sixteenth century illustrates these four "senses" of scripture:

> *Littera gesta docet, quid credas allegoria, Moralis guidagas, quo tendas anagogia.*
> [The letter shows us what God and our fathers did; the allegory shows us where our faith is hid; the moral meaning gives us rules of daily life; The anagogy shows us where we end our strife.][2]

In applying this traditional mode of interpretation to the Parable of the Good Samaritan, the *literal* sense would be what the text says. Perhaps the interpretation would include a discussion of its Greek vocabulary and grammar, as well as any relevant historical data. The actual geographic locations of Jerusalem and Jericho, the fact that Jews and Samaritans detested each other and that it would be extremely odd to find a Samaritan in Jewish territory—all are pertinent to the literal meaning.

Allegorically, the parable would have different hidden meanings that could be deduced by the sensitive interpreter. Jerusalem, for example, would be the City of God.

The *moral* sense of the parable is basically given in the context in which Luke places it. The believer is to imitate the deed of the Good Samaritan, as he or she is to imitate Christ.

The *anagogical* meaning is that which is the source and end of faith. Humankind has come from paradise ("Jerusalem"), has fallen, but if aided by God (the Samaritan) will return there. Anagogical interpretation is heavily dependent on allegory. It focuses on the ultimate meaning or hope for the believer.

The dominant mode of traditional Christian interpretation was allegorical. It enabled learned believers to feel that they could live relevantly in their own time while remaining faithful to the scriptural witnesses. Augustine's interpretation of the Good Samaritan is an apt example of allegory. Here is a selection from his exegetical notes: [3]

"A certain man":	Adam
"Jerusalem":	The city of God from which Adam fell
"Thieves":	The devil and his angels
"Left him half-dead":	Man is dead insofar as he lives in sin, alive insofar as he knows God
"Priest," "Levite":	Ministry of the Old Testament
"Samaritan":	"Guardian," the Lord himself
"Inn":	The Church
"Morrow":	After the Lord's resurrection

MODERN CRITICAL METHODS

Textual Criticism

Textual criticism entails establishing the language of the text, comparing manuscripts, delineating thoughts or ideas, and dividing the original text. Some of the most interesting textual criticism of the parable of the Good Samaritan has to do with the attempt to work out an Aramaic original of the parable. (The New Testament is in Greek, but Jesus and his earliest followers spoke Aramaic, which is closely related to Hebrew). This Aramaic would reflect word play on the Hebrew Bible and other Jewish sources. For example, to a Greek-speaking person "Samaritan" (*samarites*) would signify only someone from the city or province of Samaria. But to a Jew raised on the Hebrew Scripture, Samaritan (*shomroni*) would evoke a network of allusions, ranging from the enmity between Samaritan and Jew to the connotation of *shamar* ("keep, observe") and *shomer* ("keeper, shepherd") and including all that was historically associated with Samaria (*Shomron*) geographically and politically.

Source Criticism

Source criticism is one of the chief interpretative methods of the historian. It involves delineating relationships between different texts, hypothesizing concerning earlier documents or collections that lay behind the present texts, and tracing the relationship of historical events to the development of scripture.

In studying the Good Samaritan the source critic would note that the parable itself is found only in Luke and would be part of L (Luke's special source). But the context, the lawyer's questions (Luke 10:25–28), is paralleled in Matthew 22:34–40 and Mark 12:28–31. Matthew and Luke are presumably dependent on Mark, but the changes made by Luke are significant.

	Luke	*Mark*	*Matthew*
Questioner	* lawyer	* scribe	* Pharisee
Question	how to inherit eternal life	* supreme commandment	* greatest commandment
Question answered by	lawyer himself	* Jesus	* Jesus
Content of answer	* Deut. 6:5; Lev. 19:18	* Deut. 6:5; Lev. 19:18	* Deut. 6:5; Lev. 19:18
Concluding comment	Jesus: do this and you will live	no commandments greater than these	on these commandments depend the law and prophets

The asterisks (*) indicate that there is no essential difference among the Gospels. The absence of an asterisk indicates a significant difference, even if a given meaning is within the range of what the others say. In this instance Luke's "eternal life" is a non-Jewish expression presupposing a Graeco-Roman audience. The lawyer in Luke answers his own question and answers it well; Luke's Gospel shows that the "answers" were already to be found among the Jews. Yet the concluding comment that Jesus makes in Luke presupposes an attempt to remove Christianity from the context of the Jewish ethos. Incidentally, the concluding comment in Matthew is illustrative of Matthew's continual, overt effort to show how Jesus and his message fulfill the law and the prophets.

Form Criticism

The emergence of form criticism early in the twentieth century had a tremendous impact on Biblical studies. Form criticism asks about the form of smaller literary units employed by the authors, their prior circulation (often oral), and the setting (*Sitz in Leben,* "seat in life") in which they arose.

The Good Samaritan has a controversy setting in Luke, although we can see how Luke has attenuated it by casting a rather favorable light on the Jewish lawyer. The original setting of the lawyer's question would have been a situation—either the situation of Jesus or that of early congregations—in which Jewish opponents of the newly born movement in Judaism questioned the basis of the new religious way in the Hebrew Bible. The setting as established in the Gospels prepares the way for Jesus to make a pronouncement. These pronouncements, whether actually uttered by Jesus or not, would have great authority in Christianity.

But Luke does not stop there. The lawyer asks, "Who is my neighbor?" so Jesus replies with the parable. The parable itself comprises only verses 30–35; verses 25–28 and 36–37 form Luke's context (vv. 25–28 were revised from Mark). The parable itself is a kind of *midrash* in the form of a folk tale. As such, it obeys many of the laws of the folk tale: All the characters are anonymous; sets of three (priest, Levite, Samaritan; had compassion, bound wounds, poured on oil and wine) are frequent; the situation is one of danger or extreme need. The story is different from the usual folk tale in that it is extremely brief; the initial subject (the traveler) receives little attention and is in no sense "heroic"; and the helper (the Samaritan) is an outsider who would not usually be accepted in the world of folk tale. Form criticism would result in the conclusion that the parable is so distinctive that it must come from Jesus (such tales are not invented by the folk) or someone on whom Jesus left his mark.

Redaction Criticism

The redaction critic is concerned with the formal redaction (editing) of a literary work. He or she shifts the emphasis from smaller units (as in form criticism) to the theological perspective and setting of the final editor/redactor of a work.

Redaction criticism would place the Good Samaritan within the context of the Gospel of Luke as a whole. After drawing upon the work of textual, source, and form critics, the redaction critic would point out the shift in Luke-Acts (originally one work) from a specifically Jewish setting while it simultaneously draws on the Jewish tradition as the sacred history prior to Jesus Christ. So the lawyer's question is asked in a Hellenistic manner; a Jew would have said, "What shall I do to inherit the world to come?" (*olam ha-ba*). The compassionate helper in the parable is a non-Jew, which fits in well with the Lucan emphasis on the universal presence of God (see Acts 17:28) and the mission to the gentiles.

Literary-Structural Criticism

Literary-structural criticism is so named here because it is concerned with literary expression and structure in and behind the text. "Literary critic" and "structural critic" could be distinct, even separate, but often the interpreter who does one of these two kinds of criticism also does the other. The kinds of methodology already discussed, while varying in focus, are all the offspring of historical study. Literary-structural criticism is more concerned with enduring structures and the relationship of literary form to human experience and religious expression.

The problem in discussing this method is that it is relatively new in Biblical criticism and there is still much disagreement on basic points. It is so important, however, that one brief example of the method is given here, namely, one particular form of literary-structural criticism that entails analysis of narrative in terms of roles. There are six basic roles: sender, subject, object, recipient, helper, and opponent. In the Good Samaritan parable the roles can be identified in the initial sequence (vv. 30–32) as follows:

Sender:	? (God?)
Subject:	traveler
Object:	to reach Jericho
Recipient:	?
Helper:	donkey; (the priest and the Levite)
Opponent:	robbers

But this sequence aborts because the possible helpers, the priest and the Levite, "pass by on the other side." A new, successful sequence begins thus:

Sender:	?
Subject:	Samaritan
Object:	health of traveler
Recipient:	wounded traveler
Helper:	ability of Samaritan, oil, wine, donkey, innkeeper, etc.
Opponent:	robbers and effects of beating and theft.

The story of "some man" going down to Jericho, robbed, beaten, left half-dead by robbers, then not receiving help from the clergy becomes the story of a detested outsider who graciously aids an insider, and we are not informed why an outsider (Samaritan) would be in our territory in the first place. The ideal religious person, the "keeper" or "shepherd" (Samaritan), and the thieves are all outsiders. There are outsiders who break in and rob and those who enter in to help and heal. The parable invites the hearer to see himself or herself as the Samaritan; this is not to imitate but to *become* the Samaritan in one's own context.

Midrash Criticism

Midrash is a Hebrew word that means "seeking, exposition," specifically, interpretation of scripture. Midrash criticism seeks out the way in which some Biblical stories and passages are commentaries on other Biblical stories and passages, even if this is not explicit. Indeed, it is often a matter of allusions, and probably at times they are deliberately subtle and ironic.

Luke 10:25–37 is, as it stands, a sort of midrash on Deuteronomy 6. Eternal life is a matter of living Deuteronomy 6:5 as well as Leviticus 19:18. But the lawyer sought to put Jesus "to the test" (Luke 10:25), whereas the Israelites were warned not to "put the Lord your God to the test" (Deuteronomy 6:16). For Luke, the "Lord" of Deuteronomy 6:16 was an earlier type of Jesus Christ. Inheriting the promised land (Deuteronomy 6:18) is a foreshadowing or earlier type of inheriting eternal life (Luke 10:25, 28). In Deuteronomy Israel is told to "be careful to do" the words of the Lord (Deuteronomy 6:3). Now the "careful one" appears as the *shomroni*, Samaritan, in Jesus's story (Luke 10:30–35). Or is the *shomroni* the Shepherd of Psalm 23?

If one were to pursue midrash criticism of Luke, it would demonstrate that the whole of Luke's central section, 9:51–18:43, is a midrash on the Book of Deuteronomy. Jesus is presented as the New Moses, fulfilling Deuteronomy 18:15.

SUMMARY

In summary, scripture is the sacred literature of a religious community, sometimes conveyed in a language that itself is believed to be sacred. Scripture originates in times of community crisis. Through it the most pressing questions are asked, while at the same time it supports and maintains the convictions of the people. People in the community believe the scripture to be of divine origin and find their own personal and cultural story—and thus their identity—mirrored in that literature. As students of religion we seek to understand scripture as though we were members of the community. At the same time, we seek a historical perspective and attempt to interpret scripture by using all of the scholarly methods available to us.

NOTES

1. See James Sanders, *Torah and Canon* (Philadelphia: Fortress Press, 1976), p. xvi.
2. R. M. Grant, *A Short History of the Interpretation of the Bible* (New York: Macmillan, 1963), p. 119.
3. C. M. Dodd, *The Parables of the Kingdom* (New York: Scribners, 1961), pp. 1–2.

QUESTIONS FOR STUDY, REFLECTION, AND DISCUSSION

1. State in your own words the understanding of scripture presented in this chapter. Be prepared to give an example of one or two writings that function as scripture, whether or not they are usually viewed as "religious."

2. What are some of the connections between the three scripture religions? It may aid you to begin with reflecting on the way the Qur'an views Jesus and Moses, continuing with the ways the New Testament views the scriptures of Israel.

3. Sometimes people within a religious tradition resent anyone making a historical-critical study of their scriptures. They believe that the uniqueness and sacredness of the holy writings are destroyed by such a study. In a discussion group, cooperate in listing and developing supportive arguments favoring a historical-critical study. Then make a list with supporting arguments opposing such a study. Then see if there is any consensus in the group regarding which position is the strongest and why.

PROJECTS

1. The author makes the following associations:
   Qur'an—scripture religion—Messenger of God.
   New Testament—basically avatar religion—God became flesh.
   Hebrew Bible—basically scripture religion—Messengers of God.
   Write an essay in which you explain why such associations are made and provide a justification for those associations.

2. The author stated that the Torah is teaching, which comprehends mythos and ethos. Expand this theme into an essay or a topic for a group discussion.

3. Controversy continues, especially in Christianity, about scriptural interpretation. Those who are called literalists insist that each word is inspired by God and is literally true. Thus no interpretation is needed. The opposing group claims that every spoken or written word must be interpreted if it is to be meaningful. Organize a simulation game in your class in which all the members are part of a PTA in a local high school. The issue being discussed is as follows: The school has decided to introduce an elective course for seniors entitled "The Bible as Literature." What approach should be taken in teaching this course, and what methods of interpretation should be used?

4. Reread Luke 10:25–37. Decide which method of interpretation is most helpful in understanding the parable. Write a paper in which you give a

thorough interpretation according to the method you adopt. Explain why you chose that particular method of interpretation.

SELECTED BIBLIOGRAPHY

Bruce, F. F., and E. G. Rupp, eds. *Holy Book and Holy Tradition*. Grand Rapids, Mich.: Eerdmans, 1968.

Buttrick, G., ed. *The Interpreter's Bible, vol. I: General Articles on Israel's History and Scripture*. Nashville, Tenn.: Abingdon, 1952.

———, ed. *The Interpreter's Dictionary of the Bible, vol. I, Canon of the Old Testament*. Nashville, Tenn.: Abingdon, 1962.

Dodd, C. H. *The Parables of the Kingdom*. New York: Scribners, 1961.

Freehof, S. B. *Preface to Scripture: A Guide to the Understanding of the Bible in Accordance with the Jewish Tradition*. New York: Union of American Hebrew Congregations, 1950.

Gibb, H. R., and J. H. Kramers, eds. "Kuran," in *Shorter Encyclopedia of Islam*. Ithaca, N.Y.: Cornell University Press, 1953.

Grant, R. M. *A Short History of the Interpretation of the Bible*. New York: Macmillan, 1963.

Hereford, T. *The Ethics of the Talmud: Pirke Aboth*. New York: Schocken Books, 1962.

Laymon, Charles M., ed. *The Interpreter's One-Volume Commentary on the Bible*. Nashville, Tenn.: Abingdon, 1971.

Montefiore, C. G., and H. Loewe, eds. *A Rabbinic Anthology*. New York: Schocken Books, 1974.

Nasr, Seyyed H. *Ideals and Realities of Islam*. Boston: Beacon Press, 1972.

Patte, Daniel. *What is Structural Exegesis?* Philadelphia: Fortress Press, 1976.

Rahman, Fazlur. *Islam*. Garden City, N.Y.: Doubleday, 1968.

Rowley, Harold H. *The Growth of the Old Testament*. New York: Harper & Row, 1963.

Sanders, James A. *Torah and Canon*. Philadelphia: Fortress Press, 1972.

———. "Torah and Christ." *Interpretation* 29 (1975).

———. "The Banquet of the Dispossessed," in J. L. Crenshaw and J. T. Willis, eds., *Essays in Old Testament Ethics*. New York: Ktav, 1974.

Van Der Leeuw, G. *Religion in Essence and Manifestation*. New York: Harper, & Row, 1963, vol. II.

CHAPTER 7

Art

JAMES W. KARMAN

Imagine for a moment that you are inside a cave. You have just turned a corner and can no longer see the opening through which you entered. There is still some light, but the cave is dim; farther down the passageway all you see is blackness. It is cold and damp. You hear, faintly, the echo of drops of water falling into a pool; somewhere, far within the earth, the water moves—each drop adds to those that have fallen for centuries. Just as the silence, the mystery, the fearsomeness begin to overcome you, you see on the cave wall the print of a human hand. Its sudden appearance before your eyes both chills and warms you.

The print is like those found in caves all over the world. Africa, Europe, and North America all have caves in which humans, as many as 30,000 years ago, self-consciously pressed their palms against the wall. Some scholars say that in such prints we can find the beginning of art.

In France, for instance, there is a cave called Gargas in which over 150 hand prints have been found. Two techniques were used to make them. Either the hand was smeared with black or red mud and then pressed against the stone, or the hand was placed against the stone first and then "paint" was blown around it. The first technique would produce a positive image; the second, a negative one. We do not know who the people were who placed their hand prints there nor what their lives were like, but we do know that they forever changed the cave in which they stood. Their works of art—simple, direct, powerfully expressive—endowed the cave with human presence. For thousands and thousands of years their hand prints have extended a silent greeting to any fellow human being who has entered into their midst.

Imagine that this is the cave into which you have come. You look at the prints in bewilderment, perhaps in awe. You begin to wonder about the people who had moved among these passages so many years before. You can almost hear the echoes of their voices, the sound of their feet on the stone. You look closely at one of the prints and then place your own hand against it, realizing that just as you are reaching out to it the print is reaching out to you.

This is one of the mysteries of art. It opens up the possibility of communication between people who are separated by distances of space or time. The print on the cave wall reaches out to you with a message perhaps as simple as "Look, I too was human. I stood where you are standing 30,000 years ago; remember me." For your part, you are reaching out toward and making contact with a person you could never know except through the print that he or she has left. You are reaching out toward and entering into someone else's experience of life. What you take from this contact is up to your own powers of empathy, intelligence, and imagination.

In some ways it is a long step from a hand print on a cave wall to Michelangelo's frescoes in the Sistine Chapel, but in other ways it is a short one. If we can say that art is tied, in part, to humankind's desire to give expression to the experience of life, to the desire to reveal the meaning it has found, or to the desire to commemorate its presence in the world, then we can say that there is a similarity between the simplest form of expression and the most complex. We can also say that the Sistine Chapel, with all its complicated majesty, reaches out to us with the same straightforward gesture as the print on the cave wall. The frescoes that adorn the chapel provide us with the opportunity to enter into the world of the artist and his or her time and to return to our own time with a deepened understanding of what it means to be human in this world.

In the following pages these and other characteristics of art will be discussed within the context of three main themes, (1) "Art, Religion, and Culture: The Concept of Style," (2) "The Artistic Style of Our Time," and (3) "Art as an Expression of Faith." We will focus primarily on the visual arts—painting, sculpture, and architecture—but we will refer to other arts as well. This chapter is designed not to answer all questions about the relationship between religion and art but to open avenues for further thought.

ART, RELIGION, AND CULTURE: THE CONCEPT OF STYLE

If one desires to understand the spirit and inner life of a people, one must look at its art, literature, philosophy, dances, and music, where the spirit of the whole people is reflected.   —WILLIAM FLEMING, *Arts and Ideas*

When we make ourselves aware of the history of human life, we realize that people in different times and places have interpreted life differently. We also realize that these differences are reflected in artifacts that are left behind. Just as the Parthenon tells us something about ancient Greece and Chartres Cathedral tells us something about medieval France, the Empire State Building tells us something about ourselves. Thus the art of a culture, whether it takes the form of painting, sculpture, or architecture, reveals something about the "spirit and inner life"—in short, the religion—of a culture.

At the beginning of our reflection on art, religion, and culture we should remind ourselves of the definition of religion proposed in the opening chapters of this book. It was suggested that religion is "the varied, symbolic expression of, and appropriate response to, that which people deliberately affirm as being of unrestricted value for them." This definition can be applied to three areas of human experience.

It can be applied, for instance, to the effort each of us must make to find meaning in our lives. Though we might not always think about them, such questions as, Why was I born? What am I supposed to do? and What is the meaning of things? provide a backdrop for our day-to-day experiences. The ideas we think about, the goals we pursue, the values we have, even the clothes we wear are tied to our personal attempt to make sense of our existence.

The definition can also be used to describe something that organized religions have in common. Religious traditions like Judaism, Christianity, or Buddhism offer people a way of understanding and affirming the aspect of life that has "unrestricted value." When a person joins a religious community or continues to affiliate with the religion in which he or she was raised, we can say that that person affirms what the tradition represents. Every religious tradition provides its believers with answers to the basic questions about life, and the believers, accepting these answers, subscribe to the meaning that is contained in them.

Finally, the definition can help us understand the religious dimensions of cultural life. *Culture,* according to one dictionary, refers to "the sum total of ways of living built up by a group of human beings and transmitted from one generation to another." *Culture,* therefore, is a word used to describe the distinctive identity a group of people has; its meaning is reflected in such adjectives as *ancient Roman, American,* or *Japanese.* A culture has a distinctive identity because it too is shaped by the answers it gives to the basic questions about existence, answers that are revealed in all areas of creativity. The spirit and inner life of a culture, we have said, is reflected in its art, literature, philosophy, dances, and music. It is also reflected in its social structure and value system.

The way a culture gives expression to its experience of life can shift and change over time. For instance, the Revolutionary War, the Civil War, the period during which the settlers moved west, the first half of the twentieth century, and the present moment all contribute to the history of the American people. Each period not only has its own distinctive identity but also adds to the American identity as a whole. When we seek to understand American culture, therefore, we have to define the limits of our inquiry—we can focus on a particular period or try to consider the entire history.

In either case, when we ask ourselves what characteristics define a certain group of people we are asking an essentially religious question. Wanting to know what knowledge a group of people possessed, what values they had, what things made them afraid or happy takes us into the area of their unrestricted value, or what Paul Tillich calls their "ultimate concern"—the area in which religion and culture become one. As Tillich has said, "Religion as ultimate concern is the meaning-giving substance of culture, and culture is the totality of forms in which the basic concern of religion expresses itself." Tillich refines this idea into the following formula: "Religion is the substance of culture, culture the form of religion."[1] The meaning of this statement should become apparent in the pages ahead.

One of the ways we can define and interpret the ultimate concern of a culture is to study its art. A study of other aspects of cultural life—philosophy or science, for instance—would also provide us with insight. But art takes us to the heart of a culture most quickly. It is somehow able, better than anything else, to express the general needs, fears, and values that are behind everything the culture is and does. As Tillich says in an essay titled "The World Situation," "The aesthetic realm always furnishes the most sensitive barometer of a spiritual climate."[2] By "spiritual climate" he means any cultural situation in which men and women are struggling to articulate the meaning of their experience of life.

The ideas behind two words, *paradigm* and *style*, might help us see the relationship between art, religion, and culture more clearly.

For a straightforward definition of the word *paradigm* one should turn to a dictionary (where it is defined as an example, a pattern, or a model), but for an understanding of the role paradigms have in human consciousness one should turn to Thomas Kuhn's book *The Structure of Scientific Revolutions*.[3] Although Kuhn restricts himself therein to a discussion of the function paradigms have in scientific communities, his findings can be and have been applied to other spheres as well. His work is especially relevant to the study of art, religion, and culture.

According to Kuhn, a paradigm represents a way of "seeing" the world. For scientists, this means that professional inquiries begin with a set of assumptions about reality. These assumptions determine the scope and direction of exploration and experimentation. An example would be the Ptolemaic system of astronomy. Ptolemy's system, in which the earth was believed to be the center of the universe, was paradigmatic for 1300 years (ca. 200–1500 A.D.)

An important characteristic of paradigms, Kuhn points out, is the way one paradigm gives way to another. A paradigm is believed in until evidence begins to appear that calls its validity into question. At this time a crisis develops and continues until a new paradigm—one that solves the emerging problems—can be set forth. The realization that Ptolemy's system was incorrect, for instance, caused a crisis that the Polish astronomer Copernicus had to overcome. Copernicus, as we know, argued that the earth revolves around the sun. Though this is obvious to us today, his way of seeing the world—his paradigm—caused a revolution in human consciousness. Albert Einstein's theories have had a similar effect during our time.

The concept of paradigms is especially useful for our purposes because it gives us a tool for approaching culture. It enables us to fix the horizons of a particular world view and to explore how it affected the lives of the people who believed in it. Also, with the idea of transiency of paradigms in mind and recognizing the crises that necessarily result, we are better able to understand moments when people have felt that they were stranded with nothing to believe in, moments when—as we will see in the next section of this chapter—people have felt that they were suspended over an abyss with no support from the past and no certainty about the future.

If we say that a paradigm is a way of seeing the world, then we can say that *style* refers to the way this vision is expressed in a culture. In England's history, for instance, there was a period (ca. 1660) during which the scientist Isaac Newton, the philosopher John Locke, the poets John Dryden and Alexander Pope, the musician Henry Purcell, and the architect Christopher Wren all shared as their paradigm the belief that natural laws govern every aspect of life and that these laws can be discovered by human reason. This way of seeing the world expressed itself outwardly in a concern for order, harmony, and decorum—a concern that helped give this period its characteristic style. We can also refer back to our discussion of the moment of crisis in a culture's history when it has no paradigm to believe in. This too would manifest itself in a characteristic style. Style would be exhibited in the way a culture manages itself when it is faced with the meaninglessness of its conceptions.

The idea of cultural style is important to Tillich. He writes that

every style points to a self-interpretation of man, thus answering the question of the ultimate meaning of life. Whatever the subject matter which an artist chooses, however strong or weak his artistic form, he cannot help but betray by his style his own ultimate concern, as well as that of his group, and his period. He cannot escape religion even if he rejects religion, for religion is the state of being ultimately concerned. And in every style the ultimate concern of a human group or period is manifest.[4]

Karl Kerenyi, an author of several books about ancient Greece and Rome, agrees with Tillich. In outlining his approach to religion he stresses his concern for style. According to Kerenyi, a culture represents *bios*, that is, "characterized existence." This is distinguished from the other Greek word for life, *zoon*, which means "an unspecified living thing." A culture *is* something; it has its own way of life, its own particular personality. To summarize his views, Kerenyi says, "Myths and doctrines, rites and institutions, ways of life and community, pictures and buildings—all . . . exhibit a style."⁵ The task, then, as Kerenyi sets it for himself, is to discern the religious attitude of a culture as it is evidenced in that culture's style. This is, of course, a task we can set for ourselves as well.

THE ARTISTIC STYLE OF OUR TIME

It happens that the stage sets collapse. Rising, streetcar, rising, streetcar, four hours in the office or factory, meal, streetcar, four hours of work, meal, sleep, and Monday Tuesday Wednesday Thursday Friday and Saturday according to the same rhythm—this path is easily followed most of the time. But one day the "why" arises and everything begins in that weariness tinged with amazement.

ALBERT CAMUS, *The Myth of Sisyphus*

When, as individuals, we are suddenly confronted with the "why" of our existence we react, according to Camus, with weariness and amazement— amazement because we might think the question is presumptuous or somehow irrelevant, weariness because we immediately sense the burden that has been placed on us. How can we answer such a question, and how, without an answer, can we continue in the tedium of our daily lives?

When, as a culture, we are suddenly confronted with the "why" of our existence, a similar reaction occurs. Scientific and technological advancements, crowded cities, worldwide wars and localized battles, hunger, and widespread misery have all been part of our experience in the twentieth century. When we ask ourselves "why" it is difficult to find an answer. In fact most of the thinkers and artists of our time have said that there is no answer.

Camus suggests, however, that there have been times when people have lived within a view of the world that has provided their lives with meaning, a view of the world that is represented by a faith like Christianity, for example. Recalling Shakespeare's line, "All the world's a stage," we can say that it has been possible, at times, for people to experience themselves as living within a drama, a drama that has character, plot, and significance. But, Camus would add, this has become impossible in our time. We have realized, suddenly, that the drama into which we have been born is only make-believe; we have discovered that the scenes that have surrounded us—the ones that enclosed our lives and gave them meaning—are composed only of canvas and paint. "It happens," he says, "that the stage sets collapse." It has been widely held that we as modern men and women have suddenly found ourselves on a stage with no story, with no purpose, with nothing to do or to say, and with no reason for being here at all.

These are dark and troublesome thoughts—yet these are the thoughts

that have preoccupied the thinkers and artists of our time and have contributed to the formation of our "characteristic style."

We find such thoughts expressed early in this century in the work of a group of men and women who called themselves "Dadaists." Dadaism was a philosophical and artistic movement that flourished between 1916 and 1922, during and just after World War I. The artists who belonged to this movement were disillustioned by the war. The senseless slaughter of millions of people, the destruction of villages and cities all over Europe, and the general loss of human self-respect all contributed to their belief that life has no meaning. They chose their name, Dada, after one of their members thumbed through a French dictionary and stopped, by accident, on the page where this word was found. The word means "hobbyhorse" and carries the connotation of childishness and nonsensicality. This fit perfectly with the aims of the group; the Dadaists were playful, destructive, serious, funny, and belligerent, all at once.

In essays titled "Dada Manifesto" and "Lecture on Dada," Tristan Tzara, a poet who was also a spokesman for the group, stated some of the group's primary concerns. Reflecting the attitude he and his friends had toward life generally, Tzara says, "The beginnings of Dada were not the beginnings of art, but of a disgust"—a disgust with all the artists and thinkers over the centuries who have made us believe that things are better than they are and a disgust with the way our leaders, in all areas of life, have consistently used and abused us. An antidote to this situation, Tzara believed, was to sweep aside all pretensions and forms of oppression and to begin anew with spontaneity and complete freedom. Existence, after all, is absurd—"The acts of life have no beginning and no end. Everything happens in a completely idiotic way." He adds, "There is no ultimate truth."

Accordingly, the concerns of the Dadaists were nihilistic (extremely skeptical) in principle and anarchistic (destructive of existing order) in action. Tzara defines Dada as "a protest with the fists of its whole being engaged in destructive action" and asserts, militantly, that "I destroy the drawers of the brain and of social organization: spread demoralization wherever I go." His methods of destruction, however, were not those of physical force. Rather, through the deliberate debasement of art and through the conscious pursuit of the unbeautiful and the commonplace, he and his friends attempted to shock their contemporaries into realizing that "everything one looks at is false" and that "everything in life . . . is useless."

Tzara says to his readers, "You explain to my why you exist," and adds, "You haven't the faintest idea." Such requests and statements are destructive in that they are deeply disturbing. They call into question our understanding of who we are. Tzara adds, mockingly, "You will never be able to tell me why you exist but you will always be ready to maintain a serious attitude about life."

The Dadaists played with seriousness. Marcel Duchamp exhibited toilet

fixtures, bottle racks, and open doorways as sculpture. Jean/Hans Arp made biomorphically shaped constructions out of pieces of wood that he painted and glued together. Kurt Schwitters made collages out of wine labels, newspaper clippings, and strokes of paint. The work of each of these men and of all the other artists who gathered under the banner of Dadaism sought to be both playful and enigmatic. As such, their work attempted to overthrow any pretensions that we might have about either life or art. In one symbolic gesture Duchamp added a moustache and a beard to a reproduction of Da Vinci's "Mona Lisa." His addition produces an effect that is both funny and disconcerting. According to Tzara, this kind of effect was exactly what he and his friends were after. As he says, summarizing the aims of the group, "Nothing is more delightful than to confuse and upset people."[6]

Perhaps it would be good for us if we could dismiss the work of the Dadaists as an isolated phenomenon that lost currency when the group disbanded in 1922. But the fact is that the ideas of the Dadaists survived and continued to have influence throughout the twentieth century. Their ideas, in fact, have never been more influential than in recent years. Much of the art that has been produced since 1960 (e.g., Pop Art, Minimal Art, Conceptual Art) can be called Neo-Dadaist in character insofar as much of this art recapitulates Dadaist themes.

Pop Art, a movement that flourished throughout the Sixties, can be taken as a case in point. Andy Warhol, for instance, a leader in the Pop movement, was aware of the connection between his work and the work of Tzara and his friends. He says in an interview that "Dada must have something to do with Pop—it's so funny, the names are really synonyms."[7] Warhol's preoccupation with commonplace objects, objects that we would not normally associate with art, gives credence to this claim. Just as Duchamp exhibited bicycle wheels and bottle racks, Warhol painted pictures of Campbell soup cans, Brillo boxes, and Coca-Cola bottles. And just as Duchamp's work contains a hard edge of cynicism, Warhol's playfulness hides a more somber comment on the emptiness, artificiality, and absurdity of our time.

We find Dadaist themes expressed in the words and works of other Pop artists as well. Robert Indiana's assessment of the troubled life of modern men and women is Dadaist in tone. As he says, Pop art conveys "the artist's superb intuition that modern man, with his loss of identity, submersion in mass culture, beset by mass destruction, is man's greatest problem." He adds, again characteristically, that "art, Pop or otherwise, hardly provides the Solution." Robert Rauschenberg, whose collages owe a debt to the work of Kurt Schwitters, echoes a Dadaist principle when he says, "It is extremely important that art be unjustifiable." Larry Rivers reports that he feels an "embarrassment with seriousness," an attitude that is also reflected in the cartoon strip art of Roy Lichtenstein. Finally, Claes Olden-

berg reveals a Dadaist disposition when he says, "I am for an art that takes its form from the lines of life itself, that twists and extends and accumulates and spits and drips, and is heavy and coarse and blunt and stupid as life itself." Among other kinds of art that he affirms, he adds, "I am for an art that grows up not knowing it is art at all."[8]

Since the Sixties more and more art has been produced that would seem to fit Oldenberg's description. The twisted pieces of metal that we see both inside and outside galleries, the chairs covered with grass and debris, the wall hangings made of string and little trinkets, the paintings that appear to have no identifiable content—all seem uncertain of their status as works of art. One critic suggests that this points to a crisis in our time:

The artist who has left art behind—or what amounts to the same thing—who regards anything he makes or does as art, is an expression of the profound crisis that has overtaken the arts in our epoch. Painting, sculpture, drama, music, have been undergoing a process of de-definition. The nature of art has become uncertain. At least it is ambiguous. No one can say with assurance what a work of art is—or, more important, what is not a work of art. Where an art object is still present, as in painting, it is what I have called an anxious object: it does not know whether it is a masterpiece or junk.[9]

This crisis—which is part of our experience today—is not something that has happened overnight. Early in the century the Dadaists gave expression to ideas that many of their contemporaries shared. The Surrealists—Max Ernst, Giorgio de Chirico, Salvadore Dali, and others—developed the ideas of the Dadaists and took them a step further. T. S. Eliot, a poet who surveyed the contemporary situation from his own perspective, pronounced our world a wasteland. "We are the hollow men/ We are the stuffed men/ leaning together/ Headpiece filled with straw"[10] he said of us, describing our lack of inner substance. The playwright and novelist Samuel Beckett explored the strangeness of our condition in his play *Waiting for Godot*. Vladimir and Estragon, the play's two main characters, do not seem to know where they have come from, what they are doing, or where they are going. They only know that they are waiting for something to happen or for someone to come. At the end of each of the two acts in the play, one of them says "Well, shall we go?" The other answers, "Yes, let's go." But the stage directions say, "They do not move."

This kind of experience of life leads a character in one of Jean-Paul Sartre's novels to a deep-seated feeling of nausea. Sartre was one of the leaders in the philosophical and artistic movement known as Existentialism. This view also leads a character in one of Albert Camus's books to commit a capital crime. The title of Camus's novel is *The Stranger*, a title that is suggestive of alienation and despair. In *The Myth of Sisyphus* Camus describes the absurdity of the human condition. Sisyphus, a figure of Greek mythology, is condemned to forever roll a boulder up a hill. Just as he gets to the top the boulder rolls back down the hill and he has to start all over again.

In the next section of this chapter we will perhaps find an antidote to the disturbing nature of these thoughts. Now, however, one more observation needs to be made. Previously we said that the way a culture sees the world (through a paradigm) is reflected in the culture's style. We also said that when a culture experiences itself as living in a crisis situation its style will reflect the turmoil it is going through. The arts will give expression to the situation as it is, and they will give evidence of a search for conceptions that will stabilize and sustain the culture's life. As Conrad Aiken writes,

> We need a theme? then let that be our theme:
> that we, poor grovellers between faith and doubt,
> the sun and north star lost, and compass out,
> the heart's weak engine all but stopped, the time
> timeless in this chaos of our wills—
> that we must ask a theme, something to think,
> something to say, between dawn and dark,
> something to hold to, something to love. [11]

The theme (or paradigm/style) of our time, it seems, is that we are asking for, looking for a theme, a theme that will answer our questions—especially the question "why"—and in some measure give authenticity and meaning to our existence.

ART AS AN EXPRESSION OF FAITH

1. The breaking up of the soulless-material life of the nineteenth century; that is the falling down of the material supports which were thought to be the only firm ones, the decay and dissolution of the individual parts.

2. The building up of the pyshic-spiritual life of the twentieth century which we are experiencing and which manifests itself even now in strong, expressive, and definite forms.

These two procedures are the two sides of "today's movement."

—WASSILY KANDINSKY, *Concerning the Spiritual in Art*

"Poetry," Wallace Stevens says in the title of one of his poems, "is a destructive force." Poetry—indeed, all the arts—can disturb the consciousness of an individual or of a culture; it can knock down or undermine the "supports" of human life (such as the basic ideas a person has about existence). "It can," in short, "kill a man." [12] On the other hand, as Stevens has also said, "The poem refreshes life." He adds, "The poem, through candor, brings back a power again/ That gives a candid kind to everything." [13] Poetry—all the arts—can help us see things in such a way that our vision of life is deepened and transformed; it can lead us to what Stevens calls "a new knowledge of reality." [14]

These observations about art are recapitulated in Kandinsky's words. As a modern artist surveying his cultural situation, he saw that many of his associates were engaged in an attempt to tear things down. At the same time, however, he perceived that other artists, artists like himself, were engaged in efforts that could be called constructive. Art, Kandinsky believed, can deepen and enrich the inner life of man. As he says in another passage, "Painting is an art, and art is not vague production, transitory and isolated, but a power which must be directed to the development and refinement of the human soul." A work of art, he says, "has a definite and purposeful strength"; it has the "power to create spiritual atmosphere." He adds that "if art rejects this work, a pit remains unbridged; no other power can take the place of art in this activity." [15]

A study of art, from prehistoric to modern times, lends support to Kandinsky's position. Throughout the ages men and women have responded to the mysterious power of art, the power that enables it to give expression to what we have called "ultimate concerns." We see this most clearly in the art that has been produced within organized religious traditions. Such faiths as Christianity, Hinduism, and Buddhism, for instance, have depended on art to help create a "spiritual atmosphere" in which believers can live. Church and temple architecture and the sculpture that often adorns it, paintings of holy men and women or of the gods (or God), carefully crafted objects that are used in rituals—all contribute to the creation of an environment in which the "faith" of a religious tradition can be experienced and affirmed.

Art that is part of a religious tradition can be divided into two main categories: didactic and sacramental. Before discussing these two categories, however, it should be observed that distinctions between them, on close examination, would be difficult to maintain.

The function of didactic art is to teach. Every religious tradition needs to instruct its members (and potential converts) in matters concerning the faith. The history of the tradition, the important figures, both human and divine, who are associated with it, its ideas about life—all need to be communicated. Creeds can be formulated to accomplish this end; explanations can be offered; books can be written; stories can be told; but religious traditions have also found that in matters of instruction a picture can be worth 1000 words.

Key doctrines of a faith, for instance, need to be expressed in a way that appeals both to the intellect and to the emotions. The aim is to involve people existentially in that which is claimed to be true. Thus the explusion of Adam and Eve from the Garden of Eden, an important tenet of the Christian faith, has considerable impact when rendered in visual terms. When we look at a painting of this theme—the one by Massacio, for instance—we feel the torment of the couple and we learn something about the consequences of their act. The same can be said for other key doctrines. Representations of the crucifixion of Christ, in which we see him hanging on a cross and bleeding from his wounds, force us to participate in the suffering he bears. Likewise, representations of the Resurrection enable believers to witness Christ's triumph over death, and representations of the Last Judgment, the time when Christ is expected to return to judge the living and the dead, present us with vivid images of heaven and hell.

Other religious traditions also depend on art to communicate key doctrines or ideas. Zen Buddhism seeks to instill in its practitioners a sense of tranquillity and reserve. It values harmonious involvement with nature, depth of mind, and freedom from attachment to things. It aims to lead those who follow its path to self-awareness or complete awakening. Works of art that have been created by Zen masters, therefore, give expression to these themes, as we can see in the delicate Japanese landscapes and still lifes rendered by Sesshū or Mu-Ch'i.

Religious traditions have also found it necessary to teach people about the history of the faith. To meet this need, important events and the people associated with them have been brought to life in pictures. The journey of the Magi to the manger at Bethlehem and the subsequent adoration of the baby Jesus have been favorite themes in Christian art. Representations of each of the twelve disciples—rendered most dramatically in paintings of the Last Supper and most notably in the one by Da Vinci—have also been important. In addition, portraits of the writers of the Gospels and paintings of scenes from the lives of the saints (such as St. George's slaying of the dragon) have served the purpose of instruction.

We find the didactic function of religious art at work in representations of divine figures as well. Portraits of Jesus, for instance, have played an important role in the lives of many Christians. Just as our knowledge of a person can be deepened and enriched when we see a picture of his or her face, a Christian's experience of Jesus can be deepened when he or she encounters his image in a portrait. In Buddhism paintings and statues of the Buddha have served a similar function. Although the Buddha was a man and was first considered a spiritual teacher, in some locations he was eventually worshiped as divine. His familiar pose—seated calmly, knowingly, in the lotus position—presents Buddhists with an image of "one who is awake." In Hinduism also, where such gods as Shiva and Vishnu are worshiped, representations of divine figures have been essential to instruction in the faith.

Instruction can become induction, however, and it often happens that a person who encounters an image of a divine figure finds himself or herself deeply involved in the spiritual reality that the picture represents. It is in this kind of experience that we find the sacramental function of religious art at work.

A *sacrament* is a "religious act, ceremony, or practice that is considered especially sacred as a sign or symbol of a deeper reality." In the Christian faith the word is used to refer to several ritual actions that were instituted either by Jesus himself or by the church. An example would be the bread and wine that is offered during Communion. But the word also has a broader meaning. It refers to "something that is sacred in character or significance" and implies that things of this world—bread, wine, an image of a divine figure—can stand for something more. Thus, something that is sacramental has the quality of being two things at once. It is what it is in its actual form, but it also stands for and reveals a greater, spiritual reality.

In religious art an icon is a case in point. In an Eastern Orthodox church, for instance, an icon is a panel of wood on which is painted an image of God, Christ, Mary, or the saints and events from their lives. The paintings are done in carefully stylized ways and are not intended to be lifelike. Rather, they are intended to present the viewer with a symbolic representation of a holy figure. The symbolic representation serves to bring the figure—Christ, for example—immediately before the viewer. A person has something in front of him or her to look at, to think about, and to revere. At the same time, the symbolic representation provides the viewer with an opportunity to see through the image and, as in prayer, to make contact with the figure who stands behind it.

In the history of the Christian faith icons have often been controversial, and at times they have been banned. During the eighth and ninth centuries the issue of whether icons should be permitted was hotly debated. In fact there were times when icons were systematically destroyed. The controversy was based on the supposed idolatry of icons. The Iconoclasts (icon smashers) based their claim on Biblical injunctions against making images of any kind. When God gave Moses the Ten Commandments, for instance, Moses was told that he and his people could not make images of things of this world (Exodus 20:3–4). This injunction is underscored in another passage, in which Moses tells his people, "See that you do not act perversely, making yourself a carved image in the shape of anything at all: whether it be in the likeness of man or of woman, of any beast on the earth, or of any bird that flies in the heaven, or of any reptile . . . , or of any fish" (Deuteronomy 4:15–19). To this day this prohibition has served to discourage both Jews and Muslims (Muslims also accept the Ten Commandments as articles of faith) from producing pictorial representations of sacred themes.

In 843 A.D. Christians lifted the ban on icons and they were again used in churches. Their subsequent history, at least in Eastern Orthodoxy, is summarized in this passage by Talbot Rice:

After 843, though the narrative aspect grew in importance as time passed, the icon took on a more definite character as a vehicle through which Christ, the Virgin or a particular Saint could be approached. Prayers were not made to the icon, but through its medium to the figure it depicted. The icon was sacred not in itself, like an idol, but as the representation of a sacred personage or because it depicted a religious theme.[16]

During the Reformation (ca. 1500 A.D.), however, Calvin and other Protestants renewed the attack on icons, banning them from churches once again. This move was reasserted in the seventeenth century by the Puritans and is still the rule in many Protestant denominations.

In other religious traditions, however, icons have been of central importance. In fact the term *icon* is broadened when applied to representations of divine figures in Hinduism. In India the worship of icons—both paintings and statues—is a central aspect of religious life. People literally live with their images of the gods; they worship them, pray to them, touch and hold them, bring them presents, and in countless ways use them to put themselves in contact with the divinities they represent.

There are other ways in which art can be sacramental. In Tibetan Buddhism art is used as an aid to religious practice. The execution of a painting by a Tibetan who is initiated in the complex mysteries of this faith is a form of meditation. The artist becomes absorbed in the mystery as it unfolds; the process of painting itself, therefore, takes the artist further along the path toward enlightened wisdom. The work of art can serve a similar function for others who view it. As an "external aid for pictorial meditation," a work of art—a representation of Buddha, for instance—can provide an initiate with guidance for his or her own spiritual journey. [17]

In Judaism, though there is a prohibition against making pictorial images of things, there is also a Rabbinic directive, *Hiddur Mitzvah*, that "demands that all ceremonial objects used for the performance of religious duties in the home or synogogue be aesthetically pleasing." [18] The synagogue itself, therefore, and all the ceremonial objects that are contained within it, are designed to help believers see and experience the "beauty of holiness."

In Islam the same prohibition against images has led to a concern with abstract designs. A pictorial image is "dissolved" in an arabesque (a complex pattern of interwoven shapes and lines). Through such art the Muslim is freed from concentration on the outward form of things and is presented with a statement concerning the deeper reality that undergirds all things. In both Judaism and Islam, therefore, art helps confirm the belief that life is essentially sacred.

Together, the didactic and sacramental functions of art help a religious tradition create, as Kandinsky says, "spiritual atmosphere." Art helps create an environment in which faith is possible or wherein specific articles of a faith can be expressed, experienced, and affirmed.

We can return now to the cave in which we began this chapter. The cold darkness still surrounds you; without the daylight that comes in through the opening, the cave would be completely black. You are still standing with your hand against the cave wall. You have discovered a hand print there, and with your own hand against it you are contemplating the mystery and power of art. The hand print reaches out to you just as you are reaching out to it.

You look at your own hand and reflect on its various functions. It can tear and yank, hit and grab, throw and catch. It touches, greets, and carries. It brings things to you and pushes them away. It reaches out and, in countless ways, gives you contact with the world. It is closely tied, you realize, to your self-identity. Remember when you were a child and made an impression of your hand in clay? For many of us this was one of our first art projects at school. We made a patty of clay, pressed our hand into it, let it dry, painted it, and then took it home for our parents to see. They were duly impressed and praised our accomplishment. They were no doubt also deeply moved by what they saw, for in the tiny print could be found the unmistakable sign of another human presence, a presence they themselves had helped create. We were proud of our works of art because they proved something about ourselves. They proved that we were individuals. We each saw in the print of our hand a private signature that no one else could ever make.

The hand print on the cave wall communicates a similar message. Though it does not match Michelangelo's frescoes in grandeur or a painting by Da Vinci in technical skill, it reminds us of another person's presence in this world and asks us to imagine the experience of life that person had. Through such imaginings our own life deepens.

The role art has played in human life is complex and difficult to understand. It seems, however, that in all areas of our lives art is a means through which we can discover and define the meaning of existence. As individuals, we each have to create a meaningful life for ourselves. The task can be seen as an artistic project. The words we use to express ourselves, the clothes we wear, the houses we live in, the ways we decorate our rooms all contribute to our self-definition; they all contribute to the personal style that serves as our identity—both for ourselves and for others who encounter us. As we have seen in this chapter, similar things can be said about the cultures in which we live and about the religious traditions to which many of us belong.

NOTES

1. Paul Tillich, *Theology of Culture*, ed. Robert C. Kimball (London and New York: Oxford University Press, 1959), p. 42.
2. Paul Tillich et al., "The World Situation," in Henry P. Van Dusen, ed., *The Christian Answer* (New York: Scribners, 1948), p. 9.
3. Thomas Kuhn, *The Structure of Scientific Revolutions*, 2d ed. (Chicago: University of Chicago Press, 1962).
4. Tillich, p. 70.

5. Karl Kerenyi, *The Religion of the Greeks and Romans,* trans. Christopher Holme (Westport, Conn.: Greenwood Press, 1962), pp. 11–13.
6. Tristan Tzara, "Dadaism," in Richard Ellmann and Charles Feidelson, Jr., eds., *The Modern Tradition: Backgrounds of Modern Literature* (New York: Oxford University Press, 1965), pp. 595–601.
7. Andy Warhol, "Interview with G. R. Swenson," in John Russell and Suzi Gablik, *Pop Art Redefined* (New York: Praeger Publishers, 1969), p. 118.
8. Claes Oldenberg et al., in Russell and Grabik, pp. 79–101.
9. Harold Rosenberg, *The De-definition of Art* (New York: Horizon Press, 1972), p. 12.
10. T. S. Eliot, "The Hollow Men," in *The Complete Poems and Plays: 1909–1950* (New York: Harcourt Brace Jovanovich, p. 56.
11. From *Collected Poems,* second edition, by Conrad Aiken. Copyright © 1970 by Conrad Aiken. Reprinted by permission of Oxford University Press, Inc.
12. Wallace Stevens, "Poetry Is a Destructive Force," in *The Collected Poems of Wallace Stevens* (New York: Knopf, 1972), pp. 192–193.
13. Wallace Stevens, "Notes Toward a Supreme Fiction," in ibid., p. 382.
14. Wallace Stevens, "Not Ideas About the Thing But the Thing Itself," in ibid., p. 534.
15. Wassily Kandinsky, "An Expressionist Credo," in Ellmann and Feidelson, pp. 709–710.
16. David and Tamara Talbot Rice, *Icons and Their History* (Woodstock, N.Y.: Overlook Press, 1974), p. 10.
17. Detlif Lauf, *Tibetan Sacred Art* (Berkeley and London: Shambhala Publications, 1976), p. 46.
18. Joseph Gutmann, *Beauty in Holiness: Studies in Jewish Customs and Ceremonial Art* (n.p.: Ktav, 1970), p. xiv.

QUESTIONS FOR STUDY, REFLECTION, AND DISCUSSION

1. In the future, 200 years from now or more, art historians and students like yourself might look back at the art that was produced during the twentieth century. What do you think people will say about us? How will they describe our style?

2. In a statement concerning the meaning of Dadaism, Tristan Tzara says, "Nothing is more delightful than to confuse and upset people." Do you think this is a valid aim for art? What other possible aims are there?

3. In the same statement Tzara also says, "You explain to me why you exist." He adds, "You haven't the faintest idea." What do these remarks have to do with Dadaism? Tzara's words are addressed to each of us. Do you have a response? How do his words make you feel?

4. In 1937 Pablo Picasso painted a large mural, "Guernica," in which he represented the horrors of war. The mural is filled with images of suffering and despair. How would a person who belongs to a religious tradition—Christianity, for example—respond to such a painting? Would the person's response be different if he or she belonged to a different religious tradition, such as Buddhism? What if the person did not belong to any religious tradition?

PROJECTS

1. Find portraits of men and women from each of the major cultural epochs in the history of the West. Arrange them in chronological order. What do the portraits tell you about the people who lived during the times when they were created? What are the differences between them?
2. Select a painting, a piece of sculpture, or an architectural design from any cultural epoch. How does the work of art relate to the paradigm/style of the time?
3. Working from within a religious tradition, research the ways in which a divine figure has been represented in works of art. Jesus Christ or the Buddha would be appropriate choices. What changes do you find? At what time or in which painting or piece of sculpture do you believe the image of the divine figure reaches its highest or best expression? What is the basis of your judgment?
4. If you could claim as your own creation any work of art from anywhere in the world, which would you choose? Explain what it means to you. What were you trying to accomplish? Do you think you were successful?

SELECTED BIBLIOGRAPHY

Burckhart, Titus. *Sacred Art in East and West.* London: Perennial Books, 1967.

Ellmann, Richard, and Charles Feidelson, Jr., eds. *The Modern Tradition: Backgrounds of Modern Literature.* New York: Oxford University Press, 1965.

Fleming, William. *Arts and Ideas: New Brief Edition.* New York: Holt, Rinehart and Winston, 1974.

Gombrich, E. H. *The Story of Art.* New York: Phaidon Publishers, 1974.

Gutmann, Joseph, ed. *Beauty in Holiness: Studies in Jewish Customs and Ceremonial Art.* New York: Ktav, 1970.

Hisamatsu, Shin'ichi. *Zen and the Fine Arts,* translated by Gishin Tokiwa. Tokyo: Kodansha International, 1971.

Lauf, Detlef I. *Tibetan Sacred Art: The Heritage of Tantra.* Berkeley: Shambhala Publications, 1976.

Streng, Frederick J. *Understanding Religious Life,* Chap. 12, "The Power of Artistic Creativity." Encino, Calif.: Dickenson, 1969.

Tillich, Paul. *Theology of Culture,* edited by Robert C. Kimball, Chap. 6, "Protestantism and Artistic Style." London and New York: Oxford University Press, 1964.

Van De Bogart, Doris. *Introduction to the Humanities: Painting, Sculpture, Architecture, Music, and Literature.* New York: Barnes and Noble, 1968.

Van Der Leeuw, G. *Sacred and Profane Beauty: The Holy in Art,* translated by David E. Green. Nashville, Tenn.: Abingdon, 1963.

CHAPTER 8

Accents of the World's Religions*

HUSTON SMITH

Inescapably, a person is involved in three basic encounters: with nature, with other people, and with himself or herself. Roughly, these may be identified as humanity's natural, social, and psychological problems.

The great surviving cultural traditions are also three: the Far Eastern, the Indian, and the Western. It is the thesis of this chapter that it helps us understand and relate the unique perspectives of these three traditions in their religious as well as other dimensions if we think of each as having attended to one problem more diligently than to the other two. The decision to do so represents each tradition's fundamental option, the main direction each has chosen in its ceaseless pursuit of salvation and the real. Thus, though in one sense the language of the human spirit can be regarded as a universal language in that wherever it is spoken it must attend to some extent to all three human problems, it is equally the case that this language has been spoken in different accents, each bespeaking a unique symphony of emphases and orientations that has constituted its culture's religious self-identity.

Specifically, the religions of the West (Judaism, Christianity, and Islam) have accented the problem of humanity's relationship to nature; those of the Far East (Confucianism, Taoism, and Shinto) have stressed its social problem; and those of India (Hinduism, Buddhism, and Jainism) have attended primarily to its psychological problem.

If this is true, the question immediately arises, What gave these traditions their distinctive slants? I do not think this question admits of a com-

---

* This chapter was first published in *The Australian Bulletin of Comparative Religions* (1961). It was reprinted in John Bowman, ed., *Comparative Religion* (Leiden: Brill, 1972). It is reprinted here with the permission of the publishers.

plete answer, not only because too much pertinent evidence has been permanently lost but also because from the empirical standpoint the question has no final answer. That this is consonant with theories that trace religious differences to divine revelation—theories that, though this is not commonly recognised, are as prominent in Hinduism as in the West—does not displease me. But the inherent mystery of origins, if such it be, may have a human explanation as well. For if freedom is real, the individuals who first ventured their faiths in different directions may simply have chosen differently, in which case the differences would be "due" to nothing. What we seek is a balance between total explanation and none. Influences will be sought, but there will be no presumption that they can completely dispel the mystery that is hidden in all great historical, as in all great personal, occurrences.

WESTERN RELIGIONS

We begin with the West: with Judaism, Christianity, and Islam, which, despite their important differences, can be grouped together because of their family resemblances.[1] All were originated by Semites; all share a common theological vocabulary (though they use it to say different things); and all stand in a single historical tradition inasmuch as Christianity claims to be the fulfilment of Judaism and Islâm the fulfilment of both Judaism and Christianity.

The suggestion that these religions are notable for their interest in nature may come as a surprise, for we have been more conscious of their supernatural than their naturalistic components. But this is because we have heard them compared with other strata of Western culture more than with other religions. Compared with Western science, Western philosophy, or Western art, Western religions *are* differentiated by their supernatural dimensions. But when they are compared with other religions their distinguishing feature is seen to lie in their higher regard for nature and the greater extent to which they have come to grips with it.

As nature's primary ingredients are space, time, and matter, we will touch briefly on the relationship of Western religion to each.

MATTER

"Christianity," Archbishop Temple used to contend, "is the most avowedly materialistic of all the great religions."[2] Denis de Rougemont concurs: "Compared with the religions of the East, Christianity might be called materialism."[3] Judaism and Islam should be ranked beside Christianity in these judgments.

Obviously there have been anti-matter eddies in the Western stream—Manichaeanism, Gnosticism, Docetism, Neo-Platonism, Plotinus, and others. But they never take over. The first three are explicitly condemned as heretical, and Plotinus and the Neo-Platonists are bypassed in favor of Aristotle and Aquinas' acceptance of matter as altogether real. Moreover, and equally instructive for our thesis, the inspiration for the matter-disparaging outlooks usually comes from the East, and often from India itself. For India, matter is a barbarian, spoiling everything it touches. By contrast, Westerners respect matter and take it seriously, meshing nature and spirit wherever possible. Time and again they seem on the verge of slipping into the view that spirit is good and matter bad, but always they recover. The Judaeo-Christian Bible opens with the assertion that "God created the heavens and the earth," and before the chapter concludes God is portrayed as surveying all that He created, earth included, "and behold, it was very good." Good, moreover, not only for beholding but as a field for endeavor, for in the center of that crucial opening chapter of Genesis humanity is commissioned to "have dominion . . . over all the earth," a commission later assumed to have been accepted and fulfilled: "Thou madest him to have dominion over the works of thy hands; thou has put all things under his feet" (Psalms 8:6). The Incarnation pays matter its highest conceivable compliment—it can become divine. The Kingdom of Heaven, from Jewish and early Christian apocalypticism right down to the social gospel, is to come on earth. Even in death the West will not desert the body. If there is to be life after death, it too must be in some sense physical: Hence, "I believe . . . in the resurrection of the body." Throughout the entire sequence runs the effort to maintain a sense of kinship between humanity and nature that totemism had earlier pointed up. Paul sees the entire cosmos as locked with humanity in its fallen condition, groaning and travailing as it awaits its redemption with and through that of humanity.[4] An earthquake forms the backdrop for the crucifixion. "Nature also mourns for a lost good."

It is unlikely that such a high regard for matter would have emerged in regions where nature confronted people as a holy terror. But in the parts of the Near East that cradled the Western religions, nature's guise was beneficient. Ancient historians have christened the arc that begins with the Nile and moves up the Palestinian corridor, across Syria, and down the Tigris and Euphrates valleys "the Fertile Crescent," and it may even be no accident that the Garden of Eden story comes from this region, for nature here was in a most favorable mood—rich and joyous and treating humanity as a friend. To the Jews, Canaan seemed veritably to flow with milk and honey. There were problems to be met, challenges to equal. But their proportions were such as to coax rather than discourage inquiry and advances. Matter appeared to be a plausible matrix within which to continue the quest for human fulfillment.

India early ceased to think affirmatively about the material world, but China did not. China resembles the West in seeking life's solution within a material context of some sort. But this is not enough to define naturalism.

A thoroughgoing naturalism requires that not only matter but time as well be taken seriously, and Chinese religion implicates itself in time no more than Indian religion.

TIME

To take time seriously is to be conscious of (1) the directional character of history, (2) the radical novelty it can introduce, (3) the uniqueness of every event, and (4) the potential decisiveness of some. Indian and Chinese religions stress none of these points. The Indian view of time is cyclical, reducing all that occurs to the anonymous insignificance of an ephemeral passage through illusion, while the Chinese tend not to generalize about time any more than about other things. For the East, time is a placid, silent pool in which ripples come and go. For the West, time is an arrow or river: It has origin, direction, destination, and is irreversible.[5] It is not difficult to see why. Judaism, the foundational religion of the West, was instigated by a concrete historical happening—the Exodus—as the religion of India and China were not. In addition, the basic concepts of Judaism were forged while the Jews, being either displaced or oppressed, were a people in waiting—first to cross over into the promised land, then to return to Jerusalem, then for the coming of the Messiah who was to deliver them.

This built into Judaism a future-oriented character[6] that was unique[7] until it was duplicated by Christianity, which also is grounded in unique historical occurrences—the Incarnation and the Resurrection—and looks toward the future, in this case to the return of Christ and the coming of his kingdom on earth. The idea of progress, which arose in the West, and independently in the West only, is the secular offshoot of this Messianism, while the equally Western-originated Marxist vision of a classless society is its giant heretical facsimile.

SPACE

The third property of nature is space, which has religious overtones because of its relationship to individuality. What distinguishes two people most irrevocably is the fact that they are spatially discrete by virtue of occupying different bodies. It may be no accident, therefore, that the tradition that values individuality most, the one that sees humanity's destiny to consist not in transcending its ego but in continuing and developing it, is the tradition in which space occasioned fewest problems because it was most plentiful. A recent report from India reads:

Too many people everywhere! Three servants for my simple hotel room. Seven or eight men, one of whom is working, in every tiny shop. The roadway invaded by a crowd moving in all directions, so that the passage of wheeled traffic is always obstructed. The pavements thick with sleepers at night. And I saw five people on one bicycle![8]

In such an everlasting swarm there simply may not have been room for individuality to rise to its possibilities. The ideal breeding ground for individualism is the frontier, and among the world's faiths it is Christianity that has been preeminently the frontier religion, moving first into the desolate swamps and forests of Northern Europe and then across the waters into the Americas. The West's high estimate of the individual may be partly a child of this fact. In the East everything participates in everything and nothing ever gets really detached from anything, neither a son from his father nor what is dead from what is alive; what is most prized in people is the essence of their humanity, which is shared with others. The West, by contrast, considers differences and distinctions to be virtues; the infinite worth that attaches to each individual derives in part precisely from the fact that he or she is unique and irreplaceable. This is part of the meaning of Kierkegaard's description of Christians as "joyful heirs to the finite"; they not only accept the finite but rejoice in it. In death no less than in life, the West resists the East's temptation to merge the soul with the Absolute, insisting instead that it retains its identity through all eternity. The theological correlative of this concept of an individual soul is the concept of a personal God, which again contrasts with Eastern, more impersonal alternatives.

Western religion has involved itself more deeply, confidently, and expectantly in space, time, and matter, all three, than the religions of India and China. Using "natural theology" in this special sense, we can identify it as the West's distinctive theological contribution.

FAR EASTERN RELIGIONS

The Far East, on the other hand, concentrated on social ethics; so much so, indeed, that people often ask whether its basic life prescription—Confucianism—is rightly considered a religion at all.

At least two facts suggest that the Far East may have turned in this direction because nature looked less promising. The first of these is the Mongoloid physiognomy, which bears marks of having originated under conditions of severe cold, probably in Siberia and eastern Central Asia, where high winds were matched by temperatures that fell below minus 80°F. Such conditions were a far cry from the mild and sunny climes of the Mediterranean. They were so fierce that to this day the Mongoloid carries their impact on his or her face. "There is no question," writes Walter Fairservis, "that the Mongoloid face is better equipped for cold weather than any other."[9] It has more protective fat, and its most exposed surface area, the nose, is reduced by the forward extrusion of the cheekbones and a retreat of the nose itself. Its eyes are protected by an extension vertically of the eye orbits and the whole area padded with fat, while the epicanthic fold that extends from the nose area over the upper eye narrows the slit of the eye and, with the fatty padding, acts as a kind of snow goggle against glare as well as an eye shield against the cold. Breathing through the nasal passages is facilitated by the retraction of the nose area into the face, while the banking up of nasal passages with fat provides maximum heat for the air on its way to the lungs. Face hair, which is a handicap in extreme cold because the beard stores breath moisture as ice that freezes the face, is reduced more than in any other human type.[10]

The other conspicuous fact is China's rivers. Chinese culture, like that of the West, is riverine in origin. But whereas the Nile, and the Tigris and Euphrates after their first cataclysmic floods, were well-mannered and orderly, China's rivers were unmanageable. The soil in the great treeless mountain ranges where the Yellow River and the Yangtze rise washes badly, feeding into the rivers enormous quantities of yellow silt. The Yangtze dumps 400 million tons of this silt into the China Sea every year, while the Yellow River's silt content reaches 46 percent by weight and gives the river its name. Building up the river beds, this silt causes the rivers to flood inordinately. A single breach in the dikes, which in places have been built up as high as fifty feet to contain the elevated waters, can inundate hundreds of square miles and cut millions of farmers off from their sustenance. As the resultant sedimentation can be as much as six feet deep, years may elapse before flood-ravaged lands can be cultivated again. As a boy I lived only twelve miles from the Yangtze during the catastrophic floods of 1932, which inundated an area equal to Missouri, Kansas, and Iowa combined and cost 1 million lives. The record of the Yellow River is even worse. Not without reason has it been called "China's Sorrow." "More than . . . any other great river, the Yellow River presents mankind with a seemingly insoluble problem. Rulers of China have always faced but never conquered it."[11] In China the rivers very early came to be symbolized by the dragon, which was also for centuries China's national emblem.

One stands in awe of dragons; one does not expect to tame them. Thus we should be prepared to find in China a certain deference toward nature. There is a kind of naturalism in Chinese thought, but it is the naturalism of the artist, the nature lover, or the romanticist rather than that of the scientist—the naturalism of a Wordsworth or a Thoreau rather than a Galileo or a Bacon. Nature in China is something to be appreciated, intuited, communed with, or reverenced; there is no sustained notion that it might be mastered. A passage from the *Tao Te Ching* puts the point in a nutshell:

> Those who would take over the earth
> And shape it to their will
> Never, I notice, succeed.
> The earth is like a vessel so sacred
> That at the mere approach of the profane
> It is marred
> And when they reach out their fingers it is gone.[12]

Chinese science, as a consequence, did not develop.[13] For a field of constructive endeavor the Chinese turned instead to society. They may have been lured in this direction by the fact that their population was racially homogeneous and so presented no surface discouragements to the natural wish for a harmonious society. But there were also factors that forced the Chinese to attend to the social problem. One was the crowded conditions under which they lived.[14] Another may have been the extended family system under which several generations and relatives as distant as third cousins might be grouped in a single household—three of Confucius' five famous relationships are concerned with the family. China's rivers may also have figured here, for from the beginning of Chinese civilization they required vast, cooperative dike-building projects to keep them in their channels.[15] Finally, China's basic outlook was forged in the social furnace of its "Time of Troubles," the five conclusive centuries that culminated in the endemic violence of the "warring kingdoms" in which anarchy was the order of the day. In this context the burning question facing every responsible thinker was the one that, on a smaller scale but under vaguely similar circumstances, faces Plato as well: how to save Athens.

The solution as it finally emerged gathered together many strands but bore the distinctive stamp of Confucius's genius. It amounted to nothing less than an attempt to "Emily Post" an entire way of life in which human relationships were always the focus of attention. Subtle differences in relationship were delineated and prescribed to a degree that has been paralleled in tribes but in no other civilization—witness the complex vocabulary for distinguishing paternal from maternal uncles, aunts, cousins, and in-laws, and for expressing fine distinctions in seniority. The prescriptions were enforced externally by sensitizing individuals to the way they were regarded by others—*face* in the peculiarly Oriental sense of that word—and internally by deliberate self-examination.[16] Interests of family and community were given precedence over those of the individual, and tested ways of the past were honored—through ancestor worship and filial piety—above innovation and experiment.

The content of the life pattern thus secured centered in the ideal of the *chun-tzu*, or "gentleman" in the best sense of the term; the man who is completely poised, competent, confident, and adequate to every social occasion; the man of perfect address who is always at ease with himself and therefore can put others at ease. His attitude toward others is that of *jen*, usually translated as "benevolence," "man-to-man-ness," or simply "goodness." But the matter is not left thus generalized. What jen requires in specific instances is carefully prescribed by the delineation of "graded love"—that is, love for others according to one's relationship to them, the five most important relationships being those between father and son, elder brother and younger brother, husband and wife, friend and friend, ruler and subject. The sum of the conduct befitting these relationships is *li*,

meaning "propriety" but, significantly, "ritual" as well, since it amounts to
the ritualization of the entire social process, from the way the emperor
opens the doors of the Temple of Heaven on great ceremonial occasions
right down to the way one entertains the humblest guest and serves him
his tea. With scholars placed at the top of the social scale and soldiers
excluded from it altogether, learning was revered[17] and violence despised.
A system of local and imperial examinations, which made learning the
primary qualification for public office, opened the door to social mobility—
the poorest peasant's son might aspire to high public office—and produced
the closest approximation to Plato's vision of the philosopher-king as this
planet has seen. Age was respected, courtesy raised to the level of an art,
and beauty admired to such an extent that the facility of an alphabet was
rejected in favor of calligraphy, the most handsome as well as the most difficult form of written expression ever evolved.

If cross-cultural comparisons are difficult, cross-cultural evaluations are
even more so. It is easy to say that China attended to social relationships
more carefully than to science or psychology, and more carefully than India
or the West did. But did it thereby achieve more in this regard? No judgment on this question can at this point pretend to be objective; too much
depends on whether one favors dynamism, passion, tumult, creativity, and
the individual (the West) or quiet, conservative order. Avoiding comparisons, let me simply say that I find China's social achievement impressive.
Chinese culture has a flavor all its own. It is a compound of subtlety,
brilliance, and reticence that produces an effect that can be described only
as good taste. Traditionally the Chinese have exalted the life of reasonable
enjoyment and despised the destructive. As a consequence they have been
able to unite an immense area of fertility and to create—if we multiply duration by size of population included—the most extensive civilization humanity has ever achieved, one that at its height included one-third of the
human race. The political structure of this civilization alone, the Chinese
Empire, lasted under various dynasties for 2133 years (from 221 B.C. to
1912 A.D.)—a period that makes the empires of Alexander the Great and
Caesar look insignificant. Its power of assimilation was equally impressive.
Having the most open frontier of all great civilizations, China was subject
to wave after wave of invasions by cavalried barbarians who were always
ready to fall on the earthbound agriculturalists. Always at their gates were
the very Tartars whose one long-range raid inflicted a mortal wound on the
Roman Empire. But what the Chinese could not exclude they absorbed.
Each wave of invasion tends quickly to lose its identity. As the great Sinol-
ogist Arthur Waley has remarked, there is scarcely a barbarian conqueror
who came in purely for profit who within twenty years was not attempting
to write a copy of Chinese verse that his master, who is also his conquered
slave, might say was not wholly unworthy of a gentleman. And already he
is hoping to be mistaken for a Chinese. Here is a cultural furnace with

enough heat to effect a real melting pot. There is no evidence that these barbarians were ever as impressed with what they found in Europe.

INDIAN RELIGION

Turning to the third great tradition, that of India, we find neither the natural nor the social environment inviting primary attention. Geographically, India today is a land of fierce extremes, running from the icy peaks of the Himalayas to the steaming jungles of Cape Comorin. In summer, wrote Rudyard Kipling, "there is neither sky, sun, nor horizon. Nothing but a brown-purple haze of heat. It is as though the earth were dying of apoplexy." During this furnace season millions of Indian villagers lie gasping in their mud huts. Wells dry up and fields blow away. When the monsoon rains come in the fall, the torrential downpours drown the arid land in surging floods. Only in the winter months does India appear comfortably livable and nature seem kind.[18] We cannot, however, assume that nature was always this harsh. It is possible that with fruit that dripped from the trees and climate that demanded virtually no clothing, there was a time during which nature in India was so easygoing that it did not challenge humanity at all.[19]

What is clear is that for one reason or another India bracketed nature. While China turned its attention to society, India found itself facing the most devilish of all social problems, ethnic diversity. India is one of the greatest ethnographic museums in the world. An English anthropologist has likened it to "a deep net into which various races and peoples of Asia have drifted and been caught." The three main color divisions—yellow, black, and white—are represented, and these in turn have been further divided into seven distinct racial types.[20] No Indian ingenuity was equal to this problem. The caste system was in part an attempt to deal with it, but instead of caste's solving the problem, in the end the problem took over caste, turning it into a device for perpetuating social distance. Relatively early India abandoned hope of solving life's problem on the social plane.[21] Instead it turned inward, centering its attention on the psychological problem.[22] Nature? No; even at its best it drags us toward senility and death and leaves us with regrets. Society? No; as long as people are people there will be inequities and blockages on this front. But the individual—to the Indian the individual looked promising. If only we could discover who we truly are, might we not win through to an inner freedom beyond the opposites that block both nature and society?[23] The following lines from the *Katha Upanishad* will be recognized at once as typical of the Indian theme:

The senses turn outward. Accordingly, man looks toward what is without, and sees not what is within. [The wise man] shuts his eyes to what is without, and beholds the self.[24]

For the Indian, the senses are false witnesses.

The world is not what it appears to be. Behind this surface life, where we experience the play of life and death, there is a deeper life which knows no death; behind our apparent consciousness, which gives us the knowledge of objects and things . . . there is . . . pure . . . consciousness . . . Truth . . . is experienced only by those who turn their gaze inward.[25]

As this conviction spreads

such intellectual energy as had formerly been devoted to the study and development of a machinery for the mastery of the . . . forces of the cosmos . . . was . . . diverted inward . . . The cosmic energy was being taken at its fountain head . . . All secondary, merely derivative streams of energy . . . being left behind. In Indian thought . . . the whole outer world was dwindling in importance.[26]

India became, as a consequence, the religious psychologist. One evidence of its preoccupation in this area is found in the elaborateness of its psychological vocabulary. Ananda Coomaraswamy, while curator of the Oriental Museum in Boston, used to say that for every psychological term in English there are four in Greek and forty in Sanskrit.[27] Mrs. Rhys Davids lists twenty Pali words whose subtle distinctions of meaning are obscured by their single, indiscriminate English rendition as "desire" or "desires."

What India actually discovered that is of importance in psychology is, of course, a moot question. Elsewhere I have suggested eight specific insights that are remarkably contemporary to have been discovered in India over 2000 years ago.[28] Here I will confine myself to a single point and several supporting testimonials. The point concerns the subconscious, which breaks upon the West in the nineteenth century but was recognized in India before Christ,[29] with (in my judgment) two continuing advantages in India's favor: first, the delineation of several layers of subconsciousness, not just one; and second, the greater awareness of the creative potentialities of the subconscious along with pathological ones. As for tributes, I will content myself with three. It was the *Upanishads'* analysis of the self that caused Arthur Schopenhauer to stamp them "the product of the highest human wisdom" and Count Keyserling to say that Hinduism at its best has spoken the only relevant truth about the way to self-realization in the full sense of the word. The third tribute is the more impressive because it comes from the leader of the Barthian-grounded school, which insists that religious truth is contained fully and exclusively in the Christian revelation. Despite this conviction, Hendrick Kraemer grants that "the wisdom of the East possesses a greater psychological virtuosity in analyzing man, in order to teach him to manage and master himself by spiritual and other kinds of training. As is well known, Eastern wisdom and spiritual experience meet here with the great discoveries in psychology and psychotherapy since Freud."[30]

Neither China nor the West has given a fraction of the attention to the mind that India has. Historically, India rightly deserves the title of the world's religious psychologist.[31]

DEFICIENCIES IN EACH ACCENT

We have suggested that each of the three great religious traditions has shown a unique specialization—the West in "religious naturalism," China in social ethics, and India in religious psychology. It remains to point out the inevitable price of specialization: ineptness in the subjects neglected. "Nothing fails like success." In the end all three traditions are brought to the brink of disaster because each has succeeded so well on one front that it felt safe in neglecting the other two.

China and India have both neglected nature, the injunction to "have dominion." Consequently science has not developed in those countries, and the standard of living remains intolerably low. In China the problem has periodically proved to be too much even for social genius. Between dynasties there was regularly a long period of civil strife that can always be correlated with population pressure on cultivated land that failed to increase productivity because improvement of agricultural technique was negligible. As for India, its only scientific contributions to the world at large have been in pure mathematics,[32] where it was dealing not with the outer world but with the resources of the mind.[33] To its ineptness toward nature India adds social clumsiness, vividly illustrated by the present state of the caste system,[34] and China adds psychological naiveté.

Occasionally we catch glimpses in China of an interest in the mind and what it can do, as in the quietistic movement in the Chou Dynasty, the *Tao Te Ching*'s esoteric rendering of the idea of *te*, Mencius' passage on "the dawn breath," and Chu Hsi's discussion of "silent sitting." But the interest is never systematically pursued, and it usually takes a social turn: The mind is being inspected not for itself but for what it can contribute to social stability. One gets the impression that when China does get around to psychology, it is really interested only in social psychology. Its deficiencies in this field are seen most clearly in the failure to recognize the dangers of repression. The Chinese scheme had no place for emotional cartharsis, spontaneity, and unrepression. Consequently negative emotions got dammed up until eventually the dam gave way and the emotions came forth in terrifying form. The pattern carried over to Japan, where, as Robert Guillain has pointed out, a youth "received a Spartan training which developed his aggressive instincts and, at the same time, screwed down over his violent nature a sort of lid of blind obedience and perfect politeness. This made him an explosive creature, ready to burst like a bomb."[35]

The deficiencies of the West have been in the areas of psychology and sociology. Psychologically, the West has been until recently merely inconspicuous, but in sociology one wonders if it has not been delinquent. At least four facts must be faced as evidence of the West's ineptitude in social relations and lack of perceptiveness as to the forces that make for social cohesion and group harmony.

The first comes to light in simply comparing Europe's political map with those of China and India. Whereas Chinese civilization had the power to expand, uniting more and more people in a common heritage, and whereas Indian civilization could at least hold its own, the record of the West has been one of continuous secession. After the union of the Northern and Southern Kingdoms in Egypt there is no further fusion in the Fertile Crescent. Instead, fission sets in. The Hebrews divide into Israel and Judah. "The fatal danger of Greece," writes Gilbert Murray, "was disunion as many see it in Europe now."[36] The Christian Church splits into East and West, the Western Church into Roman Catholic and Protestant; and then Protestantism splinters. The Medieval Empire shatters into nations, and the process continues. Norway, Denmark, and Sweden, originally a Scandinavian unit, divide. Belgium and Holland, once united in the Netherlands, are apart. The British Isles have been plagued with separatist movements. The United States has had its Civil War and continuing North–South animosity. What has enfeebled and discredited us in our own day, writes Arnold Toynbee, "is the atrocious fratricidal warfare, within the bosom of our Western Society, since 1914 . . . We Westerners have fought among ourselves another bout of wars that have been as savage, destructive and discreditable as our earlier wars of religion."[37]

Western religion appears to have shared in this social ineptitude. The only large-scale persecuting religions have been those of the West— Judaism, Christianity, and Islam. Since the Middle Ages Christianity has been divisive by itself. To continue with Toynbee,

For 400 years and more, from the outbreak of the struggle between the Papacy and Frederick II in the thirteenth century down to the end of the Catholic–Protestant Western wars of religion in the seventeenth century, the Christian Church in the Western World was a force that made not for gentleness and peace and concord, but for violence and dissension . . . Before the end of the seventeenth century, the hatred, strife and atrocities inflicted on the Western World by Christian *odium theologicum* had become a scandal and menace to the Western Civilization.[38]

The West has invented the two things that, combined, most endanger the world's future: total war and religious nationalism.[39]

Eventually (one almost says inevitably) there emerges in Europe a social theory—or more accurately a religion, albeit a heretical one—that pushes the Western emphasis to its logical extreme. Paralleling the West's temptation to reduce psychology to physiology, Marx reduces sociology to economics. In the end, were one to believe him, there is no social problem. Once the material problem is solved, the social problem will automatically take care of itself.

CONCLUSION

We have suggested that each of the world's three great religious traditions has exercised a noteworthy influence on one of humanity's basic problems but seems to have tended insufficiently to the other two. It would appear that an adequate culture must strike all three notes as a chord. In
developing this chord of a fully adequate world culture, each of the three
great traditions appears to have something of importance to contribute.
Perhaps each has something to learn as well.

EPILOGUE

Not often in discussions as general as this does one stumble upon evidence so clear-cut as to stand as independent verification for an entire
thesis. But since this chapter was written a point has occurred to me that
seems to come close to achieving this.

What is truth? The question did not arise in our discussion. But if one
does raise it one finds the three cultures answering along the lines we
would expect. For the West, truth is essentially correspondence with a
state of affairs that exists independently in nature or history (past nature).
The Chinese, on the other hand, will feel that the primary objects to which
assertions refer, and are responsible, are the feelings of the people involved. Hence the normality of white lies and keeping one's mouth shut
when appropriate. India has a third criterion: To the Indian, truth is essentially spiritual pragmatism. One can generate little interest in India over
whether Hindu myths are "true" in our Western sense—whether Krishna
really lived, for example. The accounts are true to the needs of the human
spirit, and what could be more important?

NOTES

1. Zoroastrianism also belongs in this group, but it is too small to bring into this general discussion.
2. William Temple, *Nature, Man and God* (London: Macmillan, 1953), p. 478.
3. Denis de Rougemont, *Man's Western Quest* (New York: Harper & Row, 1957), p. 122.
4. Romans 8:19–23.
5. Though the West's time consciousness has been recognized, it has not always been admired. Schopenhauer, for example, considered Christianity's grounding in a unique historical event a weakness, contending that Buddhism shows a deeper wisdom by remaining
   aloof from such an unphilosophical encumbrance.
6. The great historian of Judaism, Salo Baron, goes so far as to define Judaism as the struggle
   between the "ought" and the "is," "the struggle . . . between the ideal and the actual."
7. Hinduism looks forward to its avatars and Buddhism to its Maitreyas, but these are archetypal rather than decisive, recurring "every time that . . ."
8. Quoted in de Rougemont, p. 13.

9. Walter Fairservis, *The Origins of Oriental Civilization* (New York: New American Library, 1959), p. 75.

10. Adapted from C. S. Coon, S. M. Garn, and J. B. Birdsell, *Races* (Springfield, Ill.: Charles C Thomas, 1950).

11. Edwin O. Reischauer and John K. Fairbank, *East Asia: The Great Tradition* (Boston: Houghton Mifflin, 1960), p. 20.

12. Witter Bynner, trans., *The Way of Life According to Laotzu* (New York: John Day, 1944), p. 43.

13. I think this statement can stand despite Joseph Needham's monumental study, *Science and Civilization in China* (Cambridge: Cambridge University Press 1956). For the general conclusion of this study appears to be that though China was far more ingenious than we had supposed in solving specific practical problems, it was disinclined to abstract from its concrete successes the general principles that might be developed into organized sciences concerned with broad domains of nature. Thus, with respect to technical and mechanical skill, China and the West remained on a par until the Ming Dynasty opened in 1368. But before that dynasty ended, in 1644, Europe was in possession of modern science and China was still going through its Middle Ages.

14. "The crowding of people upon the land and in tight walled villages is not new in China's history. The Han Empire, which was contemporary with the Roman Empire, had a population of sixty million people, most of it concentrated in North China. Throughout their history the Chinese have habitually lived close-packed in their social and family relationships" (Reischauer and Fairbank, pp. 27–28).

15. "From earliest times Chinese administrators . . . have had to construct dikes to keep the Yellow River in its channel" (*ibid.*, p. 20).

16. "Tseng-Tzu [one of Confucius's chief disciples] said: Every day I ask myself three questions: Have I been unfaithful in carrying out my obligations toward others? Have I been insincere in my relations toward my friends? Have I failed to put what has been taught me into practice?" (*Analects*, 1, 4).

17. To this day there are Chinese who will not step on a piece of paper if there is writing on it.

18. Cf. S. Levi, *L'Inde et le Monde* (Paris: Champion, 1962), p. 90: "The civilization of India, alone, has grown up between the tropic and the equator in reaction against a nature which exceeds normal limits."

19. Arthur Basham sides with this view in *The Wonder that was India* (New York: Grove Press, 1959), pp. 13, 14: "In 3000 B.C. [India's] climate was very different. The whole Indus region was well forested . . . and Baluchistan, now almost a waterless desert, was rich in rivers. . . . If the climate had any effect on the Indian character, it was . . . to develop a love of ease and comfort, an addiction to the simple pleasures and luxuries so freely given by Nature."

20. T. W. Wallbank, *A Short History of India and Pakistan* (New York: New American Library, 1958), p. 11.

21. Heinrich Zimmer, in *The Philosophies of India* (New York: Pantheon Books, 1951), p. 127, speaks of "the blank pessimism of the Indian philosophy of politics, untouched as it is by any hope or ideal of progress and improvement." T. W. Wallbank says that a "fundamental feature of the Indian traditional culture pattern has been its neglect of what we might call the science of society, and more specifically the art of government" (*ibid.*, p. 47).

22. Cf. S. Radhakrishnan, *Indian Philosophy* (London: Allen & Unwin, 1923), I, 28: "In India . . . interest . . . is in the self of man."

23. "What is the Oriental [read Indian] dream? We want to master physics, they psyche" (de Rougemont, p. 193).

24. Swami Prabhavananda and Frederick Manchester, trans., *The Upanishads* (Hollywood: Vedanta Press, 1947), pp. 30–31.

25. Swami Prabhavananda, "Religion and Otherworldliness," in Christopher Isherwood, ed., *Vedanta for Modern Man* (New York: Harper & Row, 1951), p. 200. One is reminded of Gandhi's repeated admonition to "turn the spotlight inward."

26. Zimmer, p. 357.

27. With regard to nature the ratio is reversed. Arthur Lovejoy has pointed out that there are 400 variations of the word *natural* in romantic poetry alone.

28. "Accents of the World's Philosophies," *Philosophy East and West*, April–July 1957.

29. Eastern religious philosophies "have by their own power reached conclusions centuries ago (especially in the field of psychology and mystical intuition) to which the modern Western quest for knowledge and for explanation of the enigma of Mind and Matter often seems to lead with compelling logic" [Hendrick Kraemer, *World Cultures and World Religions* (London: Lutterworth, 1960)]. Cf. also de Rougement, p. 192: "The psychology of the unconscious, as inaugurated by Freud and developed by Jung, links up with the Yogis."

30. Kraemer, p. 374.

31. India's "great contribution to the world is a clarified and discerning understanding of the spiritual psychology of man." Edwin A. Burtt, *Man Seeks the Divine* (New York: Harper & Row, 1956), p. 125.

32. Unless one includes methods of body control as imbedded in hatha yoga. But note that these were originally developed as preliminaries to controlling the mind. Characteristically the body was being investigated for its psychological consequences.

33. The Indians discovered the zero, the decimal-place system, and the numerals that we call Arabic (we got them from the Arabs, but the Arabs got them from the Hindus).

34. Nehru has asserted that when the caste system became rigid and inflexible this led to a "decline all along the line—intellectual, philosophical, political, in techniques and methods of war, in knowledge of and contacts with the outside world" (quoted in Wallbank, p. 46).

35. Quoted in Werner Bishoff, *Japan* (New York: Simon and Schuster, 1955), p. 7 Cf. also Frank Gibney, *Five Gentlemen of Japan* (Tokyo: Charles E. Tuttle, 1954), p. 33: "It has so often been Japan's tragedy that cruelty and atrocities have formed the one escape valve for the freer human feelings which a ruthlessly tight society did its unconscious best to inhibit or suppress."

36. Gilbert Murray, *The Five Stages of Greek Religion* (London: Watts, 1935), p. 81.

37. "Man Owes His Freedom to God," *Colliers*, 137, no. 7 (March 30, 1956):78.

38. *Ibid.*

39. Though his book is on the whole strongly pro-Western, Denis de Rougemont admits this. On p. 178 of *Man's Western Quest* we read that "Europe . . . certainly invented total war," and on pp. 75–78 he says some very important things about nationalism becoming a religion—for example, in the French Revolution, Hegel, and thereafter—first in the West, then in the East. Japan comes close to sharing the invention of religious nationalism, but until it caught the West's variety its form could better be designated religious patriotism.

QUESTIONS FOR STUDY, REFLECTION, AND DISCUSSION

1. This chapter seeks to highlight the distinctive emphasis of the three great enduring religious traditions, but they would not be referred to by the common phrase "religious traditions" if they did not also have

something—in all probability a great deal—in common. What aspects do all the world's religions have in common?

2. The chapter develops the position that there are distinct accents in the historic religions of the West, the Far East, and India. Accepting this point of view, what reasons might you give for the growing interest in Asian forms of religiousness such as yoga and Zen meditation in the West?

3. Are there any ways in which the modern world is changing that might lessen the differences among the world's religions? Are there any reasons to suppose that the different accents might become more sharply drawn?

PROJECTS

1. Select one book listed in the bibliography at the end of this chapter. After reading the book, summarize the major thesis of the book in no more than two pages. Following the summary, make your critical and creative response to the book. In your response you may wish to suggest successes or failures in the way the author follows through on his or her arguments. You may wish to comment on the author's adequate or inadequate interpretations of the data presented. You may find other strengths or weaknesses in the book.

2. After your careful reading of this chapter, imagine that you have been given fifteen minutes to expand on some point or theme. You may do research in the library for your task, or you may depend on your creative insights on the implications of that point or theme. Prepare notes and plan to speak to members of your class or discussion group on the topic you have chosen.

3. Part of the thesis of this chapter is that in the West humanity's relationship to nature has been of extreme importance. Nature is here understood to be composed of space, time, and matter. Furthermore, in Western civilization attention to each of the three components has led to momentous discoveries: Matter has led to modern science; time has led to the idea of progress; space has resulted in an emphasis on the individual and his or her rights. Choosing one of these three Western discoveries, write an essay in which you identify and discuss the various elements that have contributed to its development.

4. The thesis of this chapter is that in the West religions have accented the problem of humanity's relationship to nature; those of the Far East have stressed its social problem; and those of India have attended primarily to its psychological problem. Write an essay or prepare a talk in

which you show ways in which each of the three distinctive civilizations, by virtue of its particular emphasis, emerges with a distinctive notion of truth.*

SELECTED BIBLIOGRAPHY

Conger, George P. *The Ideologies of Religion.* New York: Round Table Press, 1940.

Haas, William S. *The Destiny of the Mind: East and West.* London: Faber and Faber, 1956.

Hocking, William E. *Living Religions and World Faith.* New York: AMS Press, 1976.

Nakamura, Hajime. *Ways of Thinking of Eastern Peoples;* edited by Philip P. Wiener. Honolulu: East-West Center Press, 1964.

Northrup, Filmer S. *The Meeting of East and West.* New York: Macmillan, 1960.

Otto, Rudolf. *Mysticism East and West.* New York: Macmillan, 1970.

Smith, Huston. *Forgotten Truth: The Primordial Tradition.* New York: Harper & Row, 1976.

Smith, Wilfred Cantwell. *The Faith of Other Men.* New York: Harper & Row, Harper Torchbooks, 1972.

Radhakrishnan, S. *Eastern Religions and Western Thought.* New York: Oxford University Press, 1975.

Ross, Floyd H., and Tynette Hills. *Great Religions by Which Men Live.* Original Title: *Questions That Matter Most Asked by the World's Religions.* Greenwich, Conn.: Fawcett World, 1975.

---

* This is a very difficult problem with a variety of possible answers. One hint that you might reflect on and develop is presented in the Epilogue: The West—objective fact; China—corporate human feeling; India—that which leads to spiritual growth. You may wish to develop a different group of ideas or expand the ones suggested herein.

Part III

RELIGIOUS ISSUES

Religion, in its various forms, is a lived phenomenon. The varieties of religious expression examined in previous chapters—myth, ritual, belief, scripture, and art—are central expressions that reveal the dynamic quality of religion in human emotion, action, the creative arts, and thought.

Just as religion is lived through its varied expressions, so too is it lived within the context of pressing problems. Living one's religion involves critical reflection, unless one dimension of life—that of raising questions and seriously reflecting on alternate answers—is denied to religious people. In closed societies where children are effectively socialized into a monolithic community and protected from all external influences, those children will only rarely be involved in intellectual issues. They will not feel the tensions of clashing truth claims or be aware that some people question God's reality, that there are alternate ways to view suffering and death, or even that there are ethnic groups different from their own. Such closed societies are rare at any time in history, however. Naiveté has always been threatened by the migration of peoples, by cultural interface, and by the awareness of different ideologies and life styles. Even more is this the case now, with worldwide television transmission and jet travel. Moreover, there seems to be something in human life that prompts people to reflect on the problems that press upon them: Why was I born? Is suffering a punishment for something I did? What happens when I die? Is life getting better or worse? If God is, what is God? These kinds of issues are inherent in religion because the concerns of religion are the most crucial concerns of humanity.

If religious people are inevitably immersed in problems, so too are students of religion, even though they may not consider themselves religious. The student, seeking to know as much as can be known about religion, will wish to understand the issues as fully as possible and to grapple with ways of resolving them in a manner that is appropriate to religion as well as intelligible for the student. If the student or scholar is thorough in the process of critical reflection on religious issues, a distinctive contribution may be made to scholarship itself, to the religious communities, and even to the person's own understanding.

THE PROBLEM OF GOD

Men and women who are deeply religious, who sense themselves to be related to God or the gods, whose self-understanding is that they were divinely created and are sustained by the source of all life, do not initially pose questions about the reality of God or about God's existence. It is well known that the Jewish and Christian Bible does not question the existence of God, nor does it present any philosophical argument in behalf of God's existence. Rather, it assumes that God is; it does not argue for that conviction. In the life of any person or religious community, it is not until the belief in God has been brought into conscious doubt by outside challenges or internal trauma that rational evidence for God's existence is sought.

Serious questions about God have, in fact, arisen in the Western religions. Traditional theism has been challenged, defended, denied, and reshaped. The first chapter in Part III, then, is an exploration of the problem of God and alternate responses to this profound issue.

DEATH AND ESCHATOLOGY

Within any single religious tradition, as well as among the different communities, death and its meaning haunt men and women. Despite the fact that all people die, why does our culture try to hide the fact of death from us? If death is real, is it also final? If death is not final, is it intelligible for people to believe in immortality? in reincarnation? in the resurrection of the body? If all people must die, is there the possibility of dying with dignity? And within the many alternative beliefs, is it reasonable for people to maintain hope in the face of last things? These issues surrounding death and eschatology are addressed by James B. Wiggins in Chapter 10.

EVIL AND SUFFERING

"Why do good people—righteous people—suffer?" This problem has captured the attention of humanity for thousands of years. If God is both good and powerful, why does He not protect His people from tragedy and evil? If He can and does not, He is not good; if He desires to and cannot; then He is not powerful. In either case He is not the God proclaimed in the Bible. Can belief in God be sustained in the midst of massive tragedy like the Holocaust or Hiroshima? The chapter on evil and suffering by Alan L. Berger serves as an introduction to this issue—an issue that he shows to be universal in the religions of the world.

PATHS TO SALVATION

Are all religions basically the same in belief and practice, or are the various religions fundamentally different? Some scholars claim that there is a universal metaphysical and ethical truth in all religions. Hence, each religion is an expression of the perennial philosophy. Others assert that each religion is distinct, expressive of a single culture, and must be understood only within its own context. The argument in Chapter 12 is that all religions have a similar structure but different content. Thus there are many different paths to salvation, but each path can be analyzed and understood by a model that represents the common structure found in all religions.

RELIGION AND GROUP IDENTITY

It appears strange that religious people whose ethical beliefs emphasize love and brotherhood perpetually fight with one another. The Christian Crusades and Muslim conquests are classic examples. In the modern era there is anti-Semitism, discrimination by "Christian" whites against blacks, conflict between Protestants and Catholics in Northern Ireland and Arab and Jewish wars in the Middle East. The troubling issue, "Must there be such conflict?" may be clarified, understood, and, in time, resolved if religion is seen not as a private experience but as an expression of group identity.

Milton C. Sernett, taking a historical and sociological perspective, discusses the issue of group identity, providing a point of view to help religious people understand themselves as part of some group, and suggesting as well to the student of religion that believers can be seen fundamentally as behavers. "Religion and Group Identity" is the title of Chapter 13.

RELIGION AND TECHNOLOGY

There are many other issues that have emerged in religion and religious studies during the last half of the twentieth century. Representative of these contemporary issues, and possibly central to them, is the problem of religion and technology. The facts that we live in a technological society and that our culture is being shaped by the symbols of meaning coming from technology are hardly to be questioned. But is modern technology an enemy of traditional religion or of any religion? On the other hand, can technology and the symbol system of a technological society furnish us with the language for expressing our deepest convictions? To put the issue differently, is modern technology destroying religion or is it ushering in a new religiosity? If the latter is true, is the new religiosity alien to Biblical religion or more like Biblical religion than most modern forms of Christianity? These crucial questions are addressed by Gabrial Vahanian in Chapter 14.

The chapters in Part III may be read in any order you choose. Please note the questions for study, reflection, and discussion and the suggested projects at the end of each chapter to guide individual or group study.

CHAPTER 9

The Problem of God

T. WILLIAM HALL

Belief in the reality of God is a central conviction in the great religious traditions of the West—Judaism, Christianity, and Islam. The ancient scriptures of each religion give clear evidence of the people's belief in one God and of the importance of God in their understanding of the world, society, and themselves and their destiny. For ancient religious people God was real; He truly existed.

We can suppose that there were skeptical people in the earliest communities—those who questioned the bold assertions about God. The historical record is clear that by 500 B.C. challenges to theism, along with supporting arguments, were made by Greek philosophers. By the rise of modern science in the sixteenth and seventeenth centuries, the issue, Does God exist, and if so, what kind of reality is God? had become a well-established problem in religious thought.

Even in our own time we continue to be haunted by questions surrounding belief and unbelief. The problem of God as discussed here may therefore be a problem for every serious student of religion. The issue is a difficult one involving a tough-minded examination of issues. Within this inquiry personal convictions about theism and atheism may be uncovered. It is even possible that an intellectual conviction supporting theism, atheism, or some new understanding of God will emerge for the person who is diligent in studying the problem of God.

The chapter, then, begins with a sketch of the belief in God within the Western religious traditions; it continues with the philosophical defense of theism. Challenges to belief in God are presented from natural science, psychology, sociology, and the philosophical school called linguistic analysis. Four meanings of atheism are then explored, followed by a discussion of issues surrounding secularization, the "death of God," and the "crisis of unbelief." The chapter ends with a few pages discussing new perspectives on the problem of God.

TRADITIONAL THEISM

The claim of practicing Christians, Jews, and Muslims is that there is a Supreme Being, perfect in power, knowledge, and value, who created the universe and continues in love to sustain and direct it. Such a concept of God is called *theism.*

Within the community of the earliest Jews, ancient Israel, it is clear that they came to believe in the one God, Yahweh. It was their assertion that "in the beginning, Yahweh created the heaven and the earth." It was this God who revealed Himself to Moses in a burning bush, who had concern for the slavery and poverty of the Israelites in Egypt, who guided Moses in leading them out of Egypt to freedom, who made a covenant with them that He would remain their God if they would be faithful to Him, and who gave them the Ten Commandments. Conviction about Yahweh and the people's obligation to be devoted to Him made up the central themes of the Jewish Bible. The Psalms most vividly show this passionate faith:

The heavens are telling the glory of God; and the firmament proclaims his handiwork . . .
The Lord is my shepherd, I shall not want; . . .
To Thee, O Lord, I lift up my soul . . .
Praise the Lord, all nations! . . .[1]

The Bible also reports the demands of the prophet Micah: "What does the Lord require of you but to do justice, and to love kindness, and to walk humbly with your God?"[2] The Book of Job, moreover, is a struggle with the problem of evil—why people who are faithful to God still suffer. Throughout the entire Jewish scriptures there seems to be complete confidence in the reality of God.

During the many years of Jewish history religious Jews have maintained this faith, which is ritualized in daily prayers and high-holiday services. It has been preserved in spite of dispersions, ghetto discriminations, pogroms, and the Holocaust. To this day the experience of God is recalled in every temple and synagogue when the people say the *Shema:* "Hear, O Israel, the Lord our God, the Lord is One."

Christianity, like the Jewish culture out of which it emerged, continued the monotheistic faith as Christians accepted the Jewish scriptures, along with their own New Testament, as the Bible. They were convinced that God was in the beginning, and the same God "became flesh and dwelt among us."[3] This claim was that Jesus, whom Christians call the Christ, was the incarnation of God—was in some sense God Himself. The Christian scriptures assert not only that "God is spirit" and "God loved the world" but also that Jesus and God are one.[4]

As Christianity spread north from Palestine toward Greece and Rome, there is evidence in the New Testament letters that the belief in a God who created the world, who forgives people for their rebellion from God, and who is their source of peace and hope, continued to be the central element in Christian religious faith. No one needed to argue for the reality of God. Rather, belief in God provided the foundation for Christian theology, morality, and religious ritual, and for the entire way of life of those who believed. In every moment of private devotion the Christians directed their prayers to God. In every kind of public worship belief in God was affirmed, often in the form of a creed like the following: "I believe in God the Father Almighty, Maker of heaven and earth; and in Jesus Christ his only Son our Lord . . ."[5]

Belief in the one God called Allah and devotion to this God is the central focus of the religion of Islam. In fact the meaning of the word *Islam* is "submission to the will of Allah." Those who are in the religious traditions of Islam and believe Muhammad to be the greatest prophet of God make up the third great monotheistic religion.

Just as the scriptures of Judaism and Christianity reflect a profound belief in God, the Islamic claims about Allah come from the Qur'an itself. According to the sacred book, Allah created humanity; Allah, being kind, taught people things that were not known before.[6] This God is a single being, a unified personal will who overshadows the entire universe with His power and grace.[7] John A. Hutchison writes that "any exposition of Muslim doctrine must begin—and end—with the one God, Allah, majestic, holy, transcendent, absolutely unique."[8] Belief in Allah truly permeates Muslim religious faith and practices. Even to this day, when the Muslim goes to his mosque to worship or kneels five times each day to pray as he is commanded to do, the reality of his God, Allah, is unquestioned.

Belief in one divine being, whether Yahweh, God or Allah, has dominated the religious faith of Jews, Christians, and Muslims from the beginnings of their communities and has continued in the piety of the faithful to this day. The lives of these people have been shaped by their confidence that they belong to the Divine Being, that He is concerned for them, and that the task of humanity is to follow the commands of the Holy One. This central conviction of the reality of God was not a "problem" or an "issue" to the faithful. The conviction was, rather, an essential part of the tradition, being affirmed in the scriptures and lived out in the holy rituals. To be a Jew, a Christian, or a Muslim was to know God, to love God, and to obey God.

Yet the time was to come when the audacious assertion that the supreme creator of the universe is a being who is perfect in every way and continues to nurture human life would be doubted as well as defended against doubts. When such questions and supportive arguments developed, theism had become an issue. The issue, stated simply and boldly, is as follows: Is the claim true that God, as understood in the Western religious traditions, really exists? Even more briefly, Does God exist? There are both defenders and critics of theism, but it is to a group of philosophical defenders of theism that we now turn.

THE PHILOSOPHICAL DEFENSE OF THEISM

Philosophy literally means "the love of wisdom." In the West this passionate concern for general principles that would answer the most basic problems anyone could think of emerged out of the intellectual life of Greece. By the time of Socrates and Plato a rich philosophical heritage had developed. Theories presented by the great philosophers—Thales, Heraclitus, Pythagoras, Epicurus—are known by every student of the history of philosophy.

After Christianity became established in the West, Greek philosophy continued to provide the method of inquiry and the symbol system that explained, defended, and criticized the theories of religion. Throughout a period of nearly 2500 years, from Plato's time to the present, a number of philosophers developed supportive arguments for the existence of God. Sometimes their motive was to defend belief against challenges. At other times it may have been a disinterested desire to show the power of philosophical argument. Many people in the West today, who believe in God and yet have been troubled by modern threats to that belief, turn to one of the philosophical arguments to justify their theistic conviction.

Throughout the literature of philosophy of religion three major "arguments for the existence of God" have been emphasized. They are (1) ontological, (2) cosmological, and (3) teleological arguments. A brief sketch of those philosophical arguments will follow.

THE ONOTOLOGICAL ARGUMENT

In about the year 1078, in an abbey in Normandy, the head monk, the prior Anselm, wrote a series of meditations in which he tried to provide a single basis of reasoning to support the Christian conviction of God's existence. The principle for which he was looking seemed to have appeared to him suddenly, and he wrote it in the form of a prayer. Since then his words, and the argument supporting them, have been known as the *ontological argument* and have fascinated philosophers and theologians. In brief, the statement is that "God is that than which nothing greater can be conceived." For St. Anselm, it followed that God must necessarily exist. Selections from Anselm's own words may be helpful in understanding his argument.

O Lord, you who give understanding to faith, so far as you know it to be beneficial, give me to understand that you are just as we believe, and that you are what we believe.

We certainly believe that you are something than which nothing greater can be conceived. But is there any such nature, since "the fool has said in his heart: God is not."

However, when this very same fool hears what I say, when he hears of "something than which nothing greater can be conceived," he certainly understands what he hears.

What he understands stands in relation to his understanding, even if he does not understand that it exists. For it is one thing for a thing to stand in relation to our understanding; it is another thing for us to understand that it really exists. For instance, when a painter imagines what he is about to paint, he has it in relation to his understanding. However, he does not yet understand that it exists, because he has not yet made it. After he paints it, then he both has it in relation to his understanding and understands that it exists. Therefore, even the fool is convinced that "something than which nothing greater can be conceived" at least stands in relation to his understanding, because when he hears of it he understands it, and whatever he understands stands in relation to his understanding.

And certainly that than which a greater cannot be conceived cannot stand only in relation to the understanding. For if it stands at least in relation to the understanding, it can be conceived to be also in reality, and this is something greater. Therefore, if "that than which a greater cannot be conceived" only stood in relation to the understanding, then "that than which a greater cannot be conceived" would be something than which a greater can be conceived. But this is certainly impossible.

Therefore, something than which a greater cannot be conceived undoubtedly both stands in relation to the understanding and exists in reality.[9]

In his book, *Proslogium*, Anselm continues at great length to develop this argument, which has led to controversy throughout the development of philosophical thought, from Gaunilo, a contemporary of Anselm, through Descartes in the seventeenth century, to Kant in the eighteenth century, and on to the twentieth-century philosopher Bertrand Russell.

Any summary of the complexity of the discussion is impossible in a few lines. If, however, Anselm is correct in assuming that existence is a predicate that can logically be included in the subject of the sentence, then the sentence "God exists" is true, existence logically following from the meaning of the word *God*. Of course not all people agree. They would probably insist that Anselm may have given an adequate definition of God but that a definition cannot prove that the one described in the definition actually exists in reality. It was Immanuel Kant, much later, who insisted that existence cannot be shown to be merely the result of an idea; existence can be known only from empirical data.[10]

Yet Anselm did make a contribution to the issue concerning the existence of God. He was seeking reasons to support his Christian faith. He seemed to believe that traditional theism could not stand without reason, nor was reason itself sufficient to deal with the question of the reality of God. Rather, Anselm sought to bring together faith and reason in an effort to make intelligible the affirmation of God in his tradition. While Anselm's formula may be inadequate for many contemporary thinkers, his "argument" remains as a clear example of "faith seeking understanding"—a motivation not absent in the modern world.

THE COSMOLOGICAL ARGUMENT

Probably more theists in the modern era appeal to the cosmological argument than to the ontological one. A man or woman might he heard to say, "Of course God exists. The world must come from somewhere; it didn't just happen without a cause." This form of argument for the existence of God can be traced to Plato's dialogue *Laws*. However, the argument itself, in various forms, is most often attributed to the theologian St. Thomas Aquinas, who lived from 1224 to 1274 A.D.

Unlike Anselm, who moves from an idea or definition of God to "prove" the existence of God, St. Thomas moves from the world as experienced to "prove" the existence of God as necessary for its intelligibility. He actually presented five approaches, all of which be believed proved God's existence in that the hypothesis that God exists is the only way to account for the empirical data.

The first argument begins with the observation that some things about us are in motion. We have also observed that whatever is in motion is put into that state by something else that moves it. Now, if everything that moves is put into motion by something else, that which did the moving would itself have been set into motion by something else. Soon we are taken back, back, and yet further back until we arrive at the conception of a first mover that was put into motion by nothing else. Such a first mover, Thomas said, is what is meant by God.

The second proof is similar to the first, but Thomas refers to the second as the argument from "an order of efficient causation." Using a theory of causation developed many years earlier by Aristotle, he presents the point of view that every efficient cause is not the cause of itself but must be caused by something prior to itself. In fact the cause of everything is something prior to that being observed. Yet in so tracing the original cause we are led to an infinite regress or else must posit a first cause if there are to be any of the intermediate causes and even the ultimate effects that we observe. Denying the possibility of an infinite regress, Thomas argued that it is necessary to insist on the reality of a first efficient cause, to which everyone gives the name *God*.

Thomas's third argument is often referred to as the argument from "contingency and necessity." We all observe that everything around us, even ourselves, is contingent; that is, everything we can experience depends on something else. Now, if everything is contingent, nothing necessarily exists, for everything depends on something else and comes into existence and goes out of existence, but is never necessary. Since this fact appears to be true, it would therefore follow in theory that at one time nothing at all existed, for nothing is necessary. But it is ridiculous to assert this, for if at one time there was nothing, then there could not be anything now. Thus we must posit a necessary being who had the power to bring about everything that is contingent.

Although there are two additional ways of stating the position taken by Thomas, the fourth based on the gradation in things and the fifth based on the governance of the world, let us for the moment rest the cosmological arguments on the first three. These do seem to have positive appeal to some believers, who thus have an answer to the question, Where did it all start? The answer is God.

Those who repudiate the cosmological arguments simply say that we do not need to affirm any first cause or first mover. We can just as intelligently believe in an endless regress of events that require no beginning at all. From this point of view it is clear that the Thomistic arguments are based on premises that can be reasonably doubted and therefore seem less than decisive in requiring rational assent. Nonetheless, the argument continues to be used by philosophers and theologians.

THE TELEOLOGICAL ARGUMENT

The term *teleological* comes from the Greek words *telos,* meaning "end" or "purpose," and *logia,* which means "the science or study of." Thus *teleological* refers to the study of final purpose, goal, or end. From the time Plato wrote the *Timaeus* through the fifth argument of Thomas about 1500 years later, arguments have been presented claiming that God must exist because the complex or intricate design in nature calls for an infinite designer. However, it was William Paley (1743–1805) who presented a modern and influential teleological argument.[11]

William Paley used an analogy in his argument. Anyone who found a watch lying on the ground would not be justified in explaining that watch, with all of its complex mechanisms, as just happening by chance. Rather, it is a better hypothesis to suppose that the watch implies a watchmaker—someone who designed it and built it. Another illustration would be as follows: suppose you take the current issue of *Time* magazine, with its many stories on approximately eighty pages. Use your scissors and cut out every single letter and punctuation mark, placing them in a basket. Then throw up the pieces until they all fall back in place, making up the magazine exactly as it was.

Such an experiment would fail, even though there might be some mathematical probability about the number of times it would be necessary for the magazine to be reconstituted by chance. It would be more reasonable to believe that the magazine was edited and written with the intention of creating a complete, logically ordered, and aesthetically pleasing volume. But the world, including nature and human beings, is infinitely more complex. Surely there must be a divine architect who planned it with the purpose or end in mind that we now enjoy.

Henri Bergson developed the same theme in his book *Creative Evolution*, using the argument that a study of the process of evolution suggests the hypothesis of a purposive being who directed the movement from simple to more complex forms of life and is responsible even for the magnificent instinctual traits in animals.

It was St. Thomas Aquinas, however, who stated the argument in a few words, as follows:

We see that things which lack knowledge, such as natural bodies, act for an end, and this is evident from their acting always, or nearly always, in the same way, so as to obtain the best result. Hence it is plain that they achieve their end, not fortuitously, but designedly. Now whatever lacks knowledge cannot move towards an end, unless it be directed by some being endowed with knowledge and intelligence; as the arrow is directed by the archer. Therefore some intelligent being exists by whom all natural things are directed to their end; and this being we call God. [12]

There are criticisms to this teleological argument. David Hume, in his *Dialogues Concerning Natural Religion,* criticized this classical argument as follows. He held that anything observed to have stability or order would seem to be designed. Yet it might have happened by chance, or by particles in random motion over a long period. To go one step further, even if we grant, as Plato, St. Thomas, and Paley insist, that there is a designer, this does not necessarily mean that the designer of the world was infinitely wise, good, and powerful, as theism asserts. Rather, there is so much tragedy and evil in the world that the designer might be some kind of devil as well as God.

Although there are weaknesses in the teleological argument for God, it continues to be used by people to express their sensitivity to order, design, and beauty and, through such awareness, to affirm their belief in a God who has created the beauty and sustains that quality in nature and in people.

CHALLENGES TO THEISM

Before 1600 there were Western philosophers who posed a serious threat to traditional beliefs about God. Indeed, there were skeptics who raised questions about the reality of God. Yet many philosophers used their intellectual skills to provide rational schemes for supporting belief in God (as we have just seen in the "arguments") and in discussing the nature and attributes of the Divine Being. The medieval synthesis was truly one in which religion and philosophy were united.

The rise of modern science in the seventeenth century, however, brought a new challenge to theistic beliefs. In fact science threatened the intelligibility of both belief in God and the philosophic defense of those beliefs. It was not that the new scientists were belligerent toward religion. Rather, the emerging methodology of science and the data that were being gathered began to undermine the assumptions on which the entire medieval view of humanity, nature, and the cosmos was based.

The world view held by medieval intellectual and religious people seems to have been one in which everything was centered on humankind, this planet, and God. The earth was central, the place created for the most important creature, the human being. Although human beings were of central importance, God was omnipotent, omnipresent, and omniscient. He was above and beyond the world He had created, having as His primary concern the welfare and salvation of His children. Ian G. Barbour says that for medieval people "Everything was in its neatly arranged place in an integrated total plan. It was a 'law-abiding world,' but the laws were moral and not mechanical. This was the medieval view of the universe which the new science was to challenge." [13] The seventeenth century brought this challenge. Built on the foundations laid by Copernicus, who developed conclusively the theory that the earth hurtles rapidly through space even though people do not see this motion because they are traveling with it, Galileo moved further in his discovery of planetary movements. Galileo's scientific writings were a serious threat to the church because he questioned the central place of humanity and its world in the larger scheme of things. Other giants of the seventeenth century, such as Tycho Brahe and Thomas Kepler, were fanatic about close observation of facts and the use of mathematics to express relations among those data. [14]

More specifically, the challenge to belief in God came by way of the scientific challenge to the methods of the philosophers and, even more, a challenge to the theories of knowledge in religion. Whereas the philosopher/theologian depended primarily on reason joined with revelation, the new sciences were proclaiming a method of rigorous observation and mathematics. As a result of the new method "Man was demoted from the center of the universe to a spinning, peripheral planet. Man's uniqueness and the idea of God's particular concern for him seemed in danger." [15]

Our special concern here is that the idea of God seemed to be challenged by the implications of the new scientific method. If the way of gaining and verifying knowledge was completely empirical and mathematical, then there might not be a "necessary being," as St. Anselm had rationally argued, or a first cause, as inferred by St. Thomas. Moreover, if the world was to be viewed as some kind of particle in motion, then a mechanistic interpretation might be a more adequate explanation than any purposive theism. Thus the foundations for belief in God, although by no means refuted, were being challenged.

By the nineteenth century the biological sciences were as prominent as physics and mathematics. It was in the year 1859 that Charles Darwin published his monumental work, *The Origin of Species,* in which his theory of evolution provided a fresh scientific challenge to belief in God. Darwin's study showed that variations exist to the extent that no two living things are exactly alike. The individuals in this variation, however, are perpetually involved in a struggle for survival. In what he called the process of "natural selection," the species that are adaptable to the environment and are successful in the struggle survive. In the chain of evolution, then, there is movement toward more complex forms of life.

In 1871 Darwin published an additional volume on evolution in which he specifically discussed human beings. It is in this book that he applied his scientific theories toward an explanation of human development. By so doing he was bringing the human being, previously believed to be the creation of God, into the realm of natural law. This was truly a challenge to theism. Such a conflict was the focus of a famous trial that took place in Tennessee in 1922. At this trial William Jennings Bryan, defending the literal creation story in Genesis, debated against Clarence Darrow, who supported a general theory of evolution.[16]

The challenge to theism continued in the form of attacks by the pioneer of psychoanalysis, Sigmund Freud (1856–1939). In *The Future of an Illusion* Freud suggested that religious teachings, including those about God, do not come from careful thinking. Rather, they are "illusions, fulfillments of the oldest, strongest and most urgent wishes of mankind. The secret of their strength lies in the strength of those wishes."[17]

Freud went on to say that all children grow up in fear and with the need to be protected. Just as the child may be protected in this life by a loving parent—often a father—the adult needs the sense of being protected by a supernatural father. Thus, according to Freud, the illusion of God may be nothing more than a projection of one's desire for an earthly father on the cosmos in the form of a heavenly father. Some followers of Freud, then, are prone to discount belief in God and, rather, seek the unconscious or pathological reasons why people hold to that belief.

While Freud sought the internal motivating forces in the human being that could account for the "illusory" belief in God, Emile Durkheim (1858–1917), a French sociologist, sought to explain religion and beliefs about God as products of society—even as projections of a feeling of social power. God is not a transcendent or supernatural reality, creating the world and human beings. God, according to Durkheim, is rather the personification of the authority of society itself to order individual life.

Durkheim's position does not demand the elimination of the idea of God. In fact he seemed to believe that the collective consciousness of society is the highest type of conscious life. God is the symbol of this collective psyche. Thus Durkheim's position was an attack on traditional theism, even while it maintained a different theory about God.

A major philosophical challenge to theism comes from people in the contemporary school of philosophy called linguistic analysis, a school of thought that has been profoundly influenced by the methods of the empirical sciences. One major representative who has written widely on religious themes is the British philosopher Antony Flew. His challenge to theism is seen clearly in the presentation of his principle of "falsification."

According to Flew, statements that are meant to assert some fact must always lend themselves to empirical verification in the same way that scientific assertions are verified. In addition, they must be, in theory, falsifiable. This way of testing assertions about God has the effect, he believes, of showing that statements about God are really without meaning. Here is his argument:

Take such utterances as "God has a plan," "God loves us as a father loves his children," or "God created the world." They look at first sight very much like assertions, vast cosmological assertions . . .

Now to assert that such and such is the case is necessarily equivalent to denying that such and such is not the case. . . . One way of trying to understand his utterance is to attempt to find what he would regard as counting against, or as being incompatible with its truth. . . . And if there is nothing which a putative assertion denies then there is nothing which it asserts either: and so it is not really an assertion.[18]

What Flew is getting at is that religious people have such a deep conviction about God that they will not let anything count against their conviction. They could hear rational refutations; they might suffer tragic events; the worst possible things might happen and they would still insist that nothing can destroy their belief in God. Thus, according to the theory of falsification, the belief in God does not lend itself to falsification and hence is a meaningless statement—it asserts nothing.

Opponents of Flew would insist that we should not be quickly persuaded that statements about God are meaningless, even though they may not lend themselves to empirical falsification. In fact statements about God may not be meant to be assertions of fact but, as R. M. Hare proposes, may be meant to express a particular perspective—a "blik," as he calls it.[19] Or again, statements about God may not be refutable according to the principle of falsification because such statements are not empirical assertions. To use the word *God* is not to declare that in the real world we can observe such and such to be a fact. Rather, the idea of God is an absolute presupposition to the knowing of facts; it is not a statement of fact itself. Moreover, the idea of God cannot be held as an empirically falsifiable idea. The

God idea is held to make sense of other things, not because other things make sense of it.[20]

Thus while scientific philosophy offers a challenge to belief in God, this challenge is not conclusive, at least not for every reflective person.

Finally, one additional challenge to theism needs to be mentioned in order to provide a representative group of challenges. It is the problem of evil.[21] Now, tragedy and evil are inevitably a problem within traditional theism. In the first place, the supreme and perfect being is one, not two. Hence, all that happens must be related to the one God. Evil cannot be the product of a devil or a second demonic diety. Second, God is understood by theists to be perfect in every way. This means that God has unlimited power, goodness, and knowledge to use in lovingly sustaining and directing human life and the universe. The empirical evidence, however, shows that there is tragedy and evil. If God does not know about such evil, then His knowledge is not perfect and He is not God. If he does not wish to eradicate evil, He is not perfectly good and hence is not God. And if He does not have the power to destroy evil, He is by definition not God, for God is omnipotent in the context of traditional theism.

At first examination, then, it would appear that if there is evil, either God does not exist or, if God does exist, He is not perfect in knowledge, goodness, and power and not the kindly God that theists affirm. This problem can be stated in a slightly different way, as suggested by the philosopher Henry D. Aiken:

> If there is a being that is at once almighty, omniscient and perfectly good, it will be both able and willing to prevent evil. On the other hand, if something is evil, it must be concluded that there is no such being, since a perfectly good person would prevent it if he could, and an almighty and omniscient being could prevent it if he would. Either, then, there is no such being or nothing is evil.[22]

Neither horn of the dilemma just presented is easy to accept. The book of Job in the Bible is one of the ancient documents that reflect the struggle of holding to the reality of suffering, tragedy, and evil while still seeking to believe in God. World War II and the Holocaust continue to haunt people today. How could a good God who had a covenant with His people permit 6 million to be killed by the ruthless Nazis. Surely no one can deny the radical evil of the Holocaust. In the face of that experience, is theism possible?

Shall the believer qualify God's power and declare that God is finite? Shall the believer permit God's goodness or knowledge to be limited? Will the remaining God still be the God of theism? Or is it possible to understand evil as somehow necessary in order for God to work out the final goodness? Can one declare that tragedy builds character, or that the world is better with some evil in it? Can tragedy and evil be considered to be caused by human free will, which is itself a gift of God? Can the believer claim that evil is ultimately a mystery and that people can be sustained by God only in the face of that mystery? In short, is it possible to affirm both the reality of evil and the reality of God? This question remains one of the most puzzling of all issues for the theist.

In summary, the challenge to belief in the God of Western monotheistic religions has taken various forms. The astronomy and physics of the seventeenth century raised questions about a purposeful deity. Later biological science, especially the theories of evolution, was a threat to the idea of God as creator. The medical psychiatric theory of Freud and the sociological concepts of Durkheim provided another blow to any easy acceptance of the existence of God as conceived by theists. Twentieth-century linguistic philosophy, profoundly influenced by the sciences, has declared that statements about God are really meaningless. And the problem of evil has always been a threat to theism.

ATHEISM

If there are major objections to belief in traditional theism, then it might be supposed that intelligent people would assume a position of atheism. Such a hasty conclusion, however, is not self-evident and poses its own problems. The first problem arises with respect to a clear definition of atheism; the second follows from the implications of each different definition.

Atheism, which comes from the Greek *a*, which means "not," and *theos*, which means "god," could, in the first place, mean that some particular god is believed not to exist. It is in this understanding of the term that early Christians were called atheists. They did not believe that the roman emperor was a god.

Second, atheism may mean a denial of the literal meaningfulness of all statements about a god. For example, if all meaningful statements about existence must lend themselves to empirical verification, then statements concerning the existence of God, which are metaphysical and do not lend themselves to such verification, are literally meaningless.

A third use of the term *atheism* intends to deny the existence of God as conceived by traditional theists. Thus atheism in this sense literally means "not theism." A person who denies the existence of "a Supreme Being who is perfect in every way, who created the universe and continues to sustain and direct human affairs" would be an atheist—a nontheist.

If we use the first definition and try to see its implications, the atheist so identified becomes one who declares that a person or group claiming the existence of a particular god is making a false judgment. From this perspective every reflective person is from time to time an atheist. Such "atheism" is really a theological position that is iconoclastic about some gods.

The second meaning of atheism is not so much a definition of atheism as it is a philosophic posture. As such, it needs to be taken seriously, if for no other reason than that the posture dominates so much contemporary philosophy and theology. When the perspective is followed, however, the conclusions are indecisive and may tend to support traditional theism, encourage a nontheistic view of God, or return to the original positivistic position that assertions about God remain literally meaningless.[23]

In the third place, the kind of atheism that is a denial of the existence of the God of theism is a position taken by a number of religious people. Some might argue that theism must be modified because of one or more of the challenges to it. They could, in addition, affirm that some other concept of God is more intelligible than theism, more compatible with modern science, or more persuasive for other reasons. To be an atheist in this third sense is to be a nontheist, but belief in God is not automatically ruled out thereby.

In short, a position of atheism appears to be without merit in solving the problem of God. Focus on the first meaning is of limited usefulness unless criteria are articulated for judging the truth or falsity of particular assertions about God or gods. The second definition leads to a complex method of linguistic analysis that does not provide definitive conclusions, even though it is a useful philosophical method. Finally, if by the term *atheism* we mean "nontheism," the reality of God is not by definition repudiated. Our task, then, is to explore the intelligibility of affirming the reality of a nontheistic God. It is to this task that we now turn. In so doing, it may be instructive to remind ourselves that belief in God is by no means extinct after many centuries of criticism and numerous expositions on atheism. Moreover, belief is not confined to nonintellectuals and nonscientists. Ian Barbour, himself a physicist, is persuasive when he writes that theology can never be replaced by the sciences, since science and theology ask fundamentally different sorts of questions. He goes on to write, "In an age dominated by religion, it was necessary to assert the independence of science. Today, in an age dominated by science, it may be necessary to assert the independence of religion."[24]

A REEXAMINATION OF THE PROBLEMATIC

In the quarter-century following world War II, religious thought was in rapid transition. Whether influenced by or influencing cultural shifts, the new intellectual climate provided a different context for stating the problem of God and for arriving at alternatives to traditional theism. Three of these cultural and ideological emphases are (1) secularization, (2) the "death of God," and (3) the "crisis of unbelief."

SECULARIZATION

In the 1960s two books about secularization captured the attention of a widespread audience. These were *The Secular City*, by Harvey Cox, and

Honest to God, by Bishop John Robinson.[25] The intent of both authors was not to challenge all belief in God. Rather, it was to cast the issue in a fresh way so that people who might otherwise throw over their conviction in the reality of God might come to a new understanding of what it means to believe in God.

Cox, drawing upon the writing of a Dutch theologian, C. A. van Peursen, defines secularization as the freedom of modern people from traditional religious and metaphysical control over reason and language.[26] It is his view that most people no longer get their self-understanding and their meaning systems from classical philosophy or traditional religion. We are now free or should be free from ancient mythologies as well as from metaphysics and religious dogmas.

It is Cox's conviction that in this new age of freedom, characterized by the anonymity, mobility, pragmatism, and profanity of the secular city, people can come to a new and more powerful understanding of the reality of God. While the traditional God may be dead, while institutions of religion and their dependence on antiquated symbol systems may be moribund, it is still possible—even essential—for modern people to express convictions about God. But the God spoken of by Cox is not the well-known God of the past twenty-five centuries. It is the God who must be spoken of in a secular fashion in the language of politics. As Cox writes,

We speak of God politically whenever we give occasion to our neighbor to become the responsible, adult agent, the fully post-town and post-tribal man God expects him to be today. We speak to him of God whenever we cause him to realize consciously the web of interhuman reciprocity in which he is brought into being and sustained in it as a man. We speak to him of God whenever our words cause him to shed some of the blindness and prejudice of immaturity and to accept a larger and freer role in fashioning the instrumentalities of human justice and cultural vision.[27]

Just as Cox proposes a new way of speaking of God in an age of secularization, Bishop Robinson urges people to use the metaphor of "depth" rather than "up" or "out" in speaking of God. Robinson's major contribution is that of making available to a large audience the theologies of Paul Tillich, Rudolph Bultmann, and Dietrich Bonhoeffer. If we are living in a secular age that is characterized by the end of theism, Robinson seems to be saying, then the newer theologians may point us to a way of thinking and speaking about God. And what he calls "worldly holiness" suggests a secular way of living one's convictions rather than merely speaking, and even doing that in antiquated language forms. For Robinson, God is real, but real as the depth dimension of existence and, as with Paul Tillich, the ground of being.

"THE DEATH OF GOD"

Another theological movement in the 1960s provided a new challenge as well as an unusual affirmation of God. It was the "death of God" writers who captured the theological interest for a few years. So shocking was the phrase that by the mid-1960s bumper stickers displayed on cars owned by pious believers declared that "God is alive and well." Cartoons in magazines and even graffiti on subway walls took sides on the issue.

The first major book on the "death of God" theme was written by Gabriel Vahanian (the author of Chapter 14 in this volume) with the title *The Death of God: The Culture of Our Post-Christian Era*. This difficult but important book does not try to persuade the reader that the God of the Bible is literally dead. Rather, Vahanian asserts that in our present post-Christian culture God has been watered down and made so immanent and secular that the transcendent God is absent from the faith of most Christians. What many readers failed to understand was that Vahanian was not trying to destroy belief and faith in God. Rather, he was attempting to point to the vision of a God who is not defined or comprehended by finite humanity. On the contrary, humanity is defined and comprehended by God the Infinite, the Wholly Other.[28]

A different group of "death of God" theologians seemed to assert that God was actually dead. Thomas J. J. Altizer and William Hamilton, two of the most prolific writers on this theme, published a volume called *Radical Theology and the Death of God*.[29] Altizer claims that the death of God is a historical event and one that should be welcomed by all people. In a similar fashion, Hamilton writes that the death of God is not just something that has happened to people. It is not simply a time in which more and more people are atheists. Rather, to say that "God is dead" is to speak of the nature of the world.[30]

From the point of view developed by Hamilton, the writings of the German martyr Dietrich Bonhoeffer provided a clue to the meaning of the "death" of God. Like the German, Hamilton declares that humanity has come of age and can get along without the philosophical hypothesis of God and without the trappings of religion. In place of theism, the sincere Christian can use the person Jesus as his or her model of how life should be lived—everyone can become the "man for others."[31]

Several comments seem appropriate regarding this unusual movement of theology. In the first place, the "death of God" themes that dominated theological discussion for several years during the mid-1960s soon ceased to draw fanatic responses. The major impact seemed to be to focus the attention of people back on the issue of God in a time when theistic convictions had become difficult to affirm. While most traditional religious persons fought against the "death of God" theology, others, especially in academic circles, attempted to explore through it new possibilities for affirming the reality of God in nontheistic ways. Thus the "death" of God did not result in a destruction of belief. Rather, it provided a criticism for a kind of religiosity that was itself a dangerous threat to profound belief. It made its contribution to a new kind of religiosity that seemed to be emerging from the "crisis of unbelief."

THE "CRISIS OF UNBELIEF"

The phrase "crisis of unbelief" is used by the philosopher–
theologian–cultural critic Michael Novak. Novak writes persuasively
that just as there was once a time when many people were facing a crisis of
belief—when affirming the existence of God was difficult—now there is a
"crisis of unbelief." Novak claims that young people, not satisifed with the
attitudes and beliefs of their secular parents, are not willing to settle for the
emptiness that results from nonbelief in God.[32]

This "crisis of unbelief" has shown itself among the youth in the counterculture's use of drugs in an effort to simulate some religious experience. It
is seen in the pervading interest in patterns of Eastern religious life such as
yoga, Zen meditation, the Hari Krishna movement, astrology, tarot cards,
transcendental meditation, and the like. Within the Western tradition itself
the spread of the "Jesus movement" and charismatic Christianity, Islamic
Sufi mysticism, and the Lubovitcher movement in Judaism also support the
hypothesis that some kind of renewed belief has followed earlier skep-
ticisms.

These popular movements will probably not add measurably to the solution of the issue of God's existence. Yet they suggest that there may be a favorable cultural context beginning in the 1970s that makes possible a reexam-
ination of the God question and the redevelopment of new ways of expressing belief in God. It is to this theme that we now turn.

NEW PERSPECTIVES ON THE PROBLEM OF GOD

Students of religion who remain convinced of the truth of theism may
not wish to explore alternative concepts of God or ways of supporting such
convictions. Similarly, atheists who are pursuaded that God language is fac-
tually meaningless will probably not be open to examine alternate perspectives to theism. Yet the plethora of new religious books dealing with the
God problem, various new patterns of religious expression appearing in
both the occult and established religious groups, and a high interest in the
study of God and other religious issues seem to suggest that the problem of
God is not settled for all people. Those who find it necessary or desirable
(or both) to continue to wrestle with the issues surrounding belief in God
may find that there are alternatives to traditional theism that are intelligible and for which there are significant grounds for belief. Only a few such
approaches can be sketched here.

AT THE EDGES OF LANGUAGE

One way of initiating such a discussion about God is to inquire into the
linguistic nature of our utterances about God. We might proceed somewhat
as follows: It seems clear that religious people, within the Western re-

ligious traditions at least, do speak of God. But in so speaking they are using a word—*God*. Let me emphasize: At minimum, God is a word. Now, since this is the case, it is of critical importance to ask the question, What is meant when we speak the word *God?* Posing the question in this way is different from asking, Does God exist? We are asking about the meaning of human language.

If the problem is pursued in this way, we may take the point of view that the most characteristic thing about humans is that we are the creators of language. We are symbol-making creatures. And the language symbols we use are those of a community that shares in the making and the using of the symbols. The word *God*, then, is part of the crucial language or symbols of the religious community.

But affirming that we are creatures of language and that God is part of the language of the religious community does not go far enough. We need to ask, What does it mean to speak the word *God?* The answer to this question is complex, but for people in the religious community it is speaking of their central and deepest commitment. It is related to their hopes, fears, desires, loves, and trusts. God talk is not ordinary language, similar to speech about rocks, elephants, beefsteak, and Buick automobiles. That is, the word *God* is not so much a name but a symbol for the depths of existence—for the mystery of what makes life and love and hope and trust. Paul Van Buren calls religious language that which is "at the edges of language." [33] In developing the position we have just sketched, Van Buren writes, "The language of belief is clearly related to how we speak of purposes and plans, of thinking, knowing, remembering, and loving, of being agents of our own actions and taking responsibility for our acts." [34] To summarize this position, when the religious person uses the word *God* that person is not speaking of a supernatural being as the theists usually mean. Rather, he or she is trying to express in language what language is barely able to express—the inexpressible. He or she is using a symbol developed by the community to speak about that which is most true, beautiful, and good but is still beyond comprehension and beyond the usual meaning of language—at the "Edges of Language."

DEPTH PSYCHOLOGY

Still another way for contemporary people to deal with the issue of God is through post-Freudian psychologists. Two representatives of this view are Viktor E. Frankl and Roberto Assagioli. Frankl, a Viennese psychiatrist who was confined in a concentration camp during World War II, has written that the human being is characterized most basically as a creature in search of meaning. [35] Moreover, Frankl argues, clinical data point to the conclusion that within the deepest dimension of the individual is a spiritual unconscious or a natural propensity toward religion. This religiousness can be repressed, leading to neurosis. If it is not permitted expression, people

often become depressed, without any sense of meaning in life. Frankl calls
this condition "existential meaninglessness." While Freud called religion
an illusion and psychiatric thought was once considered a challenge to
belief in God, Frankl holds that people are naturally religious and that, just
as there is an unconscious religiousness, so we can speak of an "unconscious God."[36]

Another psychiatrist whose writings may guide an inquiry into the problem of God is Roberto Assagioli, the founder of a school of thought and
practice called *psychosynthesis*. Assagioli insists that all knowledge begins
with the observation of "facts" and moves from the known to the unknown.
Yet many people have failed to examine all the data in developing their understanding of human beings. It is his conviction, derived from clinical observation, that the spiritual dimension is as real as the physical and mental
dimensions. He writes,

Our position affirms that all the superior manifestations of the human psyche, such
as creative imagination, intuition, aspiration, genius, are facts which are as real and
as important as are the conditioned reflexes, and therefore as acceptable to research
and treatment just as scientifically as conditioned reflexes.[37]

Like Frankl, Assagioli believes that spiritual drives are as real as sexual
drives and that, as such, the spiritual propensity should be considered not
pathological but normal.

Assagioli proposes that through creative imagination and various medita-
tive techniques a person may follow spiritual needs and find that symbols
such as "light" or "warmth" become powerful in expressing the synthesis of
the psychological and spiritual. The implication of Assagioli, like that of
Frankl, is that psychiatric theory and practice may provide an avenue of experimentation, inquiry, and affirmation regarding the issue of the reality of
God. Their conclusions are that God is real. Yet their conceptions of God
are different from theism.

NEOPRAGMATISM

One final approach is expressed in the writings of an American
empiricist, John E. Smith, especially in his book *Experience God*.[38]
Smith first suggests that modern people must rediscover experience for an
adequate approach to the problem of God. Whereas the scientist often
identifies experience as that which is known by the senses, the rationalistic
philosopher considers the basis of knowledge in reason, and the mystic
believes the source of knowledge to be intuition, Smith defines "experience" as that which encompasses all of these dimensions of knowing. In
what he calls "radical empiricism," Smith asserts that experience is the interaction of what is outside of people and what is inside. More specifically,
"experience is an objective and critical product of the intersection between
reality in all its aspects on the one hand and a self-conscious being capable

of receiving that reality through significant form on the other."[39] With experience as his key category of knowledge, Smith sets forth the hypothesis
that "there is a religious dimension to human existence and that this dimension is unintelligible without reference to God."[40]

This kind of empiricism, which resembles that of William James, who
wrote in the last decades of the nineteenth century, may provide a methodological way for contemporary people to renew their quest for God and
succeed in reaffirming the reality of God. Such a search may be successful
because no data that are available to experience are judged a priori to be irrelevant or meaningless. James may thus seem strangely modern in setting
forth the point of view that anything less than God is not rational, by which
he meant that if all experience is accepted, and if one permits one's will to
be active when other data seem to dry up, then belief in God is not only
possible but even compelling.[41]

SUMMARY

It has been suggested, then, that while the problem of God has been an
issue throughout the history of the West, and whereas arguments for God's
existence or nonexistence have been inconclusive, the issue continues into
our time. Many people will wish to return to the philosophical arguments
to clarify and defend their belief. Those who tend toward nonbelief may
use some argument from the natural, biological, psychological, or sociological sciences to defend their denial of the existence of God.

It is suggested in this chapter, however, that critical believers and
thinkers in our time might find it more rewarding to look toward newer
approaches to the problem of God. These approaches will not focus on
the traditional God problem. Rather, attention will be directed to issues of
transcendence, as hinted at in religious language, in the depth of the psyche, and even in the rediscovery of experience. It may even be that the
creative imagination of men and women in our time will lead to radically
new and meaningful affirmations of God heretofore undreamed of.

NOTES

1. Selections from the Psalms, Chapters 19, 23, 25, and 117. All quotations are taken from
   the Revised Standard Version of the Bible.
2. Micah 6:8.
3. John 1:14.
4. Selected passages from John 3.
5. The Apostle's Creed. Tradition, not historical evidence, links this creed to the twelve
   apostles. However, it was used prior to the fourth century in the Christian Church.
6. Taken from the Qur'an, Surah xcvi, 1–4.
7. See Huston Smith, *The Religions of Man* (New York: Harper & Row, 1968), p. 205.

8. John Hutchison, *Paths of Faith* (New York: McGraw-Hill, 1975), p. 462.
9. Taken from John H. Hick and Arthur C. McGill, eds., *The Many Faced Argument* (New York: Macmillan, 1967), pp. 4–6. The authors used St. Anselm, *Opera Omnia*, ed. Dom F. S. Schmitt, trans. Arthur C. McGill.
10. See John Hick, *Philosophy of Religion*, rev. ed. (Englewood Cliffs, N.J.: Prentice-Hall, 1974), chap. 2, and John E. Smith, *Experience and God* (New York: Oxford University Press, 1968), pp. 122–134.
11. See William Paley, *Natural Theology: or Evidence of the Existences and Attributes of the Deity Collected from the Apperances of Nature*, ed. Frederick Ferré (New York: Liberal Arts Library, 1962).
12. St. Thomas Aquinas, *Summa Theologica*, pt. 1, ques. 2, Art. 3, ed. Anton C. Pegis (New York: Random House, 1968).
13. Ian G. Barbour, *Issues in Science and Religion* (Englewood Cliffs, N.J.: Prentice-Hall, 1966), p. 18.
14. See John Herman Randall, Jr., *The Making of the Modern Mind* (Boston: Houghton Mifflin, 1940), chap. 10.
15. Barbour, p. 33.
16. See Jerome Laurance and Robert Eree, *Inherit the Wind* (New York: Bantam Pathfinder, 1957), a popular rendition of the Scopes trial.
17. Sigmund Freud, *The Future of an Illusion*, as quoted by Allie M. Frazier, ed., *Issues in Religion* (New York: D. Van Nostrand, 1975), p. 111.
18. Antony Flew, "Theology and Falsification," in *New Essays in Philosophical Theology*, ed. by Antony Flew and Alasdair MacIntyre (London: SCM Press, 1955), p. 97, 98.
19. See the debate in Antony Flew and Alasdair MacIntyre, *New Essays in Philosophical Theology*, chap. 6. The essay by R. M. Hare begins on p. 99.
20. See Gordon Kaufman, *God the Problem* (Cambridge, Mass.: Harvard University Press, 1972), chap. 10, and J. Brenton Stearns, "A Priori Argument in Theological Disciplines," *Journal of the American Academy of Religion*, 44, no. 2 (June 1976): 269.
21. See Chapter 11 for a thorough discussion of evil and suffering.
22. Henry D. Aiken, *Reason and Conduct* (New York: Knopf, 1962), p. 175. Quoted by Dewey Hoitenga, "Logic and the Problem of Evil," in Keith E. Yandell, *God, Man and Religion* (New York, McGraw-Hill, 1973), 334–335.
23. See Flew and Macintyre, op. cit.
24. Barbour, p. 51.
25. Harvey Cox, *The Secular City* (New York: Macmillan, 1965), and J. A. T. Robinson, *Honest to God* (Philadelphia: Westminster Press, 1964).
26. Cox, pp. 1–12.
27. Ibid., p. 223.
28. Gabriel Vahanian, *The Death of God* (New York: George Braziller, 1961), p. 231.
29. Thomas J. J. Altizer and William Hamilton, *Radical Theology and the Death of God* (Indianapolis: Bobbs-Merrill, 1966).
30. Ibid., p. 28.
31. Ibid. See especially the chapters by Hamilton, "American Theology, Radicalism and the Death of God" and "The Death of God Theologies Today."
32. Michael Novak, *Belief and Unbelief* (New York: New American Library, a Mentor Book, 1965), p. 34.
33. Paul M. Van Buren, *The Edges of Language* (New York: Macmillan, 1972).
34. Ibid., p. 88.
35. Viktor E. Frankl, *Man's Search for Meaning* (Boston: Beacon Press, 1959).
36. This position is developed in Viktor E. Frankl, *The Unconscious God* (New York: Simon and Schuster, 1975), see esp. chap. 6.
37. Robert Assagioli, *Psychosynthesis* (New York: Viking Press, 1971), p. 193.
38. John E. Smith, *Experience and God* (New York: Oxford University Press, 1968).

39. Ibid., p. 12.
40. Ibid., p. 11.
41. These comments are the author's interpretation of the lengthy discussion by William James in his essay "The Will to Believe," published under the title *The Will to Believe and Other Essays* (New York: Dover Publications, 1956).

QUESTIONS FOR STUDY, REFLECTION, AND DISCUSSION

1. If a person asks you the question, Do you believe in the existence of God? which of the following answers would you give and why?

    a. That depends on what you mean by *God*.
    b. Yes, and I'll tell you why . . .
    c. No, God does not exist. God is the ground of existence itself.
    d. No, I only believe that which is scientifically verifiable, and the fact of God cannot be thus proved.

2. Schubert M. Ogden, in *The Reality of God*, states that "the reality of God has now become the central theological problem." Do you agree or disagree with this statement? Why or why not?

3. Suppose you are with a group of people discussing the problem of God and one person says, "This is a foolish discussion. God is a private and personal belief which cannot be talked about." How would you respond to that person?

4. As you reflect on your own self-awareness, would you tend to support or reject Frankl's belief that there is an unconscious spirituality in us all? What evidence can you share from your own experience to clarify your point of view?

PROJECTS

1. Select one of the classical philosophical arguments for the existence of God. Read thoroughly the argument as presented by the originator and commentators on it. Study also those who have rejected the argument. Then write an essay in which you state, in your own words, the argument for God, important refutations of the argument, and your own conclusions regarding the validity or nonvalidity of the argument.

2. The word *God* is sometimes a handicap to a discussion of the central religious issue to which the word *God* refers. Therefore write a short story or a drama in which the central theme has to do with theism or atheism. However, write the story without using the words *God* or *divine* or similar religious words.

3. In chapter 3 of *Belief and Unbelief* Michael Novak states that inquiry after God does not begin with objective philosophical inquiry but begins with reflection about our own selves. Thus if we are to inquire after God we must seek to know who we are.

Let us, for the moment, assume that Novak has a fruitful insight. For a period of fifteen minutes each day for at least two weeks, practice simple, quiet meditation, focusing your attention on how it feels to be a person. Then read Chapter 3 of *Belief and Unbelief* and write a brief paper in which you summarize the chapter and support or reject the author's conclusions, given in the last paragraph on page 90.

4. Friedrich Nietzsche, the German philosopher, in an essay called "The Gay Science," has a madman declare, "Whither is God. I shall tell you. We have killed him—you and I." Write an essay in which you discuss Nietzsche's meaning. Criticize and evaluate this point of view from the perspective of one author who affirms the reality of God.

5. Assuming that secularization will be a dominant characteristic of culture in the next 100 years, and assuming that scientific technology will continue to be prominent, write an essay in which you discuss the nature of belief in God for the future.

6. Select a science fiction book that imagines religion in the future. Prepare a review of that book with special attention to the concept of God presented in it. Provide a critique of that point of view.

SELECTED BIBLIOGRAPHY

Barbour, Ian G. *Issues in Science and Religion.* New York: Harper & Row, Harper Torchbooks, 1971.

Flew, Anthony G., and Alasdair MacIntyre, eds. *New Essays in Philosophical Theology.* New York: Macmillan, 1964.

Hick, John. *Philosophy of Religion.* Englewood Cliffs, N.J.: Prentice-Hall, 1973.

Macquarrie, John. *God-Talk.* London: SCM Press, 1967.

McClendon, James W., Jr. *Understanding Religious Convictions.* Notre Dame, Ind.: University of Notre Dame Press, 1975.

Miller, David L. *The New Polytheism: Rebirth of the Gods and Goddesses.* New York: Harper & Row, 1974.

Novak, Michael. *Belief and Unbelief.* New York: New American Library, Mentor Books, 1967.

Ogden, Schubert M. *The Reality of God.* New York: Harper & Row, 1966.

Robinson, John A. *Honest to God.* Philadelphia: Westminster Press, 1963.

Smith, John E. *Experience and God.* New York: Oxford University Press, 1974.

Vahanian, Gabriel. *The Death of God.* New York: George Braziller, 1961.

Van Buren, Paul M. *The Edge of Language: An Essay in the Logic of Religion.* New York: Macmillan, 1972.

Walsh, Chad. *God at Large.* New York: Seabury Press, 1971.

CHAPTER 10

Death and Eschatology

JAMES B. WIGGINS

Many students having recently begun their study of religion will be unfamiliar with the word *eschatology*. In contemporary American culture a surprisingly large portion of college-age people have never experienced contact with a dying person or even attended a funeral. Although these generalizations undoubtedly do not apply to some, they are a sufficiently safe set of presuppositions to warrant including a few very fundamental considerations before turning to some of the more extended implications to be considered.

A cultural context that so effectively shields so many of us from experiencing the death of friends and loved ones marks contemporary America as radically unlike most of the historical cultures of mankind. Regardless of violence of many sorts all around us, many of us rarely experience the shock of recognizing that each of us lives toward death. Since dying is a unique and absolute experience, the only ways of coming to any sort of terms with death are of necessity vicarious. When grandparents are shunted off to "rest homes" and left to die, and when the number of people who die in hospitals increases annually, from whom do we have an opportunity to learn how to die? Apart from the costs exacted from the people who reside in them, the "humaneness" of rest homes and hospitals is perhaps nowhere so self-evidently put to the test as in what it robs from us, the living.

It may be objected at this point that a culture develops its institutions as responses to the deepest desires and needs of its participants. By this analysis, then, it might appear that this culture wants most deeply to avoid contact with death and dying, and that the institutions that accomplish this are masterfully efficient. In the area of cultural analysis we must differentiate between describing the realities of a given culture and comparing these realities with those of other cultures. Such comparisons may be used to discard pertinent differences and to glean insight into alternative institutions, and perhaps to evaluate their respective strengths and weaknesses.

We find a concern with death at the very center of some of the most ancient religiomythical records available to us—stories such as "The Descent of Ishtar to the Nether World" and the "Gilgamesh Epic." The latter is most poignant and universally representative of the human desire to escape death. In summary, the hero Gilgamesh, after the death of his beloved friend Enkidu, begins the quest for immortality. Having consulted the gods, he is told of a plant that guarantees eternal youth to whoever eats it. The plant grows on the floor of the sea, and although Gilgamesh obtains it, it is lost before he can eat it, leaving him with the realization that he too must die. The awakening of consciousness not only of mortality in general but specifically of one's own mortality is a mark of human maturation. Fantasies of escaping death or frantically avoiding the consciousness of one's own death are but marks of an underdeveloped consciousness. As Gilgamesh became aware of his mortality, so must all of us.

Every religious tradition of which I am aware acknowledges the stark reality of death as the given limit to individual lives. This is a mark of the maturity engendered by religion wherever it appears and in whatever form. Many (but not all) religious traditions also affirm, however, that the reality of death is not the final word. Caution is necessary here. It is not a contradiction (claims to the contrary notwithstanding) to acknowledge maturely the reality of death and at the same time to question the finality of death. Two examples may help make this clear. The devout, literalistic Hindu who affirms a belief in reincarnation knows full well that in any particular incarnation death is the terminus. The belief that the spirit will find another life form in another incarnation may function to enable the believer to accept the reality of death in a manner unavailable to someone who does not share this expectation. But the actuality of death in this life is no less real, despite these expectations of another incarnation. The traditional Christian view of the resurrection of the body and life in the kingdom of God may very well function to relieve some anxiety in the face of death for the believing Christian. But death remains real, even if it is not ultimately victorious. Death is real, and any belief regarding something beyond or after death, while it may alter the believer's attitude toward death, was never, I believe, intended to encourage the illusion of escaping the reality of death.

In the immediately preceding paragraphs the link between death and eschatology has already been forged. The etymological (i.e., having to do with the origin and development of a word) derivation of eschatology is a combination of the Greek words *eschaton* and *logos*. Literally, it can be translated as "discourse (*logos*) regarding the last things (*eschaton*)." In its literal origins, then, eschatology is not confined to a relationship with death, nor, it must be clearly noted, is it a peculiarly Christian idea. For example, the etymology of eschatology would allow it to be used with reference to the end of the planet earth in an ecological discussion. If ecologists propose that the earth may be destroyed by alterations in atmospheric conditions, they are by definition thinking eschatologically. To some readers such a suggestion will seem strained or fanciful. I make this point, however, as an attempt to begin releasing our imaginations from rigid definitions.

In Christian theology, where (on purely quantitative grounds) the idea of eschatology has most frequently appeared, the word *eschatology* represents a fairly consistent set of ideas. Most frequently it has had to do with discourse on the four last things: death, judgement, heaven, and hell. Thus in the first of the "Notes on Eschatology" Hans Schwartz represents accurately what Christian theologians have most frequently meant when they have spoken of eschatology. I must, however, underscore my own conviction that such a representation by no means exhausts the possibilities inherent in the idea—as I will demonstrate later in this chapter.

In summary, it has been asserted that death is inevitable and real; that our culture tries to deny or at least to camouflage the reality of death; that religions foster maturity in recognizing the reality of death; and that some religions have propounded beliefs that may reduce anxiety in the face of death by asserting that even though death is real it is not to be feared. The degree to which traditional religions have declined in their influence is noted in the degree to which fear of death in our culture has contributed to the development of so many devices for avoiding death.

ALL MUST DIE

In the history of thought one may trace two distinct views toward the reality of death and dying. On the one hand, Socrates remarked that all philosophy (and all serious search for meaning) is a "meditation on death." This sentiment may be traced through the centuries to the present, when the German philosopher Martin Heidegger contends that humanity lives toward death. On the other hand, the opposite view has had its equally staunch defenders. Spinoza spoke for the opposing tradition when he observed that all philosophy is a meditation on life, since life is all that is knowable and death is the unknown and unknowable. The most that one can know about dying, in this view, would be the reactions, feelings, and thoughts of people in the throes of dying (e.g., terminal cancer patients). Though this is not quite to the point but tangentially related, one may also know the reactions of living people to the death of people close to them.

A crucial distinction has just been drawn between death and dying. Dying is, of course, a process as long as life itself. Consciousness of this, however, is generally less acute until some crisis arises that raises mortality to consciousness. It is possible to learn much from people who are in such states of heightened consciousness about the human experience of dying. However, what we cannot learn about the other side of the reality is what it is like to be dead. Therefore we resort to images and visions in order to describe death. In medicine a difference is drawn between various signs of death (e.g., cessation of heartbeat and brain waves, which may not be concurrent), all of which must be observed before a person is legally pronounced dead. The sum of the stages, however, can be said to be a total condition characterized by the absence of vital life signs. We are able to describe death only as the negation of life. It is gratuitously assumed that we know how to define it adequately. The point is that just as the dead tell no lies, death tells no truths. And if the living have any claim whatsoever to knowing the truth about death, it is precisely truth addressed to the living that leaves death an inexorable mystery. Surely this realization of its mystery underlies E. E. Cummings's lines:

> I wouldn't like death *if it were real*
> But, *dying*, oh baby! [emphasis added]

The experience of dying and people's responses to the recognition of death's mystery are matters of present concern. If your attention is limited to these matters, the selected readings listed at the end of the chapter suggest some ways in which religions have developed attitudes and practices relating to these phenomena. On the one hand, you can read portions from *The Wheel of Death*, edited by Philip Kapleau, in which are assembled practical aids from the Buddhist tradition for helping dying people through the process leading to death. It will be extremely helpful to read portions of *The Tibetan Book of the Dead*, or *The Book of Martyrs* of Protestant Christian origin. These works demonstrate the traditional religions' concern for "ministering" to dying people. On the other hand, in "Traditional Attitudes Toward Death," by Arnold Toynbee, and "Attitudes Toward Death in Eastern Religions," by Ninian Smart, in Toynbee's *Man's Concern with Death*, and in Joseph Matthew's essay "The Time My Father Died," in Nathan Scott's *The Modern Vision of Death*, you may read of some religious cultic behaviors occasioned by death—funeral customs, burial, cremation, and so forth, which function both to honor the memory of the dead person and to give expression to the grief and sense of loss felt by the living. In both instances very concrete practical aspects of religions are demonstrated as they give sustenance to the dying and cultic support to the bereaved.

A further issue must be mentioned. As the traditional religious practices have declined in the degree of support they apparently offer to the dying and the bereaved in our increasingly secularized world, the secular surrogates for the religions have begun to manifest an increasing concern for these matters. One of the better books in this field is Dr. Elizabeth

Kubler-Ross's *On Death and Dying*, in which a psychiatrist describes her work with hospitalized dying patients. She has traced several predictable stages through which the dying patient passes: (1) denial and isolation, (2) anger, (3) bargaining, (4) depression, and (5) acceptance. No one familiar with the traditional religious manuals on spiritual guidance for the dying should be surprised at the discovery of these stages in the psychology of dying. But each age appropriates and interprets the wisdom of the centuries in its own fashion and expresses it in its own language. Whereas family members, friends, and professional representatives of religion— shamans, clergy, rabbis—have ministered to the dying in traditional cultures, in ours it is different. Today the service professions—social workers, nurses, doctors, psychologists, and the like—are often forced to fulfill these tasks. Their attempts to develop appropriate skills leads them into a discovery of wisdom as old as humanity, even if it often goes unrecognized as such.

Kubler-Ross's work has been directed primarily toward developing seminars in which nurses, interns, residents, and physicians learn about the possibilities of more effective ways of working with dying people. Over several months the participants witness Kubler-Ross interviewing terminally ill patients. The interviews are recorded, transcribed, and studied in depth by the seminar participants. Kubler-Ross has reported generally successful results of these seminars from her point of view. This kind of study has been expanded by many others in other places around the world and is one of the most helpful developments in the sensitivity training of the "service professions."

Not only have the dying been benefited by such increasing sensitivity among the helping professions, but other avenues of exploration have been opened by such considerations. Dr. Raymond Moody's best-selling book, *Life After Life*, is a symbol of some of the new directions in this area. In this work Moody reports his conversations with a significant number of people who either had been declared clinically dead but had subsequently been resuscitated or had had experiences during very serious illnesses or accidents that they describe as death experiences. Moody creates a typology within which to arrange such experiences. None of the reports corresponds in detail to the typology, but the typology does offer an intelligible model on which to reflect in responding to the reports as a group.

In a foreword to Moody's book Kubler-Ross observes the remarkable congruence between Moody's material and her own recent work. Both are insistent that the reader not misunderstand what the reports of such experiences offer. They do not constitute scientific proof of life after death. After all, medical judgments notwithstanding, the people in question were not really dead. The most that can be concluded is that some people experience the approach of the mystery of death as something very different from the fearful prospect that it is for many others. Such terms as "beauty," "peace," "rest," but also "full consciousness," "panorma of one's life" abound in these testimonies. And there is a consistent report of regret at having to "return" to the body and be resuscitated or recover from the coma or illness. Virtually all report that they subsequently have no fear of death; many positively anticipate it.

The significance of these studies for religion may lie in the importance that living assumes. If dying offers the possibility of the survival of the soul, then the richer that soul's living experiences have been, the more glorious it will be in its "life after life." The mystery of death is not thereby reduced, but the wisdom of many religious traditions in insisting on the importance of the quality of life in the present is strongly underscored in such reflections.

Finally, the cultic function of funerary practices must be mentioned. Allusion was made earlier to the cultic support that funerary and burial or disposal rites provide for the bereaved family and friends. The function of rites of this sort seems to be to repeat in a religious context the story of life's meaning (including the experience of dying), within which the dead person and his or her heirs live and by which they are sustained. It is entirely inappropriate to question the "truth" of the story to which all cultic acts (i.e., rituals and liturgies) collectively and separately give witness. The acid test of all rites and cultic behaviors is whether or not they enable those who participate in them to experience reality as meaningful. If they do not function in this way, the story that is enacted cultically is a dead story. To illustrate, the Jewish and Muslim traditions have steadfastly insisted on burial as the only way to dispose of the bodies of the dead. This has a certain consistency vis-à-vis the use of certain passages from Genesis (e.g., "from dust to dust . . . "). There is a behavioral and cultic common denominator therein. Christians, however, using the same passage from Scripture, more and more frequently use cremation for disposing of the body. There then tends to be an inconsistency between the "story" used in the funeral rites and the mode of treating the body. The story itself becomes dead and ineffectual.

ESCHATOLOGY AS HOPE

When one moves from the reality of death to the idea of eschatology, one is making a gigantic step—or so it would appear. Nobody seriously doubts that all must die. But to many people the notion of eschatology, traditionally viewed, is a source of great incredulity. Whether the vision be of Hades, sheol, heaven, nirvana, the kingdom of God, or whatever, living people frequently regard this vision as a matter of vain speculation at best or as a cowardly delusion at worst. If, with Freud, all religion is regarded as a necessary illusion, intimations of immortality and aspirations for eternal life will seem the most illusory of all. Or if, more open-mindedly, one is prepared to say that, because it was unique, the resurrection of a dead man is at least theoretically possible, the fact that it has never occurred again leads many people to conclude that a general resurrection is immensely improbable and hardly to be counted upon.

The more penetrating question is, Are all the concepts just listed really what is important about eschatological thinking? I am prepared to argue, in agreement with Jurgen Moltmann in *Theology of Hope,* that such a reading fundamentally misses the point of eschatology. This is a bold claim indeed, for it runs counter, in the Christian instance, to the weight of traditional theological thinking. Stated as plainly as possible, it is my conviction that the central concern in eschatological thinking, whether Christian or some other form, is the human capacity to hope. Any concern for the future, whether it be the future of the world or my own personal future, is of necessity possible only to the degree that I am able to hope. What is needed, then, is the ability to recognize in the images and symbols of any vision of the future that those images and symbols are manifestations of humanity's ability to hope. For example, the image of heaven or nirvana is less important for its content than as a demonstration of humanity's aspiration for the future. Hope is to the future as memory is to the past. Just as imagination is required to enliven memory and breathe vitality into the past, so it is needed to enliven the future.

It comes as no surprise to me that in her study of the psychology of dying Kubler-Ross, after tracing the five stages through which the dying typically pass, adds a chapter entitled simply "Hope." Her point is that through all of the stages hope is a constant thread. Conversely, when it becomes clear that a dying patient has lost all hope, death is inevitably near, usually within twenty-four hours.

There are some distinctions that are basic in any consideration of hope. One is that hope must be seen as serving more than strictly utilitarian purposes. Important as it is, when we think of hope only in terms of "hoping for this or that" we have not yet plumbed the most significant depths of the phenomenon of hoping. There is a level of hoping that we may characterize as having no object, that is, a level at which, instead of hoping for something, one simply hopes. This distinction is characterized in Josef Pieper's "What Does Hope Mean?" in *Hope and History.* As you may discover, Pieper differentiates what he calls "everyday hopes" from "fundamental hope."

My own interpretation of this distinction is between "utilitarian hope" and "ontological hope." In the case of utilitarian hope the object hoped for is always given greater attention than the human capacity to engage in hopeful activity. It is always hope in order to achieve something else. But in the case of ontological hope the full focus is on the ability to hope as a fundamental human capacity.

Now, it is clear from the study of the history of many religious traditions that utilitarian hope has typically received more attention than ontological hope. But changes in cultural circumstances may allow us today to see certain things from perspectives that have not been readily available in previous times. Perhaps an analogy will help. In Christian theology one of the three greatest virtues has always been faith (along with love and hope). Through the centuries great attention has been given to faith. Indeed, enough attention has been given to it to make it a commonplace to assert theologically that faith is at bottom a state of being. Faith is not simply a matter of giving intellectual assent to a set of beliefs in the form of propositions. Rather, it is a state of confident trusting. In the Book of Job these words are uttered: "Even if He slays me, yet will I trust in Him." These words come close to what I am trying to say. Nothing, according to this saying, could alter the trust by which the speaker lives. Hope of an ontological kind is like that. Just as faithlessness no doubt is the true opposite of faith, so hopelessness is the real opposite of hope.

All along, then, religions, even when they have appeared most directly to be engendering and propounding utilitarian hope, have significantly contributed to evoking ontological hope. Is this not true, for example, in the case of Hinduism, in which what is hoped for ultimately is entering into nirvana? Even at the most literal level the entering into nirvana will only finally occur after the last death, beyond which the spirit is never again destined to be reincarnated in any form. The function of such a hope is ontological even if the form is utilitarian, simply because what is hoped for could by definition never occur under the conditions of mortal life. Utilitarian hope, by contrast, is always subject to confirmation or disconformation. Either one marries the partner of one's hopes or one does not. If one does not, one's hopes are unfulfilled. But the hope for something beyond death can never be either fulfilled or not fulfilled in this life.

Of course some critics of the human capacity to hope make their strongest case just at this point. If there is nothing that could occur in this life to fulfill one's deepest ontological hope, they say, it is foolish and vain to so hope. What the criticism presupposes, however, is precisely what is at issue, namely, that the important point is what is hoped for. If the interpretation of eschatology being offered here has anything to recommend it, it is that hope itself is of central importance in contrast to what is hoped for.

CONCLUSION

The issues associated with death and eschatology are by their very nature ultimately mysterious. For as long as people have been self-consciously aware of the transience of human existence, death has been among the greatest of concerns. It has evoked fear, avoidance, repression, and most of all ignorance. But the mortality rate remains 100 percent. In response to the reality of death, many religious traditions have evoked a firm conviction, in one form or another, that the spirit of humanity, no matter how realistic the view of death may be, is not confined to reflections on this life alone. The daring of utopian dreams and eschatological hopes, however, does not depend on the literal actualization or realization of those dreams and hopes. What they do reveal is the greatness of humanity, even when people live in the full awarness of their own mortality.

QUESTIONS FOR STUDY, REFLECTION, AND DISCUSSION

1. What feelings do death and dying, either your own or a loved one's, evoke in you?
2. Does your own religious tradition, if you identify with any, offer hope to you regarding death and dying?
3. What do you expect to be able to learn from the study of death and eschatology?
4. Does any religious tradition other than the ones you already know about offer a vision of eschatology that you find particularly attractive? If so, which one(s) and why?
5. Why do you believe American culture has taken its typical attitude toward death?
6. Is it helpful to study death and dying through religion? If so, why? If not, why not?

PROJECTS

1. In order to clarify your own thinking, write a brief essay on death and another on eschatology. Use your own experiences and feelings as data as well as other ideas that are familiar to you. Discuss these essays with others. Note: No ideas in this subject should, at this point, be judged "right" or "wrong." We should, however, strive for clarity of expression and authenticity.
2. Subject: Death, its meaning and religious attitudes toward it.
    Read the pages suggested in the following list (see Selected Bibliography for complete citations). Make notes on ideas that impress you. Write an essay expressing at least two different religious attitudes or beliefs regarding the meaning of death. Be prepared to discuss your essay with others.

    a. Arnold Toynbee, "Traditional Attitudes Toward Death," in *Man's Concern with Death*, pp. 59–94.

b. Ninian Smart, "Attitudes Toward Death in Eastern Religions," in *Man's Concern with Death,* pp. 95–115.
c. Ninian Smart, "Death in the Judeo-Christian Tradition," in *Man's Concern with Death,* pp. 116–121.
d. Paul Tillich's essay in *The Meaning of Death.*
e. Philip Kapleau, *The Wheel of Death,* pp. 1–29, 37–46, 61–75.
f. Joseph Matthews, "The Time My Father Died," in *The Modern Vision of Death,* pp. 107–122.

3. Subject: Eschatology, what it is and how it functions in religious consciousness.

Read the pages suggested in the following list. Make notes on ideas that impress you. Write an essay on the subject "Eschatology—Despair or Hope?" Be prepared to discuss your essay with others.

a. Mircea Eliade, *Myth and Reality,* pp. 54–73.
b. Jurgen Moltmann, "Introduction: Meditation on Hope," in *Theology of Hope,* pp. 15–19.
c. William Lynch, "On Hope" and "On Hopelessness," in *Images of Hope,* pp. 23–50.
d. Josef Pieper, "What Does Hope Mean?" in *Hope and History,* pp. 13–28.

4. Arrange to see the film "Occurrence at Owl Creek Bridge." Discuss the film with others. You may wish to view the film a second time. Write an interpretive review of the film in which you deal with the story, film techniques, important images, and suggestions about death and eschatology.

SELECTED BIBLIOGRAPHY

Becker, Ernest. *The Denial of Death.* New York: Free Press, 1973.
Capps, Walter. *Time Invades the Cathedral.* Philadelphia: Fortress Press, 1972.
Eliade, Mircea. *From Primitives to Zen.* New York: Harper & Row, 1967.
———. *Myth and Reality.* New York: Harper & Row, 1963.
Feifel, Herman, ed. *The Meaning of Death.* New York: McGraw-Hill, 1959.
Hick, John. *Death and Eternal Life.* New York: Harper & Row, 1977.
Heidel, Alexander. *The Gilgamesh Epic and Old Testament Parables.* Chicago: University of Chicago Press, 1967.
Irish, Jerry A. *A Boy Thirteen.* Philadelphia: Westminster Press, 1975.
Kapleau, Philip. *The Wheel of Death.* New York: Harper & Row, 1974.
Keleman, Stanley. *Living Your Dying.* New York: Random House, 1974.
Kubler-Ross, Elizabeth. *On Death and Dying.* New York: Macmillan, 1969.
———. *Questions and Answers on Death and Dying.* New York: Macmillan, 1974.

Lynch, William. *Images of Hope.* New York: New American Library, a Mentor–Omega Book, 1965.

Massanari, Jared and Alice. *Our Life with Caleb.* New York: Fortress Press, 1976.

Matson, Archie. *Afterlife: Reports from the Threshold of Death.* New York: Harper & Row, 1977.

Mitford, Jessica. *The American Way of Death.* New York: Simon and Schuster, 1963.

Moltmann, Jurgen. *Theology of Hope.* New York: Harper & Row, 1967.

Moody, Raymond A. *Life After Life.* New York: Bantam Books, 1976.

Neale, Robert. *The Art of Dying.* New York: Harper & Row, 1973.

Pieper, Josef. *Hope and History.* New York: Herder and Herder, 1967.

Scott, Nathan, ed. *The Modern Vision of Death.* Richmond, Va.: John Knox Press, 1967.

Toynbee, Arnold. *Man's Concern with Death.* New York: McGraw-Hill, 1969.

CHAPTER 11

Evil and Suffering

ALAN L. BERGER

Evil and suffering are universal human experiences. Apparently unwarranted cruelty and pain, as well as the inevitability of death, are as inextricable a part of the human condition as birth, growth, and pleasure. Attempts to come to terms with evil and suffering have been part of the belief system of every world religion.

The problem of evil and suffering in Western monotheistic religions has two focuses—God and humanity—and involves a tension between a God conceived as good and the existence of injustice in His creation—*Si deus bonus, unde malum?* Theodicy, the attempt to justify God's goodness in spite of the existence of evil and suffering, is therefore a fundamental concern of people in the theistic religions. The motivation for an adequate theodicy is crucial because it is a search for meaning in the midst of otherwise unexplained evil.

Two primary modes of the experiential dimension of the problem of evil are expressed by the age-old questions, Why do innocents suffer? and, in Jeremiah's words, "Why does the way of the wicked prosper?" Suffering, for religious people, implies a transcendent cause; it is never viewed as merely a random occurrence, for everything is related to God. Consequently suffering involves a radical challenge to one's fundamental assumptions concerning the divine–human relationship, membership in the human community, and self-understanding.

Responses to evil and suffering have varied with different philosophies, literary works, and religions. For example, St. Augustine and Maimonides both attempted to deny the independent reality of evil. St. Augustine's classical definition of evil as a "privation of good" and Maimonides's assertion that there is more good than evil in the universe typify the attitude of Western philosophical speculation. Neither answer has been particularly satisfying when human despair has struck.

Literary attempts to treat the issue often provide a powerful and profound grasp of the reality of suffering and evil. Works such as Dostoevsky's *The Brothers Karamazov*, Camus's *The Plague*, Wiesel's *Night*, and Wallant's *The Pawnbroker* are gripping portraits of evil and suffering.[1] One must, however, analyze specifically religious responses to the problem in order to comprehend the urgency and fear that are experienced in the attempt to wrestle with these central issues of existence. The question is not one of God's existence but, rather, one of His justice.[2] "How I sympathized with Job!" observes Elie Wiesel. "I did not deny God's existence, but I doubted His absolute justice."[3]

Within some strands of religion evil may be viewed as a powerful reality independent of God. Gnosticism in the West and Eastern Zoroastrianism clearly assert a dualistic view of the universe. Even monotheistic traditions have shown the powerful influence of Gnostic thought in their mystic systems. Jewish mystical speculation, for example, asserts that certain acts are performed for the benefit of the *sitra achra* (the other, "evil" side) in order to soothe or bribe the power of evil. Judaism is not dualistic in its orthodox—*halakhic*—expression. Nevertheless, Jewish mysticism as expressed in the kabbalah and in Hasidism was able to provide a theology that explained what the rigidified rabbinic ethos dismissed as a nonproblem, that is, the reality of evil.

Monistic, or nontheistic, religious traditions have suggested alternate explanations of why people suffer. Focusing on Buddhism and Hinduism as representative, it is possible to discern two basic responses: craving and ignorance. The first, the motif of craving or desire, is seen in Buddhism. Theravada Buddhism, the Buddhism of the elders, postulated as the *sine qua non* of the problem of suffering the four noble truths: (1) Existence is suffering (*dukkha*); (2) suffering is caused by craving (*tanha*); (3) the cure is cessation of tanha; and (4) the way the cure can be achieved is the Eightfold Path. Through disciplined practices, suffering that is caused by craving can be overcome as nirvana is achieved.

Ignorance is a key response in the Hindu tradition. Summarizing Hindu thought on any given issue is, owing to the astounding variety of thinking in this tradition and its eclectic nature, at best a risky undertaking. Nonetheless, it may fairly be stated that the doctrine of maya represents a major component of the Hindu response to the problem of suffering. According to this doctrine, it is illusion or ignorance to believe material things are ultimately real.

The poetic tale of Vishnu and Nārda reflects the subtlety of the problem. Lord Vishnu grants the wish of Nārda (a godlike, holy seer) that he be shown the secret of maya. Before revealing the secret Vishnu requests Nārda to bring him a glass of water. The disciple goes to a nearby village seeking to fulfill the lord's request. While there he falls in love, marries, has three children, and heads the household of his departed father-in-law. Twelve years pass. A severe flood carries away his wife and three children.

Grief stricken, Nārda "collapses into darkness." Upon awakening, he hears the voice of Vishnu asking him a question: "Child, where is the water you went to fetch for me? I have been waiting more than half an hour."[4]

Historically, the problem of theodicy has appeared most pressing when calamities, either natural or man-made, have occurred: the Lisbon earthquake in 1755, which destroyed thousands of lives, the gas warfare of World War I, and the most diabolical and least explicable event in the history of cruelty—the Holocaust, in which 6 million Jews were slaughtered. In fact it may be the Holocaust that has made the problem of evil and suffering one of the most crucial, if not *the* crucial, problems of our day for both secular and religious people. Hannah Arendt, commenting on the Holocaust, suggests that we see evil not as a metaphysical principle, nor as a mythological devil or demon; rather, she speaks of the "banality of evil." In her book, *Eichmann in Jerusalem* (1963), Arendt describes the man who was the bureaucratic overseer of the Nazi death camps as representative of the banality of evil. Another writer, Richard Rubenstein, questions the possibility of belief in God after the Holocaust.[5]

Thousands of books on subjects related to evil and suffering, ranging from the Holocaust to the more personal concerns of pain and death, indicate that the problem with which we are concerned here is an issue on the individual, personal level as well as on the collective or societal level. The death of a child, prolonged and mysterious illness, severe misfortune as well as societal tragedies need explanation in order for people to live in an ordered world with continued trust in God or at least some semblance of meaning.

EXPLANATIONS OF THEODICY: THE QUESTION OF TYPES

The sociologist Peter Berger, in *The Sacred Canopy*, offers a typology that is helpful in differentiating among various kinds of theodicies. Moreover, the general vocabulary used by Berger provides a hermeneutical tool for interpreting the theodicy in various religious traditions as well as the theodicy implicit in such writings as Job and the novel *The Pawnbroker*.

A theodicy is the part of a belief system that serves to maintain religious meaning in spite of evil and suffering. In Western theism, this means justification of belief in God's goodness even in the face of evil. In the monistic traditions, theodicy is the attempt to reconcile evil with the central meaning of existence as affirmed by the religious community.

Theodicies vary in type from an irrational identification of the self with a society, as in primitive religions, to the more rational type of theodicy found in Indian religiosity—the "karma–samsara complex." In the latter, one is rewarded or punished in successive incarnations according to the degree to which one has been faithful to the tasks imposed by former lives.

Intermediate types include "this-worldly" messianic–millinarian notions (ranging from Jewish Sabbatianism to cargo cults), "other-worldly" compensations (exemplified by the elaborate mortuary beliefs and rites of ancient Egypt and ancient China—even in our own day), and dualism, in which "all anomic phenomena are . . . ascribed to evil or negative forces"[6] (Zoroastrianism, Mithraism, and Manichaeism are exemplary). More common types, especially in the West, are those that emphasize submission to God's will (as in the book of Job) or the redemptive power of the suffering of God incarnate (Christianity).

Two necessary components of any theodicy, Berger contends, are self-transcending participation and masochism. The former is found in any religion in which people fully identify with their society, finding their total orientation to life and death in the religious community. Mystical union with the divine is also an important example of self-transcendent participation. Religious masochism, on the other hand, is not to be confused with psychological concepts. Masochism in religion is "the attitude in which the individual reduces himself to an inert and thinglike object vis-à-vis his fellow man, singly or in collectivities or in the nomoi established by them."[7] Masochism is essentially a twofold transformative process: The self is transformed into nothingness, and the other is transformed into absolute or ultimate reality. The example *par excellence* of religious masochism in the West is provided by the book of Job, which will be discussed later.

Berger's contribution to the study of theodicy is at least twofold: First, while basing his discussion on the pioneering efforts of Max Weber, he considerably broadens the range of data pertinent to the discussion by providing a conceptual framework that includes primitive religions—something Weber did not treat.[8] Second, Berger has correctly stressed that theodicies are by no means concerned with happiness or even with redemption. "Indeed," writes Berger, "some theodicies carry no promise of 'redemption' at all—except for the redeeming assurance of meaning itself."[9]

VARIETIES OF THEODICIES WITHIN TRADITIONS

Religions are multifaceted. Characterizations employing rubrics such as monotheistic/theistic or Western/Eastern supply only a partial image of the religion in question. Nevertheless all traditions have at least two basic components, "elite" and "folk," or what anthropologists term "great" and "little." Beyond this distinction, however, there exist both "orthodox" and "heterodox." By the latter we mean the mystical elements in every religious system. In Judaism, for example, orthodox theology does not speak of transmigration of souls. Yet the twelfth-century *kabbalah* (one historical expression of Jewish mysticism) emphasizes this notion, utilizing the word *gilgul* ("revolving") as descriptive of the process. Moverover, at least part of the reason for this transmigration was the opportunity to eradicate the sins of one's former existence. In this chapter we will suggest a variety of positions maintained by several world religions in their orthodox and mystical expressions concerning the problems of suffering and theodicy.

PRIMITIVE RELIGIONS

Primitive religions viewed suffering as having many causes: (1) the magical action of any enemy, (2) the breaking of a taboo, (3) the entering of a baneful zone, (4) the anger of a god, or (5) the will or wrath of a Supreme Being.[10] Having suggested possible causes, there appear to be two major ways of combating or treating suffering: utilizing the prowess of a priest or sorcerer and, if this proves insufficient, having recourse to the memory of a creator God who, although a *deus absconditus*, may be propitiated by sacrifices. Suffering, for primitive religion, always has meaning. In fact suffering is positively evaluated when it is part of the initiatory process involved in becoming a *shaman* (i.e., a primitive mystic). Here

Certain physical sufferings find their exact counterparts in terms of a (symbolic) initiatory death—for example, the dismemberment of the candidate's (the sick man's) body, an ecstatic experience that can equally well be brought on by the sufferings of a "sickness-vocation." Or by certain ritual ceremonies or, finally, in dreams.[11]

The shaman is also a "doctor of the soul," one who is believed to be able to treat both physical and spiritual types of suffering.

Basically, the response of primitive religion to suffering is found in a "depersonalization" of the problem. The individual does not exist apart from the tribe or collectivity. Therefore the welfare of the entire group is at stake in overcoming suffering or the eruption of anomic forces. While it is true that a virtuoso (i.e., the priest, shaman, or sorcerer) is called upon to intervene, his success or failure will have repercussions on the collectivity. Personal consciousness of sin, as expressed in Biblical religion, is not a normative component of primitive religious orthopraxis.

JUDAISM

Judaism is the oldest of the monotheistic faiths in the West, as well as the generator of both Christianity and Islam. Orthodox Judaism, as expressed in the Torah (Law) and the various commentaries and reflections thereon (e.g., Mishnah, the two Talmuds, Gemorrah, and Midrashim, as well as various rabbinic writings) suggests a twofold explanation of the origin of sin: the rebellion of humanity, which is caused by excessive and unwarranted *hubris* (pride), and the presence of an evil *yetzer* (impulse). People are created with two *yetzrim* (impulses), *yetzer tov* (good impulse) and *yetzer ra* (evil impulse). Talmudic thought is understandably reluctant to attribute evil to the work of God. When there appears to be no option, however, this attribution is carefully hedged: "God created the Evil Impulse, but He also created its antidote, the Torah" (Kiddushin 30b). The orthodox explanation of suffering is punishment for sin. But the matter is not without ambiguity. Judaism is replete with instances of protests to God when suffering is thought to be unwarranted, for example, Abraham, Job, the eighteenth-century Hasidic movement [especially the sayings of Levi Yitzhak of Berditchev (d. 1809)], and the profound theological reflections occasioned by the Holocaust.

The antidote for suffering in traditional Judaism has been prayer and penance, based on the assumption that suffering results from sin. Judaism is, in addition, a tradition committed to deeds (*mitzvot*). The good person must live the righteous life, which is expressed not merely in words but in performance: "Everyone whose deeds are more than his wisdom, his wisdom endures. And everyone whose wisdom is more than his deeds his wisdom does not endure" (Avot III.12). Judaism is, moreover, a covenant religion. This covenant implies that life is constituted primarily of relationships on both the vertical axis (God and humanity), and the horizontal plane (interaction among people). The Israelites and each successive generation of Jews are called upon to hear the word of God in the recitation of the *Shema*—"Hear O Israel, the Lord our God, the Lord is One" (Deuteronomy 6:4)—and to accept responsibility for their actions.

Mystical Judaism presents a response to the problem of suffering in a richly mythological mode. The sixteenth-century kabbalah of Isaac Luria, for example, endowed exile, the synonym for suffering *par excellence* in Judaism, with a sense of cosmic mission. Jews have been dispersed throughout the world in order to aid in elevating divine sparks (*aliyath hanitsotsoth*), which, owing to a primal "accident" (*shevirath ha-kelim*, "breaking of the vessels" designed to hold divine light), are scattered everywhere. When the process of restoration (*tikkun*) is completed, owing to humanity's achieving proper intention (*kavvanah*) in prayer, the Messiah will come—symbolizing harmoney between the upper spheres (macrocosm) and the lower world (microcosm).

The Lurianic kabbalah was greatly influenced by Gnostic currents. Nonetheless, Luria assumed an optimistic evaluation of humanity's role in restoring cosmic harmony, thereby eliminating exile/suffering. Luria also posited the daring and unrabbinic notion that God is a savior in need of salvation. Kabbalistic *mitzvot* are therefore presumed to have cosmic implications as far as the elimination of disunity and suffering are concerned. Jewish mysticism, with the exception of certain outstanding ecstatics, never advocated union with God, and thus is differentiated from other forms both Western and Eastern. Rather, the goal is communion or *devekut*—adhesion to God. Even though union with the divine was not the goal for Jewish mystics, it involves self-transcendence. In fact the ecstatic and enthusiastic Hasidism of the Baal Shem Tov (Besht) necessitated extinction of the self (*bittul ha-yesh*), a type of masochism as well.

CHRISTIANITY

Mainstream Christianity contends that humanity suffers because of the original sin occurring with the Fall as reported in Genesis. The essence of the Christian response to suffering, according to John Bowker, is the "realization of God as Father."[12] The Synoptic Gospels require Jesus's disciples to exhibit the two attitudes exemplified in the founder's life: "supreme confidence that even the furthest extremes of suffering do not defeat the possibility of God" and "an active and practical response to suffering wherever it occurs."[13] Essential to the Christian understanding and response to suffering is the acceptance of the life, death, and resurrection of Jesus. Orthodox Christians are required to "accept suffering, as did Christ, e.g., as devastatingly real, but as not the final word."[14]

The central event of Christianity is, of course, the person, passion, and resurrection of Jesus. The creative-murder and creative-suffering motif attributed to Jesus is not unique in the history of religions. Dema-deities of Polynesian mythology also were killed for the benefit of humanity. The Hainuwele mythologem, for example, tells of a heroine, Hainuwele, who is killed and from whose body springs life-giving crop plants. Christ, however, plays a dual role. He is both victim and victor.

In the history of theology there are two types of Christian approaches to the problem of evil and suffering: the "Irenaean" model, which argues that humanity's capacity for goodness has not yet achieved maturity, and the "Augustinian" response, which contends that evil results from the misuse of free will. The Augustinian position concerning theodicy exhibits a "profoundly masochistic shift from the question about the justice of God to that about the sinfulness of man."[15] Christ as victim tends to mitigate the severity of the Christian view of fallen humanity.

The normative Christian response to evil and suffering embraces elements of both the Irenaean and Augustinian prototypes. Christianity maintains the tension between humanity as redeemable and humanity as sinful. Orthodox Christianity posits a theodicy that accommodates suffering, often by affirming that it is the "will of God," which is itself mysterious and unknowable. Nonetheless, the true believing Christian can, in imitation of Christ, accept suffering with strength and courage, thereby finding in it a meaning. This acceptance is made possible by an affirmation of the divine Presence (Christ) as well as through the support of the Christian community. The latter, as fostered by communal worship and the reception of church sacraments, aids the Christian in the effort to heed Christ's call, "Abide in me." In fact the entire sacramental system of Roman Catholicism, as well as Protestantism's demythologized concept of holy community, serve to provide the context within which the Christian can accept evil and suffering and eventual redemption—whether gradual or sudden, this-worldly or other-worldly—from the basic cause of evil and suffering, human sin.

The Christian mystical tradition clearly exhibits the "total surrender" characteristic of religious masochism. "I have been crucified with Christ; it is no longer I who live, but Christ who lives in me." (Gal. 2:20). Pauline and Johanine Christianity speak of union with Christ, a Christ-mysticism. Moreover, Paul, who refers to himself as one untimely born (I Corinthians 15:7–8), is the recipient of an auditory and visual mystic experience of the master (Acts 9:3–9). Consequently one can locate the origins of a mystical monistic tradition in the Christian scriptures. Union with Christ meant, for primitive Christianity, a kind of corporate mysticism—a brotherhood of believers who had become part of the transcendent order. Theodicy per se ceases to be a problem for the Christian mystic who is in union with Christ.

ISLAM

The fundamental attitude of Islam toward evil and suffering is submission (*aslama* means "to submit") to the right relationship with God. Suffering in Islam is therefore viewed largely in instrumental terms as (1) punishment for sin and/or (2) a trial or test. John Bowker suggests that the "hard" response of Islam requires patience and endurance. "Suffering," he writes, is "part of God's strict justice." [16] The wicked merely seem to prosper. The Qur'an, the sacred text of Islam, indicates that ultimately the wicked suffer, albeit in an unending agony of punishment after death—an "other-worldly" judgment.

Central to Islamic practice is the *shahādah* or confession of faith: *lā ilāha illa'llāh muhammadun rasūlu'llāh*, "There is but one God, [and] Muhammed is the Apostle of God." The Qur'an treats suffering as a practical reality, rather than a theoretical proposition about which one may speculate. Basic to Quranic argument is the assumption that God is in control of everything that occurs. One hastens to add the caveat that this assumption placed a great burden of proof on the Qur'an to demonstrate that suffering was in fact part of a plan, the intention of which was beyond human understanding. "Much Quranic material is devoted to substantiating and exemplifying exactly that God is in control, and that suffering must . . . be a part of God's purposes." [17] Suffering, for mainstream Islam, occurs when people forget that God is omnipotent. Repetition of the *shahādah* coupled with retelling of *hadiths* (traditions concerning the life and teachings of Muhammed) serve to remind the faithful that God (Allah) knows in advance of all sufferings. In short, there are neither anomic phenomena nor ambiguities about theodicy for strict Islamic theology. Allah's providence is absolute.

Sufism, the Islamic mystical tradition, also treats the issue of suffering. Sufis, who evidently received their name from the rough wool garments (*suf*) they wore, were originally a group of ascetics. However, Sufism early became synonymous with Islamic mysticism. Suffering, according to Sufi doctrine, meant separation from God's love. *Dhikr*, the ritual repetition of Quranic and other religious literature, characterized the Sufi attempt to become united with God. Tension soon emerged between orthodox Islam and Sufism. Mansúr al-Hallaj, a fourth-century mystic who identified himself with God, was martyred in an especially cruel fashion by orthodox Islamic theologians. Even the suffering of a martyr like Hallaj was, for the Sufis, more a problem for the soul than one for the body. The soul, according to Abū Yazīd of Bistām, is both humbled and suffers agony when visited by God. Nonetheless, the soul by virtue of this agony is prompted to strive for closer contact with the divine. Achieving such contact means the cessation of all suffering.

In summary, in Western monotheistic religions suffering tends to be viewed as a form of pedagogy or punishment. Human pride or the Fall or forgetting God's omnipotence are the causes of suffering. The condition is remedied by a type of masochism in which the individual acknowledges his or her insignificance *vis-à-vis* the Creator. The trial of God is reversed and becomes instead the trial of humanity. It is people who are being judged and who suffer because of their sin.

Nevertheless, deeply imbedded in this kind of a theodicy, which does protect God's goodness and power, is the deep conviction and undaunting hope that finally evil and suffering will be overcome. "Not now but in the coming years" are among the words of a Protestant hymn that expresses this hope. God, the creator of the universe and of humankind, will, in the end, preserve final meaning, whether expressed as the kingdom of God, a heavenly reward, or the messianic age, or in some kind of self-extinction and/or union with God.

Hinduism and Buddhism

Indian spirituality exhibits a different response to the problem of evil and suffering. People are believed to suffer not because of sin but, rather, owing to ignorance (*avidyā*). The cure, accordingly, is not penance but knowledge. Mention has been made of the karma–samsara complex. *Karma* is the indisputable law of cause and effect that governs everything in the universe. *Samsara* refers to the wheel of rebirths that people must endure.

Every human action has its necessary consequence and every human situation is the necessary consequence of past human actions . . . The individual has no one to blame for his misfortunes except himself and, conversely, he may ascribe his good fortune to nothing but his own merits . . . Every conceivable anomy is integrated within a thoroughly rational, all-embracing interpretation of the universe.[18]

Moreover, for the Hindu, yoga is the primary spiritual technique for escaping the limitations imposed by the human condition of ignorance. Yoga itself (*yuj,* the root, conveys the meaning "to bind together," "hold fast," "yoke") is expressed in a variety of forms: *jnana* yoga (the way of knowledge), *raja* yoga (the royal way of contemplation), and *bhakti* yoga (devotion) are three of the disciplines available.

Still another related emphasis in Hinduism comes from the *Upanishads* (appendages to the *Vedas,* which are among the earliest significant religious documents). Here an identification is made between *atman* (individual soul) and *brahman* (divine soul). Yoga may be seen on one level as an attempt to overcome all obstacles to achieving this union. In brief, yoga and its various techniques may be understood as the Indian attempt to come to grips with the very structure of human consciousness. By reorienting the individual so that the illusion of selfhood is dissipated, yoga achieves its goal of overcoming ignorance—the cause of suffering. Yogins, for example, are able to control supposedly involuntary physiological functions such as heart rate and blood pressure. This serves as "empirical proof" that the yogin has eliminated dependence on the physical world and the suffering involved in ignorant devotion to it. In these ways it is believed to be possible to achieve *moksha* (spiritual release from suffering).

The Buddhist way may be understood as a kind of diagnosis of a disease. The disease is suffering, which is caused by clinging to the illusion that the self and the material world are real objects. The self, contended the Buddha, comprises five *skandhas* ("heaps"): (1) the body, (2) feelings (3) perceptions, (4) impulses and emotions, and (5) acts of consciousness. Nirvana, the goal of Buddhism, is achieved when the "individual," who is composed of these heaps, disappears. This cure has prompted the witticism that the Buddha advocated "spiritual suicide"—he gets rid of the disease by eliminating the patient. Nevertheless early Buddhism carried out with logical rigor the implications of its own teachings on the cause of suffering. Cessation of craving and the nonpermanence of the ego (*an-attā* = not-self) were advanced as necessary steps to achieve the Buddhist goal, nirvana and an end to the round of rebirths.

Mahayana ("Great Vehicle") Buddhism modified the rigid demands of Theravadin tradition by positing as an ideal type, not the reclusive and monastic *arhat* but the *bodhisattva* or enlightenment being. The bodhisattva was one who, on the brink of achieving nirvana, paused in order to assist others in their own quest for salvation. Mahayana liberalized Buddhist teaching, thereby making salvation available for all. The bodhisattva is a compassionate figure who emphasizes the importance of community.

It should be reemphasized that while both the Hindu and the Buddhist aspiration is to escape the wheel of birth and rebirth, their day-to-day orientation, and thus a crucial element in their theodicy, is their belief in reincarnation. They thus "solve" the problem of evil and suffering in the long run, since after many rebirths suffering and evil can be overcome.

These observations suggest that Eastern as well as Western religions have sought to cope with evil and suffering in a way that will preserve meaning for the individual and the community in the face of whatever is tragic. In every case the problem of evil gives rise to a theodicy that either recognizes and accepts the suffering or seeks to overcome it through some religious discipline. In the Western monotheisms, evil and suffering are most often viewed as a result of human sin or pride and are considered to be punitive or redemptive or both. In the East, the cause is viewed as craving or ignorance and can be overcome.

In the mystical aspects of the great religions the emphasis has been on a personal experiential mode of surmounting the problems of evil and suffering. The Hasidic *zaddik,* the Sufi *shaihk,* and the Buddhist *bodhisattva* are exemplary mystical figures who serve as intercessors and aids in the struggle against suffering.

TWO WESTERN MODELS: CLASSICAL (JOB) CONTEMPORARY (THE PAWNBROKER)

The Biblical book of Job is an engrossing, compelling, and baffling document. It is engrossing because it deals with the problem with which every person is confronted at some time in life—evil and suffering. Evil and suffering may seem to be inherent in the human condition, may result from illness of body or mind, or may follow from natural calamity. But evil and suffering are the lot of every person.

Moreover, Job is compelling in that all people, at least within the Jewish and Christian traditions, are haunted by the problem of evil. If God is good and just, why does He allow suffering and evil, especially among the righteous? In the case of Job, why was he, a righteous and God-fearing man, being punished? Is there no divine justice? The answer to these questions for Job transcends religious affiliations, for Job is not necessarily a Jew. He is everyman questioning the rule and maintenance of the cosmos.

But Job is also a baffling book in that it proposes no clear theodicy—at least there is no single theodicy that is clear to all scholars. And if a theodicy can be ascertained, is that view of suffering, which still preserves God's goodness and justice, one that is intelligible to twentieth-century people reflecting on Hiroshima and the Holocaust? Nevertheless Job stands in Western religious literature as an undisputed model of the problem of evil and the struggle to discern the omnipotence and goodness of God.

Now, Job is sorely afflicted. He loses children, wealth, and property and suffers severe bodily agony. Yet he refuses to renounce his faith. The three friends cannot understand his protestations of innocence. Job is determined to sever all connection between piety and expectation of reward (17:9–9). This move results in double isolation, for he is estranged from human society (the three friends) as well as being isolated from God. Job's suffering is intensified because his friends are quite unable to conceptualize suffering apart from the traditional notions of sin or separation from the will of God. Job's afflictions are thus manifestations of anomic phenomena. Eliphaz's assurance that he will intercede with God on Job's behalf, if only Job will confess, is an attempt to make these afflictions conform to the contours of meaning by which the society has defined the problem of suffering. The book has now set the stage for God's response and for Job's new self-understanding.

In a series of hierophanies and kratophanies God speaks to Job out of a whirlwind (38–41). He reminds Job of their respective positions. "Who is this that darkens counsel by words without knowledge?" (38:2). There follows a stirring and poetic recapitulation of God's cosmological activities. In the midst of rehearsing the beauty, majesty, and mystery of His creation, God acknowledges the existence of certain imperfections in the cosmos (40:11–13). He might even be willing to abdicate if someone else could do better (40:14). Clearly the question is rhetorical.

After God's speeches Job reverses his understanding of what has happened. He refuses to accept traditional theodicies—that suffering is a test or that suffering is divine punishment for sin. He also refuses to take the position that rewards may be expected in an afterlife (7:7–9). Job turns to self-accusation. It seems that Job's direct personal experience of the divine shatters his human arrogance. While God fails to answer Job's question (29:1–31:40), the question is turned against Job, proving his insolence. He is confronted by the numinous majesty of the Lord and responds in what has become the *locus classicus* of religious masochism, "I despise myself, and repent in dust and ashes" (42:6). Providing an interpretation for this dramatic shift in Job's position, Berger writes,

The Biblical God is radically transcendentalized, that is, posited as the totally other (*totaliter aliter*) vis-à-vis man. In this transcendentalization there is implicit from the start the masochistic solution *par excellence* to the problem of theodicy—submission to the totally other, who can be neither questioned nor challenged, and who, by his very nature, is sovereignly above any human ethical and generally nomic standards.[19]

Berger's interpretation, then, is a contention that "the book of Job presents . . . the . . . pure form of religious masochism."[20] Job's declarations, including the responses "Though he slay me, yet will I trust in him" and "Now my eye sees thee; therefore I despise myself and repent in dust and ashes," represents the thinking of aristocratic Israelites. It was these people who accepted the Talmudic position: "It is beyond our power to understand why the wicked are at ease, or why the righteous suffer" (Avot 4:15).[21] Repudiating the other traditional theodicies, and finding it impossible to locate his remedy on the "horizontal plane" of relationships among his fellows, Job's position seems to be one of complete submission to God's will—a radical masochism. From this perspective the problem of theodicy is transformed, and in its place appears a problem of anthropodicy. "The question of human sin replaces the question of divine justice."[22]

The Pawnbroker, by Edward Lewis Wallant, is the story of Sol Nazerman, a Jewish survivor of the Nazi death camps, and his black assistant Jesus Ortiz, a petty criminal. Sol has undergone unspeakable horrors in the camps, suffering the loss of his entire family and himself the victim of a Nazi medical experiment. Each year he commemorates the anniversary of his family's murder with nightmares of intense terror. Isolated from all human feeling, Sol has been described by one literary critic as "the scar tissue of man." Before the war he was a university professor specializing in Western intellectual history; after the war he works for the United Jewish Appeal in Paris assisting refugees. Arriving in America, he operates an East Harlem pawnship owned and financed by a major crime figure whose income is derived from drugs, prostitution, and other illicit activities. The book reflects in an extreme manner the problem of secularization—the "collapse of the plausibility of traditional religious definitions of reality,"[23] including, one notes, a definition of the meaning of suffering.

Unlike Job, Sol has no God to question and no divine source of response. God has either been slaughtered in the death camps or become a *deus absconditus* to the extent that He is no longer recoverable. Consequently the story emphasizes secular, human relationships. But Sol is no longer able or willing to open himself to the possibility of human communion. The meaning, if there is any, that he constructs for himself is essentially private. "I am safe within myself. I have made an order for myself and no one can disturb it."[24]

Throughout the story Sol's apparent abandonment of religion abounds in religious symbolism. Confronted by a customer wishing to pawn a velvet Torah cover, Sol erupts in anger. "Take it out of here, you and it together" (p. 81). Elsewhere Sol sarcastically compares himself to a priest giving absolution in hard cash (p. 108). The pawnship itself is described as a "holy place" having "the sacramental aura of a church, a place of penance and redemption, where Sol and his assistant Jesus dispense with ceremonial judgment, 'in exchange for the odd flotsam of people's lives,' small loans of cash—the artifact of grace."[25]

Sol, however, unwittingly begins to assume some responsibility for his fellow humans. He carries, but does not yet share, the burden of their plan.

He stretched on the rack of his sight and smell and hearing, saw all the naked souls ready to spill blood over him. And it began to seem to him that they all were making a profit on him, that they found ease from their individual pains at the sight of his great aggregate of pains, that they looked around at the stock of the store and saw it all as a tremendous weight on him. And that seemed to awe them, too, for as they added their own small item it was as though they piled on weight to prove his immense power, so that some of them even went out laughing, having left him a piece of their pain. (p. 189)

The origin of evil and suffering for Sol is not some divine or transcendent realm. Rather, they are caused by illusions about the perfectability of humanity and the invincibility of technology. The latter is an especially vicious source for Sol in that technology was manifested in the deadly efficiency of the crematoria and the gas chambers. Sol no longer trusts "God or politics or newspapers or music or art." Beyond this, however, he no longer trusts "people and their talk, for they have created hell with that talk," proving that they "do not deserve to exist for what they are" (p. 87). Both physical and spiritual suffering are depicted, but there appears to be a qualitative difference between the two. Ortiz, the assistant, emphatically states the case. "Niggers suffer like animals. They ain't caught on. Oh yeah, Jews suffer. But they do it big, they shake up the worl' with their sufferin' " (p. 24).

Sol's relationship with Jesus Ortiz is one of master and disciple. Through this association and its traumatic conclusion Sol is enabled to inhabit a meaningful world. Having told his assistant that money is the only thing of value, Sol has unknowingly set the stage for his escape from anomy. Jesus and three black companions rob the pawnshop. Something goes wrong and Sol is about to be shot. Jesus steps in front of him and is killed by a single bullet.

His assistant's sacrifice shocks Sol into the realization that compassion and love, two aspects of human meaning, are not yet dead. Further, to be alive requires taking responsibility for the building and maintenance of the world, as well as for the care of its inhabitants. "All his anesthetic numbness left him. He became terrified of the touch of air on the raw wounds. What was this great, agonizing sensitivity and what was it for? Good God, what was all this? Love? Could this be love:" (p. 200). Released from his isolation, Sol telephones his nephew and says simply, "I need you." The novel concludes with Sol uttering a prayer for his dead, finally able to weep for them. "He took a great breath of air, which seemed to fill parts of his lungs unused for a long time. And he took the pain of it, if not happily, like a martyr, at least willingly, like an heir" (p. 205–206).

The Pawnbroker protrays suffering as isolation from the human community. This isolation was the consequence, for Sol, of the anomic event *par excellence*, the Holocaust. Sol's estrangement and bitter suffering lasted as long as his separation from his community—from any community. In his state of anomy he is alone, denying or failing to find his part in a society that could heal the wounds of despair. Sol's suffering is stamped on him physically and spiritually.

Yet Sol's suffering is no longer destructive when he becomes part of a community. His redemption from the paralysis instigated by the Holocaust comes through the sacrifice of his assistant. In a secular way the community is his redemption in the midst of evil and suffering, even as in the religions the Christian *koinonia*, the Muslim *'umma*, the Buddhist *sangha*, and the Jewish covenant community provide the context for salvation from whatever is tragic in the human condition. Whereas Job excluded the possibility of finding a meaning in suffering on the horizontal plane and focused his efforts on the vertical, Sol reverses the process. For Sol meaning can come only via membership in the human community.

The theodicy implied in *The Pawnbroker* is that suffering and evil are real. Whatever their causes, the cure is found in community. Only then is ultimate anomy relieved; numbness leaves and meaning is restored in spite of even the Holocaust.

CONCLUSION

Explanations of theodicy and the problems of evil and suffering vary according to a tradition's orientation toward the divine and expectations of various social groups within a particular tradition. God, or some divine concept, and humanity are the focuses. As Weber long ago wrote, solutions to the problem of theodicy "stand in the closest relationship both to the forms assumed by the god-concept and to the conceptions of sin and salvation crystallized in particular social groups."[26] The basic issues, regardless of geography and theology, are imperfection in the world and the fact of death. Humanity is required to construct and maintain a meaningful world in order that anomic phenomena—that is, chaotic random events—be overcome. Theodicy becomes ultimately a search for meaning.

This search remains central for contemporary men and women. Technology, sometimes celebrated as the new deity, is the "god that failed." While it has provided part of humanity with increased ability to manipulate, dominate, and destroy, technology has not supplied any dependable assurance that suffering and evil can be destroyed, or any overarching meaning in the face of continued suffering. Humanity does not view matters *sub specie aeternitatis*. This limitation implies a search for other resources, both secular and religious in nature. Responses that are apparently in the process of being rediscovered include the possibility of human community, new forms of mysticism, and God concepts other than theism. Nevertheless the emergence of vast and terrifying nuclear arsenals intensifies the feelings of dread and uncertainty concerning the meaning and duration of human existence. The irrefutable facts of suffering and death remain. "Theodicy," writes Berger, "represents the attempt to make a pact with death."[27]

NOTES

1. See the valuable comments of Thomas A. Idinopulos in "The Mystery of Suffering in the Art of Dostoevsky, Camus, Wiesel, and Grunewald," *Journal of the American Academy of Religion* 43, no. 1 (March 1975).
2. There are philosophers and theologians who believe that evil and suffering do raise ques-

tions about the existence of God as conceived in Western traditional religions. See Chapter 9, "The Problem of God."

3. Elie Wiesel, *Night*, trans. Stella Rodway (New York: Avon Books, 1969), pp. 55–56.
4. The tale is cited in its entirety by Heinrich Zimmer in *Myths and Symbols in Indian Art and Civilization* (New York: Harper Torchbooks, 1961), pp. 32–34.
5. See Richard Rubenstein, *After Auschwitz* (Indianapolis: Bobbs-Merrill, 1966).
6. Peter Berger, *The Sacred Canopy* (Garden City, N.Y.: Doubleday, 1969), p. 71.
7. Ibid., p. 55.
8. See Max Weber, *The Sociology of Religion*, trans. Ephraim Fischoff (Boston: Beacon Press, 1968).
9. Berger, p. 58.
10. See Mircea Eliade's discussion in *Cosmos and History*, trans. W. R. Trask (New York: Harper & Row, 1959), pp. 95–98.
11. Mircea Eliade, *Shamanism: Archaic Techniques of Ecstasy*, trans. W. R. Trask (New York: Pantheon Books, Bollingen Series, vol. 76, 1963), p. 34.
12. John W. Bowker, *Problems of Suffering in Religions of the World* (Cambridge: Cambridge University Press, 1970), p. 56.
13. Ibid., p. 57.
14. Ibid., p. 94.
15. Berger, pp. 77–78.
16. Bowker, p. 115.
17. Ibid., p. 103.
18. Berger, p. 65.
19. Ibid., p. 74.
20. Ibid., pp. 74–75.
21. Max Weber contended that this submission to God's absolute sovereignty over humanity served as a precursor of Puritan predestination. See *The Sociology of Religion*, trans. E. Fischoff (Boston: Beacon Press, 1968), p. 112.
22. Berger, p. 74.
23. Ibid., p. 127.
24. Edward Lewis Wallant, *The Pawnbroker* (New York: Macfadden-Bartell, 1965), p. 91. All references are to this edition.
25. Jonathan Baumbach, *The Landscape of Nightmare: Studies in the Contemporary American Novel* (New York: New York University Press, 1965), p. 140.
26. Weber, p. 139.
27. Berger, p. 80.

QUESTIONS FOR STUDY, REFLECTION, AND DISCUSSION

1. Compare the book of Job and *The Pawnbroker*. What is the origin of suffering in each? What forms do suffering take? What theodicy is given in Job? In *The Pawnbroker*?

2. Each of the major religions offers a variety of theodicies. List the different theodicies that people in your religious tradition may hold. [For example, (a) evil and suffering are God's punishment; (b) evil and suffering are caused by human misuse of freedom; (c) God is neither all-good nor all-powerful.] Are they convincing?

3. Do natural evils like earthquakes and floods provide greater difficulties

in affirming the goodness of God than social evils like war and domestic crime? Is there a difference in meaning between the two kinds of evil?
4. A theodicy in Christian Science is that of denying the reality of evil. Only the good is ontologically real. By the denial of evil God's goodness is made absolute. What kinds of arguments and evidence might be used to support and/or refute this position?

PROJECTS

1. Organize a group of people to spend a number of hours together studying the book of Job. Then spend two hours or so reading Archibald MacLeish's play "J.B." You might also get the recording of "J.B." (RCA Victor LDS 6075). Discuss the differences between Job and "J.B.," especially in the way they end.
2. The problem of evil and suffering can be discussed theologically and sociologically, as this chapter has indicated. Yet the problem can be analyzed through the methods and theories of other disciplines such as psychology or literature. Select a psychologist such as Freud, Jung, Fromm, Erickson, May, or Skinner and indicate the way each would deal with evil. Or analyze a novel such as Dostoevsky's *The Grand Inquisitor*, Wiesel's *Night*, or Camus's *The Plague*. Write an essay in which you discuss the origin and nature of evil and suffering as well as an interpretation of the meaning of evil from that perspective.
3. As a research project using the method of participant observation, become part of a family or social group in which there has been some tragedy leading to intense suffering. Through empathetic listening see if you can discover their theodicy and see if you can tell how well their theodicy functions for them. Then note the meaning that their theodicy has for you.
4. As a research project, select any major writer within one of the religious traditions, Eastern or Western. Make an extensive study of that person's thought with special concern for his or her theodicy.

SELECTED BIBLIOGRAPHY

Arendt, Hannah. *Eichmann in Jerusalem: A Report on the Banality of Evil.* New York: Viking Press, 1965.

Berger, Peter L. *The Sacred Canopy: Elements of a Sociological Theory of Religion.* New York: Anchor Books, 1969.

The Book of Job.

Bowker, John. *Problems of Suffering in Religions of the World.* Cambridge: Cambridge University Press, 1970.

Dasgupta, S. N. *Hindu Mysticism.* New York: Frederick Ungar, 1960.

Eliade, Mircea. *Yoga: Immortality and Freedom,* translated by Willard R. Trask. Princeton, N.J.: Princeton University Press, Bollingen Series, vol. 56, 1970.

Fleischner, Eva, ed. *Auschwitz: Beginning of a New Era?* New York: Ktav, 1977.

Rubenstein, Richard J. *After Auschwitz: Essays in Contemporary Judaism.* Indianapolis: bobbs-Mcrrill, 1966.

Scholem, Gershom G. *Major Trends in Jewish Mysticism.* New York: Schocken Books, 1961.

Smith, Huston. *The Religions of Man.* New York: Harper & Row, 1965.

Wallant, Edward L. *The Pawnbroker.* New York: Macfadden-Bartell, 1970.

Wiesel, Elie. *Night,* translated by Stella Rodway. New York: Avon Books, 1972.

CHAPTER 12

Paths to Salvation

T. WILLIAM HALL

RELIGION: ONE OR MANY?

The vast differences in religious myth, belief, ritual, scripture, and art
from one religion to another, and even the varieties of expression within
the same religion, can leave us bewildered. Should we think that the same
word *religion* applies to all such widely different phenomena? And if we do
use the term *religion* in relation to the staggering diversity, does it not lose
specific meaning?

On the other hand, is *religion* a generic term that has to do with a common class of things that only appear to be different but are, on closer
inspection, really the same? One version of this second point of view is
found in "perennial philosophy" as represented by Aldous Huxley. Perennial philosophy, Huxley writes, includes a "metaphysic that recognizes a
divine reality substantial to the world of things and lives in minds."[1] Moreover, those who hold to this point of view believe that there is a common
psychology and ethics in every religion. A brilliant book by Huston Smith
entitled *Forgotten Truth* presents a persuasive argument for one Truth
rooted in the unchanging depth of the universe.[2] Both scholars affirm the
similarity or near identity of the essence of all religions.

Shall we assert, as the nominalist does, that there is only each particular
religion; that we can study only a ritual or belief within a particular community because each is unique? If we take this horn of the dilemma, are we
not soon pushed to the conclusion that religion is a private personal experience for each individual? If so, religion is not a subject that can be studied
in a general way.

The second position, that all religions are really the same, may be more
attractive. Surely there must be something common to all religions for us
even to use the term *religion* in speaking of Buddhism, Judaism, Islam, and

all other religions. Even when we say something like "Baseball is my religion," the last term must refer to the common element with other things in that class. Nevertheless in taking this position is it not possible that we will uncritically accept the conclusion that all religions are at bottom the same, whether we are speaking of the Holy Eucharist as a religious sacrament or the May Day celebration as part of the communist religious ritual? And in so doing are we not always in danger of distorting the distinctiveness of each religion and each culture of which that religious expression is a part?

The issue, then, can be stated again simply as follows: Are all religions basically the same, or are they different?[3]

The purpose of the following pages is to show that there is an intermediate position between these two extremes. In fact a position between the two extremes seems necessary for the study of religion. To take the first position, that each religious experience or each religion is unique, makes a general study of religion impossible, for there would be no common framework for analysis and evaluation of a *sui generis* experience. To assume the second position would be to deny at the start distinctive characteristics in belief, behavior, or emotions in individuals and in separate religious traditions. The danger is that religion would be reduced to a watered-down common denominator.

If we wish, then, to discover a more adequate framework for exploring religious similarities and differences, a restatement of the basic issue is a place to start. If each religion is neither totally unique nor exactly the same as another religion, IN WHAT WAY ARE RELIGIONS THE SAME AND IN WHAT WAY ARE THEY DIFFERENT? A satisfactory answer to this question will open the door to a description and understanding of the similarities and differences in the religions and provide a method for identifying and interpreting any aspect of religion.

Initial observation of religions provides persuasive evidence that there are differences. Belief systems, for example, are different. In traditional Christianity a personal God and a human soul are affirmed, while in Buddhism the reality of both God and the individual soul is denied. Hindus believe in reincarnation, while certain Christian theologians defend belief in the resurrection of the body. Christians assert that Jesus was the Christ, the incarnate son of God, the anointed one. For Jews and Muslims Jesus was only a man, although he was an important prophet. The Australian myth of the great father who created the world out of nothing is quite different from the South Pacific myth of the emergence of the world from a coconut shell or the Shinto myth of Izanagi and Izanami, who descended from the heavens and by touching a spear to the water created the "self-coagulating island."[4]

Reflecting on these and many other differences, we sense that whereas beliefs and myths are markedly different, they seem to function in similar ways. Different beliefs about death and what follows may serve a similar function of helping people affirm that which is of highest value—what is ultimate—and survives even physical life. Various creation myths may speak about the limitations in the human condition as well as the sacredness of the cosmos.

I am therefore ready to suggest that amid the diversity among the religions there is a common structure. This common structure, I assert, is found in all religious communities in all cultures and is equally discernible in personal religious quests. Nevertheless, as I will illustrate later, cognitive, affective, and behavioral aspects of the religions differ markedly. In short, religions have a common structure; their content is different. The writings of three distinguished scholars help express the nature of this common structure.

John E. Smith[5] presents the hypothesis that there is a common structure and argues that "this structure makes it possible to have a genuine encounter between the world religions. . . . No experience regarded as unique within any religion need be sacrificed. . . . Comparisons with relevant alternatives can provide each tradition with a clearer understanding of itself."[6] With Smith, I am here affirming that there is a common structure in the religions.

Later in the same book Smith suggests that the common structure found in all religions includes three elements, two of which are important in this discussion: First, "Religion demands an ideal or religious object that is at once the ground and goal of all existence."[7] Smith's statement is similar to that of Alfred North Whitehead, who wrote that "religion is a vision of something which stands beyond, behind and within the passing flux of immediate things; something which is real, and yet waiting to be realized."[8] Both scholars are pointing out what we all observe—that religions have a high goal, an aspiration, a "vision" or an "unrestricted value."

Smith suggests a second element in the religious structure. "Religion," he writes, "lives in the conviction that natural existence of life as we find it is separated from the ideal or religious object by some flaw or defect."[9] Here again Whitehead's position is similar when he concludes an earlier statement: "Without this religious vision, human life is a mass of occasional enjoyments lighting up a mass of pain and misery, a bagatelle of transient experience."[10] Both writers are suggesting that all religions recognize that something is wrong in the human condition—that they have a problem to be overcome.

The point of view of a third scholar makes us a bit more confident in asserting the common structure of religions. Frederick Streng insists that religion is a means of ultimate transformation.[11] Streng seems to be suggesting, along with Smith and Whitehead, that the common element in religions is the path by which individuals and groups seek to overcome the basic human problem as they are transformed into something that Streng calls "salvation."

Beyond the problem to be solved and the aspiration to be achieved, there are a variety of other elements in the structure of religion. At least we need to be prepared to find, beyond the first two mentioned, cognitive elements, behavioral elements, and emotional aspects. The totality of the religious quest will be called the "path to salvation." From the point of view being developed, we will expect to find in our investigation a variety of paths of salvation. The structure and function will be the same; the content will be different in each religion.

In order to proceed in the task of identifying precisely the common structure of religion and using that structure to examine and interpret various religions, our next step is to create an intellectual model of the structure we believe to be within all religions.

A MODEL FOR ANALYZING PATHS TO SALVATION

A *model* is a group of related concepts that, when taken separately and as a whole, help us discover and explain complex data. In this case the model will be a model of the common religious structure. A model is a hypothesis or a construct used by the researcher. By using a model we can investigate various human expressions more easily because it enables us to handle a wide range of information and to observe the relationships of each of the elements studied to other elements.

A hypothetical model would be inadequate if it did not clarify and provide an organizational pattern for the data being investigated. If one model is found to be inadequate, its limitations must be studied and a better one constructed. For example, the concept of evolution provides a model for examining living species. The use of the "evolution" model is helpful in examining data about life on earth if the material being studied can be adequately explained. If research into the life sciences is not aided by the concept of evolution, then another model will have to be selected as a way of recording and analyzing data.

In the field of religion, the body of data being studied is vast and diverse. Types of religious expression can be observed in every culture, and these observations suggest that the belief systems, the expressions of feeling, and the behavioral patterns in each are quite different. Yet a hypothetical model will help uncover a structure that is, I believe, inherent in all religious communities as well as within the individual in his or her religious pilgrimage.

A model, which points clearly to certain data, helps organize these data in some understandable way, and explains the dynamics of religion, might be either too simple or too complex. If it is too simple, it may clarify some aspects of religion but not enough for an adequate explanation. For example, a simple "transformation model," as suggested by Streng and Whitehead and developed by Cavanagh (Chapter 4) has three parts: (1 problem, (2) transforming power, and (3) goal. In using this model the investigator would search for ideas that are believed to represent the problem, the transforming power, and the goal of religious people. Such a model might focus on the cognitive aspects of religious belief and minimize the emotional and behavioral modes of religion.

The model to be described here is also a transformational model, but it is more complex than the one just mentioned. It has been adapted from David McClelland's "achievement motivation" model.[12] This model has been chosen because each description of a religious path to salvation appears to portray a quest or journey toward some desired goal or a need for goal achievement. Moreover, observation of various paths reveals that each has beliefs (the cognitive elements), emotions (the affective elements), and actions (the behavioral aspects). The model proposed here points to each element of the path and suggests a relationship among them. This model, then, is a conceptual framework through which data can be collected, organized, and understood to show the interrelationship of the elements in each path. It is, then, the hypothetical structure of religion. However, it does not provide a way for dealing with the "truth" or "falsity" of any belief, nor does it provide criteria for evaluating the appropriateness or inappropriateness of any feeling or any behavior. Instead, it directs our attention toward the key common elements of the religious journey and to the different beliefs, actions, and feelings.

This model includes ten distinct elements, most of which will be found in every path to salvation: (1) problem—P, (2) aspiration—ASP, (3) hope of success—HOS, (4) fear of failure—FOF, (5) action—ACT, (6) internal limitations—IL, (7) external limitations—EL, (8) failure feelings—FaF, (9) help—H, and (10) success feelings—SuF. Some elements are primarily cognitive (i.e., knowing); some are essentially affective (i.e., feelings or emotions); others are basically behavioral. Each element, however, may possess two or three dimensions.

It is assumed that each journey along a path to salvation begins with a "problem." Hinkle has described this universal drive in these words: "There is one great and universal wish of mankind expressed in all religions, in all human life; the wish to pass beyond himself as he now is."[13] The origin of this awareness of limiting factors in the human condition is difficult to ascertain. An individual or a culture may have been so dominated by isolation or slavery or suffering that the need to overcome one or more factors has become the dominant passion. A person on a religious quest will believe that the tragic flaw in the human condition, as he or she sees it, is not just his or her personal limitation. Such a person believes, rather, that the flaw is the fundamental problem of all people. Thus the ini-

tial element in this model of analysis—the problem—will help the investigator search for expressions of a desire to overcome that which hinders
spiritual growth. In the model the problem of overcoming human limitations and transform the present into some desired condition is given the
abbreviation P.

Under the pressure of intense problems it is reasonable to expect that
people will form an image of that which will free them from their oppres-
sions and save them from their limiting conditions. Thus people in every
culture will have aspirations (ASP) to achieve that which will be of highest
value—that which will save them. In the model the term ASP is used to
designate statements of a people's hoped-for goal at the end of their path to
salvation. Figure 12-1 illustrates graphically an individual or cultural group
that experiences the problem (P) and conceives of aspirations (ASP) for a
goal. That shaded line in Figure 1 represents the cognitive image of some
further condition.

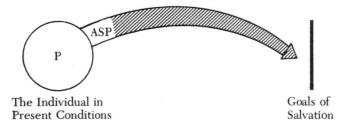

The Individual in   Goals of
Present Conditions   Salvation

FIGURE 12–1. The first two elements in the model of paths to salvation, problem
and aspirations.

With the pressure of the problem and aspirations for some possible goal,
most religions include expressions of both hope and fear relative to these
aspirations. In the model hope is symbolized by HOS (hope of success) and
is exemplified by religious expressions of confidence and trust in the expectation of achieving the goal. But this hope is often accompanied by expressions of fear of failure (FOF in the model), which are indicated by statements of the very possibility that one may not be successful, that the
aspirations may not be achieved; these statements express feelings of
dread, dismay, and apprehension. By including these two emotions (HOS
and FOF), one positive and the other negative, the model directs the
student to study religious literature with special sensitivity to the feelings
of hope and fear that are an integral part of the religious quest, just as feelings are an integral part of every human activity.

Any description of a path to salvation will surely include plans for action
(ACT) that will lead away from present conditions and toward the aspiration
and goal. The appropriate action may vary widely from one religious ex-

pression to another and even within any one religion. In one expression the appropriate action may be the following of a specific moral discipline. In some religions it will be the gaining of knowledge that is believed to take one from the present problem to the aspired achievement. In other religions the action may be ritual, or it may be the following of a personal savior like Krishna, Buddha, or Jesus. The action may be centered in community participation or in private meditation. But regardless of how it is expressed there will be action along the journey.

In Figure 12-2 the diagram of the model has been expanded to include these three themes (HOS, FOF, and ACT), which will guide the searcher in the effort to understand the nature of religious expressions.

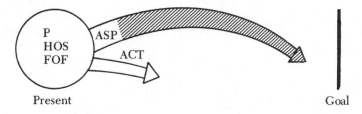

Present   Goal

FIGURE 12–2. The model, including five types of themes commonly expressed in descriptions of a path to salvation.

Achievement of any ultimate goal is never an easy task. We can expect any person or group on the journey to come across obstacles or limitations. The obstacles may be objective events that block progress, such as natural disasters, the stubbornness of other people, or the many obligations that a person must fulfill in daily life. The model suggests that we look for expressions of such external limitations (EL) in religious expressions as recognitions of the difficulties that people face in the external world. At the same time, religions have recognized that there are internal limitations (IL) within the individual or group that may block progress toward the goal, such as personal weaknesses, tendencies to yield to temptations, or the feelings of unworthiness that lead one not to try.

When action is taken toward the goal and these obstacles and limitations are encountered or believed to be present, we can expect to find accompanying failure feelings (FaF), or despair of reaching the goal because of the tremendous obstacles along the path. When Job cries out in his misery and suffering, "What is mine end, that I should prolong my life?" he is expressing failure feelings in the face of massive limitations.

The model that we can use as a guide to our exploration of religious expressions has been expanded in Figure 12-3 to include the obstacles (both external—EL—and internal—IL) to progress and the feelings (FaF) that result from experience with these obstacles.

One characteristic of every religion is that some help (H) is believed to

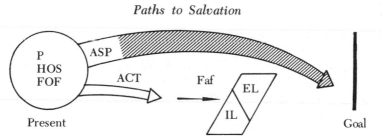

FIGURE 12-3. The model, with symbols for eight themes common to expressions of the path to salvation.

be available to every person in his or her time of greatest difficulty. This help may come from scripture, a teacher, or divine power. Help may come in any number of other ways, depending on the culture or religion involved. Including H in our model suggests that the investigator of religion look for assertions that help has come or will come to give encouragement and support in overcoming or circumventing the obstacles faced by those who continue along the path.

Finally, when action is continued and some or all of the aspirations seem to be almost a reality, as peace, joy, freedom, or enlightenment seem almost achieved, a great feeling of euphoria and ecstasy may be experience. These success feelings (SuF) may be expressed poetically, in hymns, or in exclamations of "Hallelujah." In some religions speaking in tongues is one of the expected ways to express unspeakable joy. These final two themes (help—H—and success feelings—SuF) of the religious path to salvation have also been added to the model. Figure 12-4 includes all ten elements and suggests some fundamental relationships among them.

REVISING THE MODEL

The model proposed in this chapter is, I believe, a useful one. It will be useful if it helps the student of religion interpret the mass of potentially

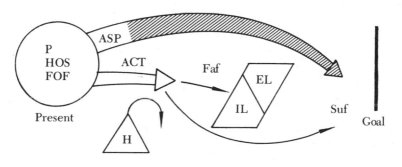

FIGURE 12-4. The model with all ten elements.

confusing data about the diverse forms and varied content of religious expression and indicates adequately the common religious structure.

As with any model, if the elements of the model do not appear in the data being studied or if the model distorts the data, then the model should be modified to include another group of concepts that explain more adequately the religious phenomena that may be uncovered by a study of the various religious journeys—the paths to salvation. In further study the student of religion should be encouraged to examine other models or methods of analysis of these paths to salvation.

ILLUSTRATION: THE BHAGAVAD-GITA

The structure of religion illustrated in the model just described can be used to explain and interpret a religious biography, the sacred scriptures of a religion, a novel that assumes a particular religious point of view, or one's own religious quest. The *Bhagavad-Gita* will be discussed here for two major reasons: (1) It is one of the best-loved and best-known of Hindu scriptures, and (2) it is brief enough to be analyzed in a few pages.*

The *Gita*, often called *The Song of God*, is the moving story and poetry of Lord Krishna and Arjuna, the Hindu warrior. The setting of the story is an ancient battle. Yet within it can be seen Arjuna's path to salvation and, hence, one path within Hinduism.

The *Gita* begins abruptly. Arjuna is troubled that he must fight against and possibly kill his relatives. He pleads, in fear, to his friend and god Krishna: "My brain is whirling . . . I can stand no longer" (p. 31). "I cannot see where my duty lies. Krishna, I beg you, tell me frankly and clearly what I ought to do. I am your disciple. I put myself into your hands. Show me the way" (p. 35).

With this introduction, in which Arjuna is expressing his failure feelings and in which he seeks help from Sri Krishna, we can reconstruct his path to salvation. It is clear that the path to salvation for Arjuna did not begin all at once on the battlefield. We have to search into the *Gita* to grasp his problem and aspiration.

PROBLEM

The Hindu tradition has one clear belief about the human condition, and this is Arjuna's problem. All people, the Hindus believe, are limited by *samsara*, the wheel of birth, death, and rebirth. Lord Krishna helps clarify

---

* Before reading the remainder of this chapter it is recommended that you read the *Gita*. All quotations from the *Bhagavad-Gita* in this chapter are taken from the Mentor Edition of *The Song of God: Bhagavad-Gita*, translated by Swami Prabhavananda and Christopher Isherwood and used with permission of the Vedanta Society of Southern California, copyright owner.

this problem for Arjuna by saying that he must "break the chains of desire . . . which will save you from the terrible wheel of rebirth and death" (p. 30). Or again, the Lord tells Arjuna, "Death is certain for the born. Rebirth is certain for the dead" (p. 38). Even more direct are the words pointing to the problem: "To be free forever from birth and dying with all their evil" (p. 79).

Moreover, Sri Kirshna reminds Arjuna that there is a tendency for a person to be limited by dualities, by anxieties for gain and safety, and by self-pride. These, too, are human limitations to be overcome.

Finally, Arjuna, like all Hindus, needs to overcome the ignorance of supposing that the material world is real when it is only *maya*. "Helpless all, for Maya is their master," Krishna says. But equally crucial is the human tendency to suppose that his body is real when it is only the *atman*, the deep soul, that is real. Thus Arjuna has the problem of ignorance along with pride and *samsara*.

ASPIRATION

The aspiration that Arjuna and all devout Hindus seek is *nirvana* (p. 65)—the aspiration "to reach union with Brahman" (p. 41). Such a goal is expressed in many words, such as *enlightenment* (p. 35), *Ultimate Truth* (p. 47), or "the peace that is in me, Lord Krishan" (p. 65), or *moksha*.

The poetic songs of Krishna are full of the dream that is Arjuna's *aspiration*.

> That innermost secret:
> Knowledge of God
> Which is nearer than knowing,
> Open vision,
> Direct and instant. [p. 79]

In Book 8 Arjuna, trying to clarify his aspiration, asks, "Tell me, Krishna, what Brahman is" (p. 74). Krishna replies that "Brahman is that which is immutable and independent of any cause but itself." And if one dies with one's consciousness united with Brahman, then one will be united with God. For this is the aspiration of the spiritual person (adapted from p. 75).

HOPE OF SUCCESS AND FEAR OF FAILURE

The two elements of hope and fear, usually expressed when one has first become aware of one's aspiration and is beginning one's quest, are not obvious in the *Gita*. We can suppose that the reason is that Arjuna is well along on his spiritual journey when the *Gita* opens. Yet a closer examination reveals these subtle and powerful emotions surging from Arjuna when he is most aware of his great aspiration to be united with Brahman—to achieve truth and *moksha*.

Arjuna expresses his hope of success in speaking to Sri Kirshna:

You are Brahman, the highest abode, the utterly holy:
All the sages proclaim you eternal, Lord of the devas:

Now I also have heard, for to me your own lips have confirmed it,
Krishna, this is the truth that you tell:
My heart bids me believe you.

God of gods, Lord of the world, Life's source, O . . . King of all creatures:
You alone know what you are, by the light of your innermost nature,
Therefore teach me now, and hold back no
. . . word in your telling,
Speak, for each word is immortal nectar: I never grow weary. [p. 88]

In his hope to achieve his aspiration Arjuna, like every person aspiring to reach a high goal, has feelings of fear that he will not succeed. Arjuna reflects on his Lord and, seeing His great power in comparison to his own feeble humanness, cries:

When I see you, Vishnu, omnipresent,
Shouldering the sky, in hues of rainbow,
With your mouths agape and flame-eyes staring—
All my peace is gone; my heart is troubled.

Tell me who you are, and were from the beginning,
You of aspect grim, O God of gods, be gracious.
Take my homage, Lord. From me your ways are hidden. [pp. 93–94]

ACTION

The action first required of all Hindus is to do their *dharma* (duty). The *dharma* is, in part, prescribed by caste. Arjuna was a soldier, so his action was to be a warrior, as was expected of any *Kshatriya*. As a Kshatriya Arjuna enjoyed pleasure, wealth, and power. Yet he had to be ready at any time to risk death in war to protect his leader or his country. In addition, he was clearly pious in that he was loyal to his chosen god, Lord Krishna. It was this plan of action—doing his moral duty according to caste rules—that brought Arjuna to the problems presented in the *Gita*. And these problems were the limitations, both external (EL) and internal (IL).

LIMITATIONS

The core of the *Gita* is Arjuna's limitations. He has been steadily progressing along his path to salvation, seeking to overcome *samsara*, pride and ignorance, while following the action of his moral duty. But he is stopped in his path by the horrible external limitation (EL) of a battle in which he must kill his own blood relatives. His own code of ethics demands that he never run from a fight. Yet when Arjuna sees the enemy he recognizes grandfathers, uncles, sons, brothers, dear friends, and many others. Lamenting to Lord Krishna, he exclaims:

> Krishna, Krishna,
> Now as I look on
> These my kinsmen
> Arrayed for battle
> My limbs are weakened,
> My mouth is parching,
> My body trembles. [p. 31]

With this external limitation facing him, Arjuna is plagued also with inner restrictions (IL). He is aware of his own guilt, uncertainty, and fear. "If we kill them, none of us will wish to live," he sobs (p. 35).

FAILURE FEELINGS

So it is no accident that the emotion of failure becomes evident as Arjuna cannot follow his plan of action in order to achieve his goal. He pleads to the Lord:

> How could we dare spill
> The blood that unites us?
> Where is joy in
> The killing of kinsmen? [p. 33]

> Let the evil children
> Of Dhritarashta
> Come with their weapons
> Against me in battle:
> I shall not struggle,
> I shall not strike them.
> Now let them kill me,
> That will be better. [p. 34]

Again Arjuna cries out: "My mind gropes about in darkness. I cannot see where my duty lies. I beg you [Krishna] tell me frankly and clearly what I ought to do" (p. 35). After Arjuna had thus vented his feelings, the *Gita* reports that he sat down on the seat of his chariot, overcome with sorrow in his heart. Yet he has asked his Lord for help, and he receives that help.

HELP

The central message in the *Gita,* like that of so many of the scriptures of the great religions, is that help is available from God or the gods when the path to salvation is stopped by limitations. The Jewish and Christian Bible reports of God's help to the people of ancient Israel and to the early Christians. In later years Martin Luther, the Protestant reformer, tells of the power of God's grace. Shingon Buddhism proclaims divine help through Kobadashi. And the *Gita* shows that Krishna, the lord of the universe, Brahman himself, gives help to Arjuna.

The help is specific, but it is in several parts. First, Krishna chides Arjuna to remember his own deeper understandings. One should not fear slaying another, even a relative, because the real person is the atman—the god in man—and this cannot be killed. Moreover, the atman dwelling within bodies is always indestructible. Therefore his advice to Arjuna is that he "ought not to hesitate, for to a warrior there is nothing nobler than a righteous war. Happy is the warrior to whom a battle such as this comes; it opens a door to heaven" (p. 38). The first advice, then, is for Arjuna to do his dharma as a warrior.

Second, Sri Krishna gives the advice of Karma Yoga, that Arjuna do his duty with no conern for the results of the action. He should fight with detachment, without anxiety, without desire for any particular consequence.

But when a man has found delight and satisfaction and peace in the Atman, then he is no longer obliged to perform any kind of action. He has nothing to gain in this world by action, and nothing to lose by refraining from action. He is independent of everybody. Do your duty, always; but without attachment. That is how a man reaches the Ultimate Truth, by working without anxiety about results. [pp. 46–47]

Lord Krishna goes on to offer his divine help by advising,

> The ignorant work
> For the fruit of their action:
> The wise must work also
> Without desire
> Pointing man's feet
> To the path of his duty.
>
> Let the wise beware
> Lest they bewilder
> the minds of the ignorant
> Hungry for action:
> Let them show by example
> How work is holy
> When the heart of the worker
> Is fixed on the Highest. [p. 47]

Third, Lord Krishna tells Arjuna that the Yoga of renunciation will help him overcome the limitations and lead him back to his path to *moksha*. Such renunciation will unite him with Brahman, free him from concern for the results of action, and set him free (p. 58).

> Absorbed in Brahman
> He overcomes the world
> Even here, alive in the world.
> Brahman is one,
> Changeless, untouched by evil:
> What home have we but Him? [p. 60]

Krishna offers Arjuna many other kinds of help, opening Arjuna's under-standing of meditation and finally leading him to the mystical vision of being one with Brahman as he is united with Krishna, who is himself the universal god.

SUCCESS FEELINGS

The *Gita* itself is not specific about Arjuna's future actions, although the stories in the *Mahabharata* tell of his life in battle. Yet Arjuna says, "By your grace, O Lord, My delusions have been dispelled. My mind stands firm. Its doubts are ended. I will do your bidding" (p. 130). It is possible that Arjuna's words mean that he returned to battle. It is clear, however, that he proceeds on his path to salvation with great joy. And without doubt Arjuna approaches the achievement of his aspirations when we hear his words of intense success feelings:

> Ah, my God, I see all gods within your body;
> Each in his degree, the multitude of creatures;
> See Lord Brahma throned upon the lotus;
> See all the sages, and the holy serpents.
>
> Universal Form, I see you without limit,
> Infinite of arms, eyes, mouths and bellies—
> See, and find no end, midst, or beginning.
>
> Crowned with diadems, you wield the mace and discus,
> Shining every way—the eyes shrink from your splendor
> Brilliant like the sun; like fire, blazing, boundless [p. 92]

The final words of Arjuna recorded in the *Gita* again show his success feelings at reaching his aspiration:

By your grace, O Lord, my delusions have been dispelled. My mind stands firm. Its doubts are ended. I will do your bidding. [p. 130]

SUMMARY

In answer to the question, In what way are religions the same and in what way are they different? we have thus far suggested that religions are the same in that they have a common structure—a path to salvation. One sacred writing, the *Bhagavad-Gita*, has been used to illustrate the path to salvation of Arjuna through the model for analysis presented in this chap-ter. The content of Hinduism expressed in the *Gita* is unique to the Indian culture and religion. The beliefs, feelings, and actions are different from those found in other religions. Yet it has served to illustrate a structure that is believed to be common to all religious quests, whether of communities or of individuals.

Further exploration of similarities and differences among various religions is urged as other religious traditions are studied through the examination of their sacred scriptures, of the lives of their founders or holy people, or of the myths or novels that grow out of a particular tradition. In
such studies, will it become clear that in each religion there is believed to
be something wrong in the human condition that needs to be overcome?
Will each religion have some high goal, some ultimate aspiration? Will
there be some plan of action to overcome the problem and achieve the
goal? Will there be a source of help? And will there be emotions expressed
during the pilgrimage—the journey to salvation?

If these questions are answered in the affirmative, then the conclusion
follows that there is a common structure in religion. Moreover, if the
problem, aspiration, action, and source of help are different, the conclusion
will also follow that the content of the religions is diverse. The questions
for discussion and the suggested projects in the following pages may be
helpful in this further study.

NOTES

1. Aldous Huxley, *The Perennial Philosophy* (New York: Harper & Row, Colophon Books,
   1970), p. vii.
2. Huston Smith, *Forgotten Truth* (New York: Harper & Row, 1976).
3. There is a corollary question: "Is there one truth or many truths?" This question will be
   postponed until the final chapter.
4. See Charles H. Long, *Alpha. The Myths of Creation* (New York: Macmillan, Collier
   Books, 1963).
5. John E. Smith, *Experience and God* (New York: Oxford University Press, 1968).
6. *Ibid.*, p. 17.
7. *Ibid.*, p. 166.
8. Alfred North Whitehead, *Science and the Modern World* (New York: A Mentor Book,
   1925), p. 192.
9. Smith, *op. cit.*, p. 166.
10. Whitehead, *op. cit.*, p. 193.
11. Frederick J. Streng, *Understanding Religious Man* (Belmont, California: Dickenson,
    1969, 1976), p. 4.
12. David McClelland, et al., *The Achievement Motive* (New York: Appleton-Century-Crofts,
    1953).
13. Beatrice Hinckle, "The Recreation of the Individual," quoted in Phillips, *The Choice is
    Always Ours* (Rinde, N.H.: Richard R. Smith, 1954), p. 4.

QUESTIONS FOR STUDY, REFLECTION, AND DISCUSSION

1. What is the problem to be overcome along the path to salvation in Buddhism, Judaism, classical Christianity, religious humanism?

2. What are different plans of action within Hinduism? within Buddhism? within Islam? (etc.)

3. Why is it difficult to identify the affective or emotional elements in a religious quest (HOS, FOF, FaF, SuF)? Where would we look for them in ancient religions? In contemporary religious quests?

4. If you were creating a new religion, what would be your problem? aspiration? action? help?

5. In your newly created religious journey, would you have any limitations in the path? Why or why not?

PROJECTS

1. Read carefully *Siddhartha*, by Hermann Hesse.

   a. Write down the two main cognitive elements in Siddhartha's spiritual journey: the problem (what flaw he was trying to overcome) and the aspiration (that which he wanted to achieve).

   b. Next, identify the behavioral element or elements that would provide the means or action to achieve his aspiration.

   c. Find illustrations of the affective elements expressed by Siddhartha. Illustrate these, trying to capture the deep emotion expressed or spoke about.

   d. Identify the various sources of help to Siddhartha.

2. Write an essay in which you present a path of salvation within Christianity. Include all of the elements as you find them in Christianity. The following selections from the Bible may be helpful: Matthew, Chapters 5, 6, and 7; John, Chapter 3; Ephesians, Chapters 1 and 2; Romans, Chapters 6 and 8; various Psalms.

3. A path of salvation representing a major religious tradition can often be seen through a novel. At the same time, the model of analysis can be useful in interpreting the main characters and themes in the novel. The following suggestion has three purposes: (1) to increase your skill in using a model for analysis, (2) to help you understand a path of salvation within Judaism, and (3) to provide a way of understanding and appreciating the book.

   Read one or more of the following books. Then write an interpretation of the book, using the model and its various elements as the interpretive principle:

   Chaim Potok, *The Chosen*
   Elie Wiesel, *Night*
   Bernard Malamud, *The Assistant*

4. Write your autobiography, a biography, or a myth in which you describe the religious quest of yourself, someone else, or a mythical character. (Be sure to include the emotional elements.) You will also need to be sensitive to the interaction among the various elements, such as the relationship among limitations, failure feelings, and help, or the relationship between success feelings and the movement toward the aspiration.

SELECTED BIBLIOGRAPHY

Eastman, Roger, ed. *The Ways of Religion*. San Francisco: Canfield Press, 1975.

Franck, Frederick. *Pilgrimage to Now-Here*. Maryknoll, N.Y.: Orbis Books, 1974.

Frost, S. E., Jr., ed. *The Sacred Writings of the World's Great Religions*. New York: McGraw-Hill, 1972.

Hesse, Hermann. *Siddhartha*. New York: New Directions, 1951.

Hick, John, ed. *Truth and Dialogue in World Religions: Conflicting Truth Claims*. Philadelphia: Westminster Press, 1974.

Malamud, Bernard. *The Assistant*. New York: Farrar, Straus and Giroux, 1967.

Nasr, Seyyed H. *Ideals and Realities of Islam*. Boston: Beacon Press, 1972.

Neusner, Jacob. *The Way of Torah: An Introduction to Judaism*. Belmont, Calif.: Dickenson, 1974.

Potok, Chaim. *The Chosen*. Greenwich, Conn.: Fawcett World, 1976.

Samartha, S. J., ed. *Living Faith and Ultimate Goals: Salvation and World Religions*. Maryknoll, N.Y.: Orbis Books, 1975.

Smith, Huston. *Forgotten Truth: The Primordial Tradition*. New York: Harper & Row, 1976.

———. *The Religions of Man*. New York: Harper & Row, 1965.

Smith, Wilfred Cantwell. *The Faith of Other Men*. New York: Harper & Row, 1972.

———. *The Meaning and End of Religion*. New York: Harper & Row, 1978.

Streng, Frederick J. *Understanding Religious Man*. Belmont, Calif.: Dickenson, 1969.

———. Lloyd, Charles L., and Jay T. Allen, eds. *Ways of Being Religious: Readings for a New Approach to Religion*. Englewood Cliffs, N.J.: Prentice-Hall, 1973.

Watts, Alan W. *The Way of Zen*. New York: Random House, 1974.

Wiesel, Elie. *Night*, translated by Stella Rodway. New York: Avon Books, 1972.

Prabhavananda, Swami, and Christopher Isherwood, trans. *Bhagavad-Gita: The Song of God*. New York: New American Library, 1963.

CHAPTER 13

Religion and Group Identity: Believers as Behavers

MILTON C. SERNETT

Is religion, as the British philosopher Alfred N. Whitehead once observed, "what the individual does with his own solitariness"[1] and, therefore, simply a personal and private experience? Or is religion most fundamentally an expression of basic group identity, given form and substance through adherence to an inherited tradition of beliefs and observances? At moments when we feel most religious we may conclude that no one else can possibly share our distinctive experience. Yet a study of religion in history suggests that all believers behave collectively. At the core of every religion is a community.

Religion is a form of social behavior. What distinguishes one religious group from another is what people do, what customs they observe, not just what they say or believe. The fact that Italians looked into the sky and saw a Catholic God while Germans found in the heavens a Protestant God says much more about their conditions on earth than what they saw up above. Religion, along with race and language, serves as a unifying principle, helping people define a sense of group identity according to the nuances of social behavior. Separating personal religion from its communal matrix would, I believe, make it unintelligible.

Religious behavior is learned behavior. One does not come into this world bearing the birthmark of any particular religious persuasion. However, many of us are baptized, confirmed, Bar Mitzvaed, or, in the case of Hindu boys, given our first haircut before the age of consent or without consciously reflecting on why it is that we are what we have become. Because religion is so closely tied to family and community, we commonly fail to perceive that "peoplehood," whether it is defined along lines of racial or ethnic origin, is the hidden skeleton or vital center of religious belonging.[2] Religious loyalties and ethnic or racial identity are so intertwined that individual believers never totally escape the bonds of affinity that give them social location.

Imagine a parade of religious caravans. The heralding of "German Lutherans," "Mexican Roman Catholics," or "East India Hindus" would strike a note of familiarity. Calls announcing the passing of "Japanese Muslims," "Obijwa Jews," or "African Buddhists" should ring disharmoniously. These pairings, something tells us, are highly implausible. Were we to map religious groups and apply the diversity index,[3] we would discover that our instincts were correct. Although it is plain to all that religion is not absorbed through the soles of our feet or in the food we eat, simply being born into a certain community predisposes an individual to a specific religious identity. What is the relationship, then, between religious belonging and group identity?

ETHNORELIGION: OLD AND NEW

In the beginning the ancestral gods lived in the ancestral lands. In folk or tribal societies there are no village atheists. If one opts out of the communal myths, beliefs, and rituals, one has, in effect, forfeited membership in the group. Ethnically and culturally homogeneous groups invoke the tribal gods, whether they are derived from ancestral geniuses, civilizing heroes, or nature's mystic book. Supported by myths of cosmic centrality, they do not concern themselves with conflicting world views, provide individual members with the option of choosing between competing religious philosophies, or seek to proselytize the outsider. Communal affiliation simply and directly determines creed and custom. Ethnicity defines faith.

We are misled by the myopia of modernity if we assume that the entanglement of religion and ethnicity is only to be found in supposedly static societies or archaic cultures. The evening news brings reports of violent conflict between Maronite Christians and Muslims in Lebanon and of guerrilla warfare between Protestants and Catholics in the streets of Belfast. Are these antagonisms nothing more than the bitter fruit of conflicts over religious doctrine? Why is it that despite the widespread diffusion of the universalizing faiths—Buddhism, Christianity, and Islam—their adherents are separated into many distinct ethnic and racial enclaves? Why is it that in America the contours of ethnoreligious identity have sharpened while, paradoxically, religious bigotry based on theological differences has declined? These questions suggest that even in contemporary pluralistic societies, where a citizen can constitutionally change religious affiliation as freely as place of residence, the kinship of religion and "peoplehood" is still a vital force.

Among closed tribal groups the gods are anchored to the familiar landscape—to local mountains, rivers, and valleys. These associations come under stress through the displacement and diffusion of the populace, are weakened by cultural syncretism and contact conversion, and may be lost entirely through the de-folking process. The international or universalizing religions of today were able to expand beyond the confines of blood ties, broke out of the seedbed society, and acquired a world parliament rather than a restricted folk character. Considered by their proponents to be proper for all humanity, the universalizing religions are usually religions of revelation and use mechanisms such as mission societies, traveling monks, and crusading armies to gather together an assortment of peoples and cultures under one religious banner.[4]

Christianity initially expanded by enlarging the concept of the family of God to include people who were not of the seed of Abraham, Isaac, and Jacob. Islam was a space-integrating religion: "Good news," reported Arab emissaries after the battle of Nehawand in 642 A.D., "the Persians have given us the soil of their country."[5] Buddhism left the rigidities of caste and the ethnic exclusiveness of the *Vedas* behind and became the export form of Hinduism. Although Judaism may be the most salient example of a closed community based on creed, it likewise became a nation, in Hans Kohn's words, "not by blood but by an act of volition and of spiritual decision."[6] Pointing the way toward this more inclusive vision, the prophet Amos refused to view the destruction of Israel as a defeat for Yahweh, as if the god of Moses were but the guardian idol of a particular tribe.

These examples give us one side of a paradox. Unlike purely ethnic religions or neoethnic sects such as Soka Gakkai in Japan or the Nation of Islam under Elijah Muhammed in the United States, the universalizing religions theoretically can strike anyone anywhere. They have attained regional, even global dimensions and embrace many varieties of humankind. Witness the racially mixed and polyglot representatives at an opening assembly of the World Council of Churches, the hosts of pilgrims from many lands fulfilling the Islamic obligation of the *hegira*, or the varied sculptural renditions of the Buddha in India, China, and Japan.

The other side of the paradox is seen in the fact that the universalizing religions are also related to specific cultures with distinct languages, customs, music, food, art, folk superstitions, and myths of common origin. For example, Buddhism was carried to China at the beginning of the Christian era and accommodated itself to Confucian and Taoist thought forms. In turn, Chinese Buddhism, introduced via Korea, moved to Japan in the sixth century A.D. and incorporated older Shinto customs. Until the modern era Protestant Christianity was almost exclusively white, of European and, derivatively, American stock. By comparison, Roman Catholicism is markedly more Mediterranean and Latin in character. Islam is so closely identified with the Arab world and Levantine civilization that Islamic religion and culture seem interchangeable. Jews in the Diaspora have taken on the language and customs of the nations in which they existed as mini-nations. As a form of social behavior, therefore, religion is inextricably bound up with all that gives a group a distinct cultural identity.

Illustrating the two sides of the paradox is much simpler than accounting for it. Perhaps psychohistorians will someday explain for us why the archives of the past overflow with examples of how religion has, on the one hand, served as a cross-cultural unifying principle while, on the other hand, it has been a means by which insiders define themselves over against outsiders. The paradox is particularly sharp when the examples are drawn from groups claiming allegiance to a common set of theological-historical creeds and symbols.[7]

On closer examination, the paradox may resolve itself if we distinguish between two ways in which people use religion as a means of affirming who they are. In the first instance, the group's identity is, in Martin E. Marty's words, "inescapable, automatic, and reflexive." In the second, it is "at least partly escapable, intentional, and reflective."[8] Some group members act out an identity that is so integral to their sense of social location that alternatives are neither available nor attractive. But individuals who are members of groups that have experienced or come into contact with the options that cultural pluralism offers must make an identity choice so as to be able to answer the question, Who am I? They want roots too.

Because religion is a cradle-to-grave experience for many people, the rediscovery of one's ethnoreligious heritage inevitably begins with the family tree. Like the faded daguerreotypes in the family album, religion seems to memorialize in our corporate and individual consciousness the times in life when human beings ritualize the acts of birth, coming of age, marriage, parenthood, old age, and death. Since biography and religious history have much in common, perhaps two brief personal vignettes will clarify the distinction we are attempting to make between the "old" and "new" expressions of ethnoreligion.

According to *Der Correspondent von und für Deutschland,* Helmut Berghöfer arrived in St. Louis with an immigrant party of Saxon Lutherans in 1839. From here he journeyed about 100 miles south to Perry County, where the Gesellschaft had purchased thousands of acres of yet uncleared but tillable farmland along the Mississippi River. Helmut preferred the hard life of this Zion in the wilderness to the more comfortable and cosmopolitan life of the "gateway to the West." For here he could practice the true faith, which he identified with Martin Luther's *Small Catechism* and the *Gesangbuch* or German hymnal. After baptism his children attended the Gymnasium and were confirmed in the ancestral faith. Helmut neither wanted nor expected anything different. He lived in the hope that he would die, like a medieval peasant, in the faith into which he had been born. The stonemason may even have chiseled Helmut's confirmation verse as his epitaph.

Heidi Jacobson is a freshman at Syracuse University. To fulfill a distribution requirement, she enrolls in a course entitled "Black Religion in American History." Here she learns how black slaves and freedmen alike hammered out a unique religious folk heritage on the common anvil of adversity. But Heidi does not think of herself as a "religious person." Her paternal grandmother once kept an Orthodox Jewish home, but Heidi's parents never resolved the ethnoreligious differences in a Russian Jewish–Scottish Presbyterian union. After much soul-searching Heidi decides that, like the children of Africa, she too wants roots. During the next semester she enrolls in a course on Jewish mysticism and joins the campus Hillel society.

These portraits are not meant to be antithetical. They suggest, however, that the functional use of religion by individuals to establish self-identity inevitably establishes linkages to some form of community. A thoroughly privatized religion is no religion at all. The Hindu mystic, no less than Christian pilgrims crowding inside a holy shrine, draws the form and substance of his religious vision from the particular tradition out of which he comes. Even in contemporary, supposedly secularized society, considerable intellectual energy must be expended in order to achieve the distance from shared religious or semireligious behavioral cues that makes possible an analysis of religious groups with the same objectivity that, for example, a political scientist uses in examining voting trends. Although we may not think of ourselves as faithful to any particular religious tradition, we are nevertheless subject to the general influence of them all, not as an identifying birthright but as a cultural legacy.

ETHNORELIGIOUS BEHAVIOR AND HUMAN RELATIONS

Once we are aware that religious belonging is a primary element of group identity, the entanglements with other equally powerful attachments, such as race and nationality, can be sorted out. When communities define themselves around a set of religious myths, symbols, and rituals, that which unites them also sets them apart from other communities. What happens when one community, thus united, comes into conflict with another community, equally united? Religion can provide a warmth of certitude and belonging. When its energy is turned outward it may express itself in acts of mercy and even saintliness. But religious conviction can also heighten the tribal instinct, a powerful emotion that can result in violent intractibility. Potential conflict situations become extremely volatile when differences in race, nationality, and social class are undergirded by a religious belief system. To be more specific, when racism is rooted in primordial prejudice, reinforced by deeply held religious doctrines, and institutionalized in religious structures, it is often immune to moral appeals and objective facts.

The medieval tradition that the three wise men of the Epiphany who came to worship the newborn Christ were, respectively, black, brown, and white expresses in a popular way the essential blindness to color that is representative of the best in the Judaeo-Christian tradition. Yet a passage in the Babylonian Talmud suggests that Negroes were the cursed children of Ham, and Christian commentators have used the story in Genesis 9 as a justification for the enslavement of Africans. As Theodore D. Weld, an American abolitionist, once remarked, "the prophecy of Noah is the *vade mecum* of slaveholders, and they never venture abroad without it."[9]

The deliberate whitening in Western religious art that transformed Christ from a Semitic to an Aryan person no doubt accelerated after Europe's contact with Africa. But religious symbolism that associated whiteness with beauty, purity, and innocence and, conversely, blackness with ugliness, carnality, and sin was already in the air prior to the arrival of the first slavers on the coast of West Africa. Cross-cultural studies suggest that symbolism associated with the colors black and white is found in many societies. The Nupe of Nigeria, for example, believe that white implies good luck while sorcery or evil is represented by black. The Gikuyu of East Africa address God as "the Possessor of Whiteness."[10]

In societies that are rigidly divided along racial lines, the ambivalence of color is lost. The original Sanskrit word for each of the four great classes in India was *varnda*, meaning "color." This suggests that as the light-skinned Aryan invaders encountered the darker-skinned aborigines on the Indian subcontinent the caste system was given religious sanction as a means of impeding assimilation. According to a portion of the *Śatasāhasvikā*, the Buddha "has no perception of difference."[11] Buddhism's attempt to surmount Hinduism's association of a light skin color with an aristocratic Brahmin status helped democratize the faith.

Claiming to be free of the onus of the "white devils," Islam made rapid gains in much of sub-Saharan African at the expense of European Christianity. Regardless of tribal or ethnic background, a Muslim apologist asserts, the African neophyte who pronounces the *Sahadah* "finds himself suddenly in a milieu which does not discriminate between African or Asian, Black or White."[12] Although Islamic ideology has not rationalized *apartheid* on the same scale as, for example, the rigid Calvinism of South Africa, it is not entirely colorblind. Historians have pointed to the low status of slaves from Bilad al-Sudan (Arabic for "the land of the blacks"); the relative absence of Negroid peoples in positions of wealth, power, and privilege; the use of Negroes as eunuchs; and the popular disproval, despite Muhammad's precedent, of intermarriage between Arabs and black Africans. Nevertheless the myth that Islam knows no difference of color has proved highly attractive to black separatist groups in America such as the Nation of Islam, founded in 1930 by Elijah Muhammed. Elijah Muhammed reversed the "curse of Ham" by teaching that "pale-faced, blue-eyed" people were devil mutations from the original Black Nation.[13]

If we accept the view that religion is but the extrapolation of group consciousness, then it would seem natural that all groups should paint the visage of the divine in their own image—red, white, black, yellow, or brown. A more defensible hypothesis is that as each group attempts to define itself over against the ultimate, seeking meaning in the universe; that which is incomprehensible becomes comprehensible by becoming familiar. Thus the Madonna and Child, for example, are given Italian features by Italian artists, black African features by black African artists, and Chinese features by Chinese artists. A powerful universal symbol of the parallels between divine and maternal love is thereby made indigenous to each culture.

This should suggest that racial prejudice, regardless of the social system, has not evolved simply from the tendency of each group to invest certain colors or physical features with positive religious value. Nor is racial prejudice simply a result of differences in creeds or doctrines. Perceived dissimilarity of belief hardly explains the exclusion of a Negro Baptist family from, for example, a middle-class Roman Catholic neighborhood. The eleventh hour on Sunday mornings may still be the most segregated segment of American life, for the vast majority of black Christians, approximately 13 million, are members of independent Negro churches. Nevertheless they subscribe to the same Protestant theological heritage that their white counterparts identify with. The fault lines separating religious communities are only the most visible of a complex set of social factors that divide people into separate voluntary associations. Such separate religious communities may disguise more basic motivations, such as fear of miscegenation, economic competition, and political rivalry.[14]

"From religion to the nation," Harold Isaacs writes in *Idols of the Tribe*, "is but a step, historically and psychologically." The adoption of Confucianism as a manifestation of the Chinese national ethos as well as the theocratic states depicted in the Hebrew scriptures exemplify this bonding of religion and nationality. In Europe, pre-Reformation societies were held together by the notion that there was a divinely appointed social order. The "religious sense" gradually shifted away from the church to the prince and finally to the people as a mythic whole. "The power and the glory," Isaacs asserts, "passed from God's Chosen Church to God's Chosen Kings to God's Chosen People."[15] The end product was the emergence of national loyalty as an "ism"—the cult of the nation. One does not need the wisdom of Solomon to understand how easily religion can be caught up in the fist into which nations harden themselves against other nations.

Frequently a beginning student of the history of religion will recoil in shock upon discovering that alongside the Twenty-Third Psalm, the Sermon on the Mount, and passages in the Koran about universal brotherhood there is a dismal record of interreligious conflict. Christianity and Islam have certainly not had a monopoly on the carnage committed in the name of religion. Pope Innocent's blessing of the Crusaders as they set out against the infidel Turk and the *Jihad,* or holy war, permitted by the Koran against polytheists are but two examples of religious conflict. More recent manifestations of ethnoreligious conflict are seen in the strife between Hindus and Muslims in Pakistan, Maronite Christians and Muslims in Lebanon, and Buddhist Burmese and Christian Karens in Burma.

"War is more humane," Roland Bainton once wrote, "when God is left out of it."[16] Unfortunately, opposing sides frequently call down the wrath of the war gods upon each other. In World War II Wehrmacht soldiers fought with *GOTT MIT UNS* emblazoned on their belt buckles while American fighting men were urged to "praise the Lord and pass the ammunition." In 1898 the Rev. George F. Pentecost told his parishioners that "the very voice of God called to us through the mouth of Dewey's guns."[17] Despite bellicose statements by such clerical crusaders, few historians have interpreted the Spanish-American War, or World War II for that matter, as a religious conflict. Even the so-called "religious wars" of the seventeenth century, in which Roman Catholics sang a Te Deum Laudamus after the death of Gustavus Adolphus, the Swedish Lion of the North, at the battle of Lützen (1632), were not simply conflicts over religious doctrine.

William James defined the problem: "Piety is the mark, the inner force is tribal instinct."[18] When an ethnic group or a nation assumes a distinctive character in which individuals invest their identity, the conclusion is that whatever serves the state is right. Encouraged by the rhetoric of absolutism, which destroys discriminating judgments about how conflicts over deep, real, material interests should be resolved, ethnoreligious groups resort to holy wars. Valiant defenders of the faith may even be promised immediate religious rewards for their participation. A premium is placed not on the individual's deep spirituality but on loyalty to the group.

Voltaire once sardonically remarked that the problem with Jesus was that he had disciples. The pure moral vision, the exalted ideals, and the holy example of the great religious figures of history inevitably suffer some slippage among their followers. The American theologian Reinhold Niebuhr argued that moral people often commit immoral corporate acts precisely because groups operate with a less vigorous code of ethics. When group survival is at stake, supernatural justification for killing overrides the dialectically opposite principle of reverence for life that is basic to Christian pacifism, the Ghandian concept of *ahisma,* and the Hebrew prophet's admonition to beat swords into plowshares.

RELIGION, GROUP IDENTITY, AND CULTURAL PLURALISM

Religion, always a receptacle for ultimate aspirations, can bring out the best and the worst in individuals. That it should appear most closely related to group identity in conflict situations, especially where differences in race, nationality, or ethnic heritage are present, says much about the nature of human society. Religion can be used to enforce an "us–them" hostility. Assuming that the tribal instinct is still part of the nature of modern social groups, we are led to ask, Is peaceful coexistence at all possible? One solution is to adopt the policy of separating opposing ethnoreligious communities, as was done in the wake of the mutually destructive battles between prelates and princes during the religious conflicts of the seventeenth century. Lutherans, Calvinists, and Roman Catholics finally decided to redraw the map so as to compartmentalize the differing religious households into different territories. While this resulted in a temporary cessation of hostilities, the ethnoreligious enclaves thus created served only to sharpen "us–them" attitudes. Confronted by a crazy quilt of ethnic and religious loyalties, the advocates of the early nation-states found that unity was possible only if spiritual allegiances were transfered from the parts to the whole.

Contemporary democratic and pluralist societies must balance loyalty to religious and ethnic groups with the common good. The United States, for example, has successfully avoided both religious wars and territorial fragmentation by dissident ethnoreligious groups. In the beginning, of course, Americans saw themselves as almost wholly Protestant, white, and Anglo. Successive waves of immigrants rejected the model of Anglo-conformity and the rhetoric of those who dreamed of creating a Protestant empire in favor of their own languages, customs, and churches. Black Americans, Native Americans, and other minorities, excluded from the notion of a single "melting pot," have long stood as social anomalies, never quite fitting into the grand schemas of those who predicted a religious and ethnic amalgamation that would bring into being a new religion stamped "made in U.S.A."

Immigrant groups sharing myths of common national origin positioned themselves on the American landscape according to ethnoreligious family trees. Some groups found room under the umbrella of religious voluntarism to fragment along ethnic and creedal lines more prolifically than was possible under the political pressures of the developing European nation-states. What kept the American experiment in religious toleration from degenerating into violent conflict? Part of the answer reflects the successful disestablishment of religion in the wake of the War for Independence. This did not result in the erection of altars to the Fatherland, as was done after the French Revolution, but led to the flowering of numerous sects and denominations. It was an experiment in cooperative separatism.

America has not been without interreligious tensions. Although the acronym WASP, if used to describe all white Protestants of North European extraction, does not correspond to a single ethnic group characterized by religious and cultural homogeneity, it does suggest a mind set that claimed to be superior to other ethnoreligious options throughout much of American history. Protestant clergy and white Anglo-American politicians kept the "religious threat" alive by raising the spectre of "popery" and "Romanism." Jewish immigrants to America, being neither Protestant nor, for the most part, of English origin, experienced a kind of double jeopardy. Ethnic diversity within American Catholicism led to the formation of independence associations, such as the Polish National Catholic Church. In the very process of getting established, immigrant groups sharing the same religious label discovered differences and divisions among themselves.[19]

Even so, the small amount of violent religious discord in comparison to other societies is a striking feature of American life. Perhaps the explanation lies in the accommodation of immigrant ethnic and religious communities to cultural pluralism as the American way of life. The same freedom to exist as a society within a society that one group claimed for itself was extended to all. Milton Gordon has argued that the key variable is structural pluralism.[20] Ethnoreligious subsocieties give individuals a primary means of answering the question, Who am I? Social restrictions against intermarriage across the boundaries that mark out Protestant, Catholic, and Jewish subgroups, along with class and racial demarcations, helped maintain separate group identities. However, individuals were free to assimilate with the transnational and transreligious cultural patterns dominant in the secondary-relations areas of political action, economic life, and civic responsibility. Thus a young college student may think of herself as both an Italian Roman Catholic and an American citizen. Her church provides spiritual and emotional security at the primary level while her sense of being an American is born of a desire to share in the economic and political opportunities promised to all citizens.

American society, then, is a mosaic of subgroups, each of which is, within constitutional limits, free to practice its ancestral faith without governmental interference or, we should add, governmental favoritism. The principle is easily stated; the implementation raises many questions. What, for example, is the proper role of legal authorities in behalf of a minor whose Jehovah's Witness parents refuse to grant permission for a necessary blood transfusion on the grounds that such an act violates their religious beliefs? Should the U.S. Congress authorize tax rebates for families whose children are sent to sectarian schools? Is the exclusion of a black Presbyterian by an all-white Presbyterian congregation, or vice versa, a violation of that individual's civil rights? Does a young man who claims no specific religious affiliation but objects to military service because of personal conviction fall within the category of "religious dissenters?" What position should the courts take when a church or synagogue divides and each side claims to be the rightful owner of the physical property? Is the definition and protection of human life with regard to abortion and euthanasia a religious issue or a judicial one? If it is religious, which group's beliefs should be determinative?

These questions raise many complex issues, not only about what has been traditionally called the church–state problem but also about how ethnoreligious subsocieties should live together in their separateness. Cultural pluralism does, however, offer the individual one clearly defined right: freedom of choice. One may choose not to belong at all or to change affiliations, in spite of parental and peer group pressure. Democratic societies should affirm the responsible freedom of individuals to express their ethnoreligious preferences by uniting with whatever group they wish or by freely cutting across traditional group lines. Those who are able to find meaning for their lives apart from any ethnoreligious ties should also be given that opportunity.

We began this chapter by observing that religion is most fundamentally a communal experience. Because communities organize themselves along racial and ethnic lines, we noted the entanglements of these factors with religious behavior. The defense of ethnoreligious loyalties can lead to social conflict, but, as we have observed, religion can also enable people to make the bricks of community out of the straw of insularity. In societies that are culturally diverse, each group must be allowed its right to singularity as long as it does not jeopardize the common good.

NOTES

1. Whitehead contrasts rational religion, which he defines as "that metaphysics which can be derived from the super-normal experience of mankind in its moments of finest insight," with the philosophically inferior "antecedent social religions of ritual and mythical belief." In denying that religion is primarily a social fact, Whitehead asserts that the collective enthusiasms, revivals, institutions, churches, rituals, bibles, and codes of behavior common to religious groups are but the "trappings of religion, its passing forms." My contention is that these phenomena are as significant to an understanding of what religion is as the interior life. Alfred N. Whitehead, *Religion in the Making* (New York: Macmillan, 1926), pp. 16–17.

2. Two attempts to rescue this theme from benign neglect are Martin E. Marty, "Ethnicity: The Skeleton of Religion in America," *Church History*, 41, no. 1 (March 1972): 5–21, and Harry S. Stout, "Ethnicity: The Vital Center of Religion in America," *Ethnicity*, 2 (1975): 204–224.

3. The diversity index measures the degree of religious dissimilarity among the inhabitants of a given space. Utah, with its high concentration of Mormons, has a low diversity index, while Colorado has a high index of diversity because of the mixing of many ethnic and religious groups in that state.

4. Louis Schneider, *Sociological Approach to Religion* (New York: Wiley, 1970), pp. 73–78; David Sopher, *Geography of Religions* (Englewood Cliffs, N.J.: Prentice-Hall, 1967), pp. 4–10.

5. Quoted in Desmond Stewart, *Early Islam* (New York: Time, 1967), p. 73.

6. Hans Kohn, *The Idea of Nationalism* (New York: Collier Books, 1967), p. 37. When Jews tie their identity to the Land of Palestine and distinguish between themselves and the world of the gentile or *goi* (a word meaning "ethnic group"), they are expressing a form of religious tribalism.

7. The fragmentation of religious communions into countless churches, denominations, and sects, an endless splitting of splits, may have more to do with social and political aspirations than with differences of doctrine. See Harold Fallding's discussion of the rise of nativistic and sectarian protest movements in *The Sociology of Religion* (New York: McGraw-Hill Ryerson, 1974), chap. 5.

8. Martin E. Marty, *A Nation of Behavers* (Chicago: University of Chicago Press, 1976), p. 164.

9. Quoted in H. Shelton Smith, *In His Image, But . . . : Racism in Southern Religion, 1780–1910* (Durham, N.C.: Duke University Press, 1972), p. 130. According to Genesis 9:21–25, Noah, recovering from a swig of wine, discovered that his youngest son Ham, the father of Canaan, had seen him naked. Deeply offended, Noah exclaimed, "Cursed be Canaan; a slave of slaves shall he be to his brothers Shem and Japheth." After much tortured exegesis this text was used to justify perpetual servitude for the African and to substantiate the myth that "blackness" was the result of a divine curse.

10. Eulalio P. Baltazar, *The Dark Center: A Process Theology of Blackness* (New York: Paulist Press, 1973), chap. 5.

11. *Satasāhasrikā* IX, 1440–1450, as excerpted in Edward Conze et al., eds., *Buddhist Texts Through the Ages* (New York: Harper & Row, 1964), p. 145.

12. Caeser E. Farah, *Islam: Beliefs and Observances* (Woodbury, N.Y.: Barron's Educational Series, 1970), p. 271.

13. Bernard Lewis, *Race and Color in Islam* (New York: Harper & Row, 1971), passim.

14. The generalization that prejudice against minorities is positively correlated with religious commitment is not altogether supported by empirical research. Although most studies have found that church members are more likely to be prejudiced than non-church members, an interesting profile appears when membership is defined so as to distinguish between intrinsic and extrinsic motivations for belonging to the religious group. The highly committed religious person is, along with the nonreligious person, one of the least prejudiced members of American society. Members who join churches in search of social status or to satisfy some other extrinsic need evidence higher levels of intolerance. See Richard L. Gorsuch and Daniel Aleshire, "Christian Faith and Ethnic Prejudice: A Review and Interpretation of Research," *Journal for the Scientific Study of Religion*, 13, no. 2 (September 1974): 281–307.

15. Harold R. Isaacs, *Idols of the Tribe* (New York: Harper & Row, 1975), pp. 170, 179–180.

16. Roland Bainton, *Christian Attitudes Toward War and Peace* (Nashville, Tenn.: Abingdon Press, 1960), p. 49.

17. Georg F. Pentecost, *A Thanksgiving Address: The Coming of Age of America* (New York: Meadon Brothers Press, 1898), p. 13.

18. James is worth quoting at some length: "The baiting of Jews, the hunting of Albigenses and Waldenses, the stoning of Quakers and ducking of Methodists, the murdering of Mormons and the massacring of Armenians, express much rather than aboriginal human neophobia, the pugnacity of which we all share the vestiges, and that inborn hatred of the alien and of eccentric and nonconforming men as aliens, than they express the positive piety of various perpetrators." *The Varieties of Religious Experience* (New York: Crowell-Collier, 1961), p. 269.

19. Additional material on these themes can be found in Charles H. Anderson, *White Protestant Americans: From National Origins to Religious Group* (Englewood Cliffs, N.J.: Prentice-Hall, 1970), David M. Zielonka and Robert J. Wechman, *The Eager Immigrants: A Survey of the Life and Americanization of Jewish Immigrants to the United States* (Champaign, Ill.: Stipes, 1972), and Harold J. Abramson, *Ethnic Diversity in Catholic America* (New York: Wiley, 1973).

20. Milton M. Gordon, *Assimilation in American Life: The Role of Race, Religion, and National Origins* (New York: Oxford University Press, 1964), pp. 158–159.

QUESTIONS FOR STUDY, REFLECTION, AND DISCUSSION

1. What differing historical and religious circumstances are implied by saying, on the one hand, "Ethnicity defines faith" and, on the other, "Faith defines ethnicity"? Give examples.
2. The universalizing religions, we have noted, are usually religions of revelation. How does revealed "truth" as found in sacred writings enable these religions to expand beyond the folk matrix?
3. Anna Levine's mother tells her, "I don't care who you marry, as long as he's Jewish!" Why are taboos on mixed marriages one of the strongest ethnoreligious group defenses?
4. Religious groups seem to emphasize their particularistic ethnic and racial identities with greatest intractability during periods of social conflict. Why is this so?
5. Would you favor a constitutional amendment that would give the federal government the power to enforce racial integration among America's churches and synagogues? Why or why not?
6. Attempt to imagine a new religion for yourself without reference to anything you have experienced as a member of any group. Why is this so difficult?

PROJECTS

1. Conduct an informal survey of the religious groups in your community, noting the ethnic character of each and its location with respect to traditional neighborhoods.
2. Investigate your family's ethnoreligious heritage. Interview parents, grandparents, and relatives and compile a brief account of their recollections, including whatever Old World roots you can discover.
3. Read one of the following with an eye to how the author uses religious beliefs and customs to establish patterns of group identity.

> James Baldwin, *Go Tell It on the Mountain*
> Willa Cather, *Death Comes for the Archbishop*
> Chaim Potok, *In the Beginning*
> O. E. Rölvaag, *Giants in the Earth*
> Leon Uris, *Trinity*

4. Visit a church, synagogue, mosque, or other place of religious assembly, preferably one with which you are not already familiar. Observe the many ways by which a distinctive sense of religious identity is reinforced among the participants, such as the use of ritual, symbol, cor-

porate worship, and such obvious features as sight, sound, color, and physical structure.

5. For one week, examine the contents of a major newspaper such as the *New York Times* for the purpose of compiling a list of both national and international events in which the religious factor seems significant. Pay particular attention to instances involving groups with contrasting ethnoreligious profiles. What generalizations concerning the significance of ethnoreligious loyalties in contemporary society does your list suggest?

SELECTED BIBLIOGRAPHY

Glazer, Nathan, and Daniel P. Moynihan, eds. *Ethnicity: Theory and Experience.* Cambridge, Mass.: Harvard University Press, 1975.

Gordon, Milton M. *Assimilation in American Life: The Role of Race, Religion and National Origins.* New York: Oxford University Press, 1964.

Hayes, Carlton. *Nationalism: A Religion.* New York: Macmillan, 1960.

Herberg, Will. *Protestant–Catholic–Jew: An Essay in American Religious Sociology.* Garden City, N.Y.: Doubleday, 1955.

Isaacs, Harold R. *Idols of the Tribe: Group Identity and Political Change.* New York: Harper & Row, Harper Torchbooks, 1975.

Lenski, Gerhard. *The Religious Factor: A Sociologist's Study of Religion's Impact on Politics, Economics, and Family Life.* Garden City, N.Y.: Doubleday, 1963.

Lewis, Bernard. *Race and Color in Islam.* New York: Harper & Row, 1971.

Marty, Martin E. *A Nation of Behavers.* Chicago: University of Chicago Press, 1976.

Niebuhr, H. Richard. *the Social Sources of Denominationalism.* New York: Holt, Rinehart and Winston, 1929.

Sopher, David. *Geography of Religions.* Englewood Cliffs, N.J.: Prentice-Hall, 1967.

CHAPTER 14

Religion and Technology*

GABRIEL VAHANIAN

Is modern technology a threat to religion? Is it destroying religion? Merely by shifting the grounds of human self-understanding, is it also proclaiming emancipation from religion?

Doubtless many a critic, viewing contemporary culture and trying to account for its disarray, feels compelled to warn against technology, contending that it is altering not only our traditional conceptions of nature, history, and man, but also man himself, body and soul. Such critics seem to consider the emergence of the technological phenomenon as a further manifestation of the movement toward secularization and the final demise of religion. They seem to imply that, unless the trend toward a technological civilization is reversed or stopped, the demise of religion will, at least with respect to Judaism and Christianity, be final.

One can understand that these critics fear for religion or even for man. But actually, to what extent are their fears justified? Really, is modern technology destroying religion or is it simply ushering in a new religious vision, a new religiosity? Rather than having come to the end of the road, perhaps, we stand at a crossroads. Rather than having exhausted man's potential for the human and his capacity for religion, we are perhaps being invited to renew this potential and to reassess this capacity.

To be sure, technology can ruin man: such a risk is not one that we will be spared automatically. Nor do I wish to minimize it. But then, have we not faced similar risks all along? Indeed we have, whether in the form of natural calamities, such as the plague, or of historically inevitable holocausts, such as World War II. In no way can we therefore build a case

* This chapter is a revision of the author's earlier essay, "Technology as an Ecclesiological Problem," published in the *Union Seminary Quarterly Review*, 29, nos. 3 and 4 (Spring and Summer 1974): 261–270. It is reprinted here with permission of the author and *Union Seminary Quarterly Review*.

merely by underestimating the apocalyptic "potential" of technology; in no way can we shore up an argument by underestimating the fact that computer technology can usher in a most perfect police state. Still, we must remember that, political or otherwise, pollution can also be controlled and attenuated, if not wholly eliminated. And I am therefore of the opinion that it is both more reasonable and more rational to argue the opposite case, namely, that through technology man is presented with a new factor of emanicipation—not from man or religion but from that which alienates man from himself as well as from religion. Preposterous as this view may seem, it is worth at least the argument; quite possibly technology might appear as the vector of a further attempt at humanizing individuals and society; in fact it might well be that nothing prevents technology from being the matrix of a new religiosity.

While the argument of the following pages could conceivably be developed in terms of any religious tradition, I will focus this essay on the biblical tradition as exemplified by Christianity.

ICONOCLASM AND THE HUMAN AS A TECHNIQUE

That technology is commonly accused of being a desacralizing factor cannot be denied. Nor would the accusation be worth contending with were it not for the fact that its implication usually is that technology must have a dehumanizing effect. As we will see, technology is not to be thought of apart from man; nor can it make sense if it is not viewed as the bearer of a technique of the human. To be sure, in thus ennobling technology by considering it the vector of a new technique of the human we seem to beg the question. The fact is, however, that there has been no process of humanization that has not been mediated by one technique or another. At any rate it is from this perspective that I propose to consider the charge that technology is a desacralizing factor and to show how, nevertheless, such an approach fails to come to grips with the real issue: the iconoclastic edge of technology.

Desacralization Versus Iconoclasm

For one thing, desacralization is quite a slippery issue. Even if we wished to agree with those who denounce desacralization, what is meant by this term is by no means clear. More often than not, what is meant is simply the process whereby nature ceases from being hostile to man, and man, thus being no longer estranged from nature, "domesticates" it. The truth is, however, that this domestication of nature is now being more readily understood in terms of its negative connotations. Not that such a misunderstanding would be entirely unfounded. However, it is not wholly free from bias, especially since it rests on the claim that desacralization can be understood only as a synonym for profanation. And inevitably, rather than dissipating any misgivings the issue is further obscured. Indeed, confusion begins as soon as profanation is viewed as the only logical outcome of desacralization and, by the same token, the domestication of nature is grasped in terms of man's alienation from nature rather than in terms of the overcoming of this alienation.

But why should that be the case? Indeed, does it follow that because nature is no longer divine it must also be profaned? Between the opposites of the sacred and the profane is there really no room for a third way?

Not only is there a third way, but biblical iconoclasm has all along built its case on exactly such a contention and has claimed, accordingly, that if God alone is holy, then nothing can be relegated to being merely profane; for everything is, then, prolepsis of that very holiness of God.

Obviously, then, it is not desacralization as such that must be denounced so much as the confusion that relates it exclusively to profanation and immediately gives it a taste of stolen fruits. Nor is it—to use a phrase that admittedly is not wholly innocent or, for that matter, wholly accurate—the "conquest" of nature that must be denounced so much as the confusion that relates it exclusively to the devastation whereby that very conquest, it is claimed, has been sealed.

Indeed, we must ask ourselves, Why should the conquest of nature necessarily imply its devastation? Is not the actual fact worthy of somewhat less tendentious an argument? It is. A more sobering reflection would not only dispel the confusion; it would also enable us to come to grips with the problem that confronts us even as the technological civilization is beginning to emerge. The fact is that not only has technology made us conscious of nature; it has also made us conscious of the limitations of nature. Nor is this meant to imply that technology is nature's last chance, but simply that, whether technological or agrarian, any civilization is capable of wasting nature.

And perhaps this is so not so much because every civilization somehow goes against nature as because it is and remains, in one way or another, bound to nature and, ultimately, because nature itself cannot quite be exonerated from the charge of being wasteful too. If it is true that agricultural methods can, because of their reliance on artificial rather than natural means, result in the "killing" of nature, it can also be argued that methods "closer" to nature can be equally dreadful: The tragedy of the Sahel region of Africa is a case in point, except that in this particular instance it was not by persons but, ironically, by nature itself that the "power to kill" was wielded.

But then, it will be asked, if desacralization must not be confused with profanation, what is the alternative? To my mind, the alternative rests on the contention that, given the context, the so-called desacralization of nature was simply meant to implement the iconoclastic implications of Biblical faith, a faith according to which, as already noted, holiness belongs only to God—and nothing that is, therefore, is per se profane but, rather, is an instrument of God's holiness and so must be approached and honored. And, consequently, whatever can be said to be sacred never is sacred per se either. Iconoclasm is thus a vindication of God's holiness, sustaining as well as sustained by the world and all that is. In other words, iconoclasm is an altogether different matter from profanation or even, for that matter, from desacralization.

Far from sanctioning the devastation of nature, as has been fantastically alleged on the grounds that Genesis understands nature in correlation with man's dominion over it, the myth of creation brings to an end nature's hostility against man and opens the possibility of considering nature as a technique of the human.

By understanding man in terms of creation, the book of Genesis advances the notion that man is not to be grasped as a mere datum, lying in nature, but in terms of that which lies ahead of man. To put it another way, man is that which takes place only by breaking away from nature even as from the past and by being thrown into the future. Not that nature then is relegated, as it were, to the past as though man could forget all about it. Creation does not deny nature. Instead, nature itself comes to its own when humanity, breaking away from it, yet comes to terms with it.

CREATION: FROM NATURE TO UTOPIA

Whatever the degree of our discontent with technology, it should not obscure the fact that our present civilization, if it is technologically determined, is so at best only halfheartedly. To put it bluntly, technological civilization does not have the religion it deserves, even while religion, today as so often in the past, has only the technology it deserves. If there remains a comforting element, it is that no religion has ever rejected technology outright: Religion has always tolerated if not actually promoted some kind of technology or another. And, consequently, the more religion has been world-facing, the richer it has been spiritually. And whenever it has rejected the world, then it has also rejected man, and its "world" has actually been one that had no room for man. Far from repudiating technology, religion has, from a different point of view to be sure, sought to cope with the problem raised by technology. The difference, which is ultimately reflected in the religious consciousness itself, hangs in the last analysis on which of the two basic existential paradigms this problem is pegged on, the soteriological or the eschatological; or which of the two basic paradigms for transcendence, the sacred or the utopian; or again, to borrow Mannheim's distinction, the ideological or the utopian.

Moreover, one could easily show that religions have differed only to the degree in which technology has been latent in them or to the degree in which they have assumed technology and "overcome" it. Just this is what is meant in observing that, from the mythological to the technological frame of reference, the religious consciousness is not obliterated; it simply undergoes a radical mutation. So much so, in fact, that one is immediately driven to remark that the emergence of technology is itself less responsible for the processs of desacralization than is this mutation of the religious consciousness for which technology simply provides a new framework. Let me illustrate this point, and carry our argument one step further, where we can see how the human, relying for its very realization on diverse techniques, today finds the optimum opportunity for this process in the humanizing vector that technology has become, replacing previous ones. Let us take the example of the American Indian.

If they shrink from ploughing the land, it may very well be that it is because they do not wish to mutilate the womb of their mother, because they do not want to be rejected by the Earth when they die and return to the dust whence they came. But commendable as filial piety or reverence for nature may be, this is not what concerns us here. More precisely, this attitude of the American Indian commands our admiration to the sole extent that it postulates an understanding of humanity according to which people are human only insofar as, given certain conditions, they live up to just what is expected of them. It does not say anything against technology as such. Indeed, if it construes technology in terms of sacredness, it does so in terms of a particular kind, namely, the sacredness of nature. And this means that nature has in fact become the bearer, the vector, of a certain technique of the human. The sacredness of nature thus appears to be a particular technique of the human, one that is fitted especially to a religious consciousness that is still "immature," technologically speaking.

By contrast with the American Indian, Adam is told, according to Genesis, that he must till the soil and earn his bread by the sweat of his brow. Whereas Adam must work, the Indians do not work: nature does it for them. In other words, technology begins where man stands out of nature and works. Far from alienating people from nature, work emancipates them. Far from leading them to depreciate nature, work leads them to appreciate it: Ultimately nature not only acquires value but becomes invaluable and turns into creation—as we seem at long last to have discovered but would have known all along had we kept in mind that creation, that work, that even what we nowadays call creativity does not devastate nature but sees in it the possibility of a land overflowing with milk and honey.

The point is this: There is no technique except where man, put into question, overcomes that by which he is alienated; except where the human consists in humanizing that which is not human. Even as a symbol is not *merely* a symbol, so is technique not *merely* technique. Unless paradise is meant as the context for work, it can indeed only be a lost paradise. Unless nature is likewise meant for a technique of the human, it can only be a mere technique if not a mere mechanism. Technique does not consist in turning man into a machine but in humanizing that which is not human.

Nor is the mechanistic view of nature to be blamed on Christianity, but on theories that claimed to be scientific only insofar as they were usurping the role of religion.

The counterpoint of folly and reason is one way of viewing the cultural unfolding of the Judaeo-Christian tradition. Another way is the counterpoint of truth and irony. Nor is this statement without its truth—I mean, its irony.

CREATURELINESS: TOWARD THE HUMAN AS THE FOCUS OF RELIGIOSITY

With the rise of technology, what comes about is a shift in the locus or, if you prefer, in the focus of religiosity. What happens is the replacement of one kind of religiosity with another. Consider the extent to which technology has "desacralized" sex; and at the same time, consider how nothing is today more sacred than sex. Or take man: The less he is understood as that which is confined within the body, or limited by it, the more is he defined or de-limited by the body. Partly owing to technology, the body is today invested with a different meaning. But remember also, in this connection, that in the Judaeo-Christian tradition what distinguishes man is not personhood or sacredness so much as creatureliness. Nor is sacredness denied to nature for the sake of being transferred to man. As a matter of fact, the Judaeo-Christian view is no more man-centered than the Indian's conception of nature as a technique of the human. And, apparently, it does not succumb to anthropocentrism, at least not until the past 400 years. Add to this the fact that the Biblical view of the world is neither theocentric nor anthropocentric but christocentric, and you can see why I am surprised by my contemporaries' dismay at the fact that technology, if anything, seems to tolerate no anthropocentrism whatever. Not to mention that, quite possibly, this anthropocentrism of the modern period was perhaps only the harbinger of the shift that religiosity was to undergo even while today's technological civilization was being born (much in the same way that, on a smaller scale, the revival of the Fifties was merely setting the stage for the demise of God in the Sixties and the ushering in of a new religiosity).

I realize that we have not yet defined what we mean by religiosity, let alone what we have in mind when we talk about a new religiosity ushered in by technological civilization. Until we tackle this point again later on, as we must, a provisional definition is the best I can provide.

By *religiosity* is meant "the conditions of credibility of any religion as well as those of its intelligibility." It is what makes a religion *both* credible *and* intelligible. Although traditionally the term has evinced individualistic overtones and, for the most part, its connotations are still rather pejorative, religiosity is, moreover, understood here not in terms of the supernatural relationship between the soul and its God so much as in terms of the utopian relationship to God grasped, if God must be *both* intelligible *and* credible, as nexus or articulation of the interpersonal structure of the human reality, a structure brought to light by technology even at the level of the human being as body. For the sake of clarification, let us note that every religiosity is conveyed by a dominant vector that gives it its particular grain. Thus a mythological supernaturalism (consisting of heaven above the earth and hell down below) corresponds to "nature" as the privileged vector of religiosity, while metaphysics or ideology will correspond to "history." In venturing that technology is today the only vector capable of conveying religiosity—which, for that reason, is a *new* religiosity—I realize the extent to which such a contention is endangered by the simplistic overtones with which it at first strikes our ears. Even so, I think its premises are basically relevant to a judicious intelligence of our contemporary problematic, of man's predicament today.

SOTERIOLOGY VERSUS ESCHATOLOGY: TECHNOLOGY AS AN ECCLESIOLOGICAL PROBLEM

Admittedly, modern technology entails a risk. But then, what kind of risk? What does it consist of? And are we not, actually, wholly mistaken when we identify it with the fact that technology threatens and undermines traditional conceptions of nature and history? Indeed, simply because technology is altering these conceptions as well as our understanding of man, simply because it is altering man himself, body and soul, does it follow that it must also be accused of alienating or dehumanizing man and of depersonalizing society? Instead, could it possibly be that through technology man is presented with a new factor of emancipation? Or could it be that, as was previously true of history or nature, technology is bound to be the vector of a further humanizing of man—and can be so without the least derogation from authentic humanity?

It bears repeating: Thanks to technology we have today become conscious of nature in a way that has had no precedent throughout the humanizing process. Once feared because it was uncanny, nature was nevertheless felt to be inexhaustible. Not only inexhaustible but also insatiable, that is, ultimately indifferent to man. As part of nature, man accordingly was, is *de trop*. Anticipating technology, creatureliness is for biblical faith the first step toward man's emancipation from a blind and anonymous nature. And God, the creator, is for this same Biblical faith man's way of acknowledging the limitations of nature, the precariousness of its jealous, avaricious abundance. "Creation" thus gives an idea of nature's finitude only by giving an idea of its utopianism. And thus, instead of thwarting the process of humanization, nature "becomes" (in both senses of the term) man. It becomes the vector of human technique. Far from disabling man, it enables him to put on his new nature. That is to say, man is no longer viewed in terms of a process from birth to death but from baptism to extreme unction; not in terms of past and future, of some *already* and some *not yet*, but in terms of fulfillment, of the fullness of time, of resurrection—destiny rather than fate. Once again anticipating technology, redemption is for biblical faith the second step towards man's emancipation. It occurs with the acknowledgment of destiny as the future of history—as the fact that here and now history is "futurable." And God, the Redeemer, is for this same biblical faith man's way of coming into his own: The new man, for whom all things are made new, is the kingdom of God—now. On this view history is no mere mythologem, nor is it mere story telling, but is prolepsis of that which precisely is untold, unheard of, unexpected. Attuned to technology, our consciousness of time has thus less to do with "story" than with "scenario"—less with gods that die and rise again than with a God who is, and was, a God who comes.

Given such premises, no longer can technology be viewed only in itself; it must also be considered as an ecclesiological problem. Two observations will help us define our approach to the twofold aspect of this problem. They will help us clarify both how we view technology and how we consider it as a church problem, that is, a problem dealing with the transfiguration of the world, its transformation.

1. The rise of technology—anticipated by the Christian tradition—corresponds with a radical transformation in the phenomenon of man. The crisis surrounding this radical transformation is what eventuates at once in the death of God (the end of traditional religiosity) and in the birth of a new religiosity, that is to say, the beginning of technological utopianism.

2. In this light Christianity is bound to be definitively obliterated, so long as it continues to understand itself soteriologically (i.e., as a religion of salvation, as evasion from the world whether through the soul or through the body). In view of technological utopianism, Christianity has no future unless it can again understand itself eschatologically (i.e., as iconoclasm of all totalitarianisms, whether of the law of nature or its laws, or whether of the order of things as established by tradition or by violence). And until or unless it can do so, Christianity will dishabilitate itself as the factor of the cultural revolution that technology will but has not yet brought about, in spite of all appearances.

TECHNOLOGY

Technology is one. It begins where man himself is put into question. The technological question is ultimately a religious question.

These three propositions are designed so as to help us achieve a definition of technology. Each represents a particular level, as if there were some kind of progression from the first to the third and, accordingly, something new unveiled at each level. And yet each stage contains the premises of the next one.

Technology is One

I make this claim to indicate what I consider to be at stake when we are driven to account for the fact that, first of all, technology as a method is no longer what technology as a tool used to be, and second, that even so, technology must be distinguished from the uses one can make of it.

Of course, I agree that there is a difference between farming land to the point of exhausting it and using a scientific method of farming in order to prevent it from being exhausted. Again, there is a difference between a hammer and a computer, even between a machine and something that already is more if not yet totally other than a machine. Let us admit that a distinction should properly be drawn between what we might call an artisan technology and, for lack of a better term, the scientific technology of today. At first sight it is evident that in the former case the hammer serves to prolong, to extend man. In the latter, man himself is already being taken over by something that is not merely a machine, that in effect begins to alter him. The former kind of technology alleviates the work that people are asked to perform. The latter kind aims at emancipating them from work—perhaps by turning them into robots, beings for whom work and labor tend to become identical if not identically tedious. Be that as it may, in the former type we seem to deal with tools, in the latter with a method.

But who does not see that this second aspect of technology—technology as a method rather than a tool—is already present in the various stages through which technology has already gone? Is not man with a hammer already other than man *tout court?* At all events it seems to me that, at least existentially, this cannot be denied. Remember the Indians: Would they not think that they would be different people and that they would alienate themselves if they were to use the plough?

By claiming that technology is one, I have tried to show that we must isolate from it, and be attuned to, what constitutes it essentially as such, namely, the particular technique of the human that lies behind it. Such a technique of the human is no less evident with today's scientific technology than it was with the tools and other instruments of earlier rudimentary stages of technology.

It is time, however, to warn against a possible misunderstanding. I am not suggesting that nothing new is brought into the picture by today's scientific technology. Nor am I ignoring that, by contrast with a technology hitherto consisting mainly in the application of science, we now face a situation in which the terms have in fact been reversed and science has become an element of technology. Quite the contrary, I have only tried to show that it is by being consistent with itself that technology has today become a vector of the human and mediates a new technique of the human.

In this light we can, but also must, say that things are no longer as they used to be. It used to be that only that which is necessary was considered possible, whereas today that which is possible is by the same token considered necessary: Technology has thus become the vector of a new humanism. And precisely this, it seems to me, is the reason why it both must and must not be distinguished from its uses. It mediates the human as a technique.

Technology Begins Where Man Himself Is Put into Question

This question of man takes a different shape from those it took in the past. Briefly, while the primitive mind sought to ennoble man by personifying nature and, subsequently, history was claimed to reflect the authentic personality of man, today, rather than depersonalizing man, technology is, it seems to me, personifying him in a radically different manner.

Undoubtedly, such a contention would meet more spontaneous approval if it were put forth on the basis of an interpretation of art, say, from Lascaux to Picasso. The more art becomes centered on man, the more nature becomes objectified, mechanistic, even while the natural law gives way to the laws of nature—and we lose nature and man as well, until there emerges a new perspective other than man himself whether as a product of nature or a product of history. Which leads me to my third proposition.

The Technological Question Is Ultimately a Religious Question

Indeed, like any other kind of civilization, technological civilization has long since begun to stumble on the question, In the name of what? It has done so, but not without having first cleared the ground of the debris of traditional, supernatural, mythological religiosity. And hence, to the extent that Christianity has become captive of that religiosity, it is invalidated, and incapacitated and dishabilitated. The death of God thus marks the end of the supernatural conception of transcendence, of the Constantinian phase of Christianity, as well as the end of salvation as an other-worldly quest, and ushers in a new kind of religiosity.

Not that, mind you, the rise of technology is to be blamed for the death of God. Not only, it was pointed out, was technology there all along, albeit in a rudimentary form, but charging it with the extinction of Christian culture would amount to contradicting a basic contention of Christianity, namely, that its conception of God and its understanding of faith is neither wedded to nor locked into a particular view of the world. Saint Paul long ago made the point by showing that it was not necessary for the pagan convert to become a Jew before he could be accepted as a full-fledged Christian.

FROM THE SACRED TO UTOPIA: THE CHURCH AS COMMUNITY OF THE ESCHATON

It seems, however, that something is still lacking in my argument that the rise of technology corresponds with the mutation from a certain kind of religiosity to another radically different one. But in trying to be more convincing, I am driven to argue not only that a new religiosity is in process but also that this very religiosity is less alien to Christianity than is usually imagined. Let me suggest two types of considerations that, I think, manifest both the shift in the grounding of religiosity and the latter's convergence with Christianity: on the one hand, the sacred and the profane; on the other, utopia.

With respect to the first item, it seems safe to observe that today the loudest advocates of the secularization of Christianity have been equally loud in their apophatic vindications of the sacred. Perhaps it would be even more accurate to say that, notwithstanding secularists and other esoteric seekers of the sacred or its vestiges, today the sacred is less than sacred while at the same time the profane is more than profane. The modern person does not seek salvation out of this world or after this world comes to an end. Technology is indeed utopian, above everything else; and the first principle of technological utopianism is that utopia is realizable, or that the possible is necessary. And if one thinks on it, one is rather quickly led to concede that this, far from diminishing the task of man, makes it even more demanding. In the Biblical tradition, it is not ignorance that is the opposite of faith, but sin. In the Judaeo-Christian tradition, furthermore, the sacred is no more understood in opposition to the profane than they are confused with one another. As Martin Buber has pointed out, the distinction actually concerns the holy and the not yet holy. And thus the task of man, which consists in hallowing the world in the name of God, is essentially an eschatological task.

But it is with respect to the second item, utopia, that the new religiosity differs from the former even more explicitly. Our case will rest on stronger foundations if we recall here that the technological view of the world seeks to obliterate both the naturalistic/supernaturalistic, on the one hand, and, on the other, the historicistic/apocalyptic views of the world. Not that they are not each utopian in their own way. But when utopia is grounded in nature it becomes identified with the quest for a lost nature, a paradise lost. Utopia is thus always descriptive of the past, of the primordial moment of time, the recovery of which can only take place by means of *anamnesis*, or recollection, achieved through the soul. Which explains why supernaturalistic utopianism is always ascetic. On the other hand, when utopia is grounded in history it becomes identified with a quest for paradise on earth, for a "city of man." But such utopianism is so anchored in the future that its realization can come about only as a result of the total negation of this world. It can occur only at the end of the world. That is why I call it apocalyptic. And that is also why the fervent advocates of the freedom of the spirit have in effect condoned the status quo in matters of personal and social ethics. Their utopianism has consisted largely in changing worlds rather than in changing the world.

By contrast, technological utopianism is not geared to the soul (as is the case when utopia is anchored in nature). Nor is it geared to the spirit (as is the case when utopia is anchored in history). Technological utopianism is geared to the body. Not, however, to the body as that which one has, but to the body as that which one is, that is to say, as that which does not belong to oneself. Who, indeed, is it that lives when I live engrafted upon someone else's heart? As Saint Paul said, "None of us lives to himself, and none of us dies to himself. If we live, we live to the Lord, and if we die, we die to the Lord; so then, whether we live or whether we die, we are the Lord's" (Romans 14:7–8). Or, to put it even more radically, "It is no longer I who live, but Christ who lives in me" (*Gal.* 2:20).

The truth is that technological utopianism shuns both the spiritually ascetic disengagement from the world, as in supernaturalism, and the spiritually aesthetic escape from the world, as in historicism. By contrast, it is centered not only on an ethic but on its radicalization. For it is rooted not in the idea of man as datum but as *mandatum*, not as a given but as a gift. How, then, can it be unwittingly said that technology is dehumanizing when, in fact, exactly the opposite seems to be the case?

Nor can I, for one, concede that technological utopianism is antithetical to Christianity.

Of course, the matter in question depends largely on how one understands the nature of Christianity. Again, at the cost of an outrageous simplification, I will say that one is confronted with two options: One may view the Christian faith either soteriologically or eschatologically, I mean either as an esoteric system of salvation centered on the individual soul or as a radical iconoclasm of nature, of history, of utopia itself. Faith, understood as eschatic existence, is indeed no quest for a new being; it is the end of this quest.

I can think of no better way of stating this as simply as possible than by saying that when Christianity succumbs to the pull of "salvation" ideology it cannot explain the reality of the new man in Christ except in terms of the dialectic of *already* and *not yet*, of the beginning and the end, the *initium* and the *finis*, the *arché* and the *telos*. By doing so Christianity succumbs either to the nostalgia of the past or to the mirage of the future. Such an approach confuses creation with the beginning and the eschaton with the end; that is to say, it either archaizes or apocalypticizes history. Time is collapsed either into the past, into some sacred mythical epoch (as Mircea Eliade says in another context), or into the future, into some apocalyptic catstrophe. Nor is what is abolished in either case history so much as eschatology, that is to say, the world as an event of God's kingdom or, in other words, the Church.

As body of the Christ, as community of the eschaton, the Church is the mode in which the kingdom of God is present in, with, and under the world; it is the way in which the Christian faith can grapple with the thoroughgoing utopianism of a technological society. For the mythical "once upon a time" (*Urzeit*) Christianity substitutes the fullness of time, just as for the apocalyptic end of the world (*Endzeit*) it substitutes the transformation of the world into the theater of the glory of God.

CONCLUSION

Technology brings to an end a certain mode of religiosity. Such a statement, perhaps, is too strong, and we should therefore qualify it by simply pointing out that the rise of technology corresponds to the obsolescence of an altogether much too mythologically laden type of religiosity. And what this implies is, of course, not merely that religion must be demythologized. What needs to be demythologized is the myth itself. Anything less than such an iconoclasm would leave us with half a myth and a halfhearted faith.

Being fundamentally supernatural, mythological religiosity is at odds with the scientific world view. It is not religion as such that is opposed to, or by, science. It is the mythology behind it. Indeed, technological persons are no less religious than mythological persons, but their religiosity is different. This difference is most clearly, most appropriately grasped when it is considered from the standpoint of the utopian dimension of the human reality. In the mythological religiosity utopia is identified with the sacred time of the origin of all origins. Or, in the apocalyptic version of mythological religiosity, utopia is identified with the end of the world as well as of time.

By contrast, technological utopianism is focused neither on the whence nor on the whither, neither on the past nor on the future, but on the now, on the fullness of time.

This emphasis on the now is how Christianity has all along understood, if not salvation, at least God's dominion over the world and His reality. It is this dominion that God performs, not only by making all things but also by making them all new—in the now of the Christ event, that is to say, in the advent of man as the event of God. This event encompasses not only Jesus but also—through the eschatological community of faith, through the Body of Christ, through the Church—man.

Obviously, by Church is meant not a natural community, nor a historical process, but the transformation of the world, here and now. Indeed, is this not, to begin with, how the early Christians understood their hope, when they stopped waiting for the end of the world and set out to change it? The history of Christianity is nothing but the record of this change, a change that Christianity undertook by adopting and adapting itself to the ambient utopianism of Greco-Roman religiosity. The task at hand is no different today. All that Christianity needs to do is to revise its understanding of the nature of the Church and adapt its structures to the utopianism of technological civilization.

QUESTIONS FOR STUDY, REFLECTION, AND DISCUSSION

1. Several terms are basic to an understanding of this chapter. Do you understand the meaning of the key words? If you have problems with any of the following terms, seek a standard definition in a dictionary; examine the meaning of the term in the context of the chapter; and compare and contrast your understanding of the meaning of the word with the meaning expressed by several other people.

   > *eschatology*   *demythologize*
   > *apocalyptic*   *iconoclasm*
   > *utopian*   *technology*
   > *desacralize*   *religiosity*
   > *secularization*   *soteriology*
   > *profanation*

2. Suppose you take a point of view opposite from the one presented in the chapter. You will then consider modern technology as a threat to religion. Develop your position as clearly and thoroughly as you can, making explicit what you mean by technology and in what ways it is endangering religion. Compare your position with that given in the chapter, showing why you believe your point of view to be more adequate.

3. Imagine that you were raised in an Amish community in Pennsylvania, living without electricity and any kind of motor-driven vehicle. All work was done by hand or with the aid of horses. Now suppose you were transplanted to New York City to live and provided with a modern apartment. In what ways would the new experience be humanizing? In what ways dehumanizing? Imagine again that as an urban dweller you were placed in a primitive rural setting to live with no scientific technology as part of the life style. In what ways would that new experience be humanizing? In what ways would it be dehumanizing? What type of religion would you expect in each situation?

4. In what ways is the technological question ultimately a religious question?

PROJECTS

1. In one form or another the question of "the good life" has been a perennial one. For example, the Greek primitivists defined it in terms of a return to nature; the Hebrews defined it in terms of Eden and the Promised Land; whether in the Greek or the Hebraic tradition, it was also defined in terms of the Just City. In each case, however, we seem to deal with a different view of humanity, echoing a different paradigm for the good life. Write an essay developing the view of humanity and the good life in at least two of the following: (1) ancient Greek civilization; (2) Hindu civilization; (3) Buddhist culture; (4) Plato; (5) early Christianity.

2. Select two of the classics of utopian literature. In a paper compare and contrast the role of religion in the two books.

3. In a research paper compare the particularly utopian dimension of various religious traditions and show what distinctive spiritual contribution each might make to humanity's future in a technological civilization.

4. Evidence seems to suggest a rise in evangelical Christianity at the same time that human sensitivity toward the ecological crisis is widening. Can the two movements contribute to each other, or are they irrevocably different and antagonistic or irrelevant to one another? This issue might serve as a project for research or for a class discussion.

SELECTED BIBLIOGRAPHY

Berdyaev, Nicholas. "L'homme et la machine," in *The Bourgeois Mind and Other Essays*, translated by Countess Bennigsen. Freeport, N.Y.: Books for Libraries Press, 1966.

Brunner, Heinrich Emil. *Christianity and Civilisation*. New York: Scribner, 1948–1949.

Bultmann, Rudolf. *History and Eschatology: The Gifford Lectures*. Edinburgh: Edinburgh University Press, 1975.

Ellul, Jacques. *Technological Society*. New York: Vintage Books, 1967.

Ferkiss, Victor C. *Technological Man*. New York: George Braziller, 1969.

Heilbroner, Robert L. *An Inquiry Into the Human Prospect*. New York: W. W. Norton, 1974.

Manuel, Frank E. *Utopias and Utopian Thought*. Boston: Houghton Mifflin, 1966.

Moltmann, Jurgen. *Hope and Planning*. New York: Harper & Row, 1971.

Mumford, Lewis. *The Myth of the Machine*. New York: Harcourt Brace Jovanovich, 1967–1970.

Vahanian, Gabriel. *God and Utopia*. New York: Seabury Press, 1977.

Part IV

PERSPECTIVES AND METHODS
IN THE STUDY OF RELIGION

Every beginning student and every seasoned scholar of religion struggle with the question raised in Chaper 2 of this book: How shall we study religion? This apparently simple question is really quite complex. Not only is the subject of "religion" vast in scope; it reaches deeply into personal lives in such a way that investigation is difficult. Moreover, the tools of inquiry available in the academic world are varied, ranging from anthropology to zoology. We have to choose from among the methods available, at least at any given time. Shall we be sociologists of religion, psychologists of religion, historians of religion, anthropologists of religion, philosophers of religion, phenomenologists of religion, or something else? Common sense suggests that all are legitimate methods of inquiry. Yet upon reflection no single method appears to be adequate for the study of all aspects of religion.

It can be claimed that only people on the inside of a given religion—those who are committed to a specific historical faith—can really "know" that religion and teach it to others. The opposite view, one that has also enjoyed support, is that only an objective person standing outside a religious faith can truly understand it and interpret it without distortion. Is either position defensible? If neither is satisfactory, what is an alternate approach to religious studies?

The author of the final chapter addresses these questions and presents a perspective that he believes avoids both uncritical naiveté and reductionism. Finally, he touches on the issue of "one truth or many truths" in religion.

Methodological Reflections

T. WILLIAM HALL

THE PROBLEM OF METHOD

Religion is as old as ancient mythologies and primitive rituals; it is as old as the human quest for meaning. The *study* of religion, however, is a new human activity, especially the kind of scholarship practiced in colleges and universities in the second half of the twentieth century. The study of religion has as its task to describe, understand, and evaluate the expressions of religion in all of its forms, to the end that the student may gain knowledge, be liberated from ignorance, and develop an appreciation for the phenomenon being studied. Religion itself, however, is more than research and thinking about something; it involves convictions, feelings, and dedicated action. It is this difference between religion as a lived phenomenon and the study of religion that leads to the problem of method in religious studies.

How shall we study religion in such a way that religion itself will be thoroughly understood and not distorted? How shall we do it so that the scholar may be free from the kind of religious involvement and commitment that make critical evaluation of religion difficult, if not impossible? In short, if we are on the "inside" of religion we may not be able to be scholarly critics because of our personal devotion. Yet if we are on the "outside" we may not be able to understand the intimate power and dynamics of religious faith and practice because of our distance from it. A brief sketch of the history of religious studies may help give focus to this problem.

General scholarship within the religious communities is not new. The rabbis who wrote the Talmud, along with the early Christian Fathers in the same period, were the intellectuals of their day. Later, medieval theologians and philosophers spent their whole lives writing and teaching within a particular religious tradition.

Yet the study of religion as an autonomous discipline—what we now call "the academic study of religion," the subject of this book—had its beginnings only in the nineteenth century. The historian of religions Max Müller characterized this new concern when he wrote that the purpose of the study of religion is "to find out what religion is, what foundation it has . . . and what follows from its historical growth." Müller believed the task of studying many religions to be extremely important, for he added, "He who knows one religion knows none."[1] Other scholars in the nineteenth century who are still famous for their contributions to scholarship in religion include Auguste Comte, Ludwig Feuerbach, Ernest Renan, Julius Wellhausen, William James, and James G. Frazer.

During the last century the church-related colleges of the Protestant and Roman Catholic traditions offered courses in religion. Yet they paid little attention to the scholars just named. The courses taught, often required of all students, were apologetic and served the purpose of indoctrinating the students into the Christian tradition. During the same period the large and well-known private universities like Yale, Harvard, Columbia, Princeton, and Chicago, except in their theological seminaries, did little to further the study of religion in a direct way. Often studies in religion were left to the classics, history, anthropology, sociology, or philosophy departments.

Beginning in the middle of the nineteenth century and continuing for 100 years, it was in the major nondenominational theological seminaries that scholarship in religion was carried on. The seminaries were able to keep two purposes alive and in creative tension—that of training professional clergy and that of educating scholar-teachers in religion. Whereas the conservative or fundamentalist seminaries limited areas of inquiry so that their doctrines might remain undisturbed, the major theological seminaries were the academic religious establishment.

The academic religious establishment, however, changed immediately after World War II, when new departments of religion were developed in state colleges and universities as well as in private universities. Krister Stendahl, while dean of the Harvard University Divinity School, said that the center for the academic study of religion is moving away from the seminaries to the departments of religion. In a major address delivered at Princeton University in 1968, he declared that

It has . . . reached a point where the question whether a religion department has a proper place within the college and graduate faculty of arts and sciences can be considered resolved in the affirmative, for state universities no less than for private schools.[2]

Such a shift in the location of the academic study of religion had a profound effect on the nature of religious studies. Departments of religion in secular colleges and universities sought for new curricular models distinct from those developed in the Protestant theological seminaries. In the new curricula, courses were changed: "Old Testament" was replaced with "History and Religion of Israel"; "Christian Theology" became "Western Religious Thought." New courses were introduced in the major traditions—Buddhism, Hinduism, and Islam along with Judaism and Christianity.

With the study of religion finding a new home in secular institutions, both public and private, the context became academic, not religious. Whereas at one time it was assumed in church-related institutions that there was one true religion and that this was Christianity (sometimes even the sponsoring denomination), the new assumption was quite different—in fact opposite. The new approach gave no preference to any particular religious claim to truth. Rather, all religions were to be studied without fear or favor. Objectivity was the slogan.

There was a potential limitation in the new stance of scholars of religion, however. In the acceptance of diverse religious phenomena as data to be investigated, that very diversity sometimes seemed to be evidence supporting the idea that religion is merely subjective and illusory. There was the danger, therefore, that religion might be studied not for its intrinsic worth but because it was assumed to be an antiquated system of bizarre thought and behavior to be investigated by more enlightened people.

If in our time we return to the older position, then the teaching of religion will be but a form of evangelism. Open inquiry, which is expected in the college or university, will be impossible. If, however, we take the latter approach, we will most likely distort religion and represent it as little else than "a curious museum within which to study the aberrations of the human spirit."[3] Rather than capitulate to either extreme position, we are now seeking methods of inquiry that will permit religion to be studied fairly and appreciatively as well as critically. These methods must be among those with approved credentials in the scholarly community. At the same time, the methods must not distort the data of religion being examined.

"INSIDE" VERSUS "OUTSIDE"

Thinking through the "inside" and "outside" approaches to the study of religion may help in dealing with appropriate methods of inquiry. Being on the "inside" means that the person who is studying a particular religion is a member of that community. As an "insider" this student is committed to the unrestricted value being examined. The scriptures, rituals, artistic expressions, and beliefs of that group are embraced by the student. He or she thinks, feels, and acts out of commitment to that particular religious faith. Such a person knows religion intimately. The obvious danger is that being on the "inside" of a religion with personal involvement and commitment may distort his or her capacity to be a critical scholar.

An "outsider" is a student of religion whose primary identification is that of a scholar who uses secular methods of inquiry created by the academic community. This person believes that religion is worth studying. Yet he or she is not a member of one of the historical religious communities but stands aloof in an attempt to be "objective" and dispassionate in scholarship.

The danger of the position of being "outside" is that the data being studied can easily be reduced to fit methodological categories. A scholar is then in danger of asserting that religion is "nothing but" that which the method can readily explain. Reductionism thus follows, with religion being reduced to secular norms.

We appear, then, to be caught in a dilemma, both horns being unacceptable. If we are to know the depths of religion, must we be on the "inside" as a devout person of faith? Yet if we are on the "inside" we may lose the possibility of critical judgment so essential to scholarly pursuits. Turning the coin, if we are an "outsider" we can be rigorous and objective; yet by being an "outsider" do we not run the risk of distorting the very stuff of religion by studying it merely as a critical scholar?

The perspective of sociology of knowledge may provide some aid in dealing with the dilemma. A major sociological assumption is that all systems of belief grow out of and are sustained within a specific community. Moreover, a community is a group of people who have developed a commonly understood symbol system and who "know" the same things because they share a common body of assumptions about what it is to know. Moreover, they share a common mythos; they understand a common group of stories about their origin, about what is important, about how people should interrelate, and about correct roles for men, women, government officials, priests and physicians, and so forth. The community of people has its sacred places and times; they share beliefs; they even develop similar ways of expressing emotion.

From this sociological point of view people on the "inside" of a specific religious community share an understanding of their religion without having to resort to "objective" inquiry. When, for example, the Jewish congregation gathers on a Sabbath evening for worship, they share pageantry. The Shema is said: "Hear O Israel, the Lord our God, the Lord is One." The Torah is brought out from the ark and read; the cantor sings; prayers are said. And those who participate in the worship, if they do so out of deliberate desire rather than some external coercion, have a kind of intuitive sense of what it all means. They seem to "know"—at least vaguely—the meaning and truth of Judaism because they are within the community. And the same kind of social dynamics are at work in the Christian community, or the community of Zen monks, or any other group that shares a common mythos and symbol system.

It would appear, therefore, that one way to know religion would be from within a specific community of people: to use its language, to join in its worship, to embrace its myths and stories as one's own, to meditate on its scriptures, to celebrate through its rituals—in short, to be an "insider" rather than an "outsider." H. Richard Niebuhr had something like this in mind, I think, when he wrote approvingly of "inner history" in opposition to "outer history" as conveying the truth of the Christian revelation to people.[4]

The student of religion is in great difficulty, however, if he or she accepts uncritically the view that being on the "inside" is a necessary condition for knowledge of religion. The academic community insists that the "insider's" claim must be qualified by some type of critical reflection. People in the academic environment will probably argue that while a religious tradition may hide some of its knowledge from the "outsider," the "outsider" has access to all the data. The "outsider," for example, may make such a thorough study that he or she can convincingly argue in behalf of a religious tradition or play the role of a priest or rabbi in a dramatic production with power and persuasiveness. The claim might even be made that a person who is outside the community may have certain insights hidden from the insider.

If we continue to turn this problem of "inside" and "outside" over in our minds, it seems reasonable to say that the scholar who is not a person of traditional religious faith is also an "insider," in a way analogous to the religious "insider." The scholar is part of a community—a community of people who are committed to the study of religion. This is a community that desires to understand, appreciate, and evaluate religion whenever and wherever it is found. The philosopher Michael Polanyi is instructive when he insists that for there to be any kind of knowledge—secular as well as religious—there must be a community of people who possess the same assumptions, use a common language, and participate in the same tradition. This "social-knowledge" principle is equally true for the scientific community as for the religious community. Scientists share a common empirical method of inquiry; they utilize the same criteria for the verification of assertions. They can continue their search for "truth" because they share the same general understanding of what it is to know.[5] Such observations drawn from the sociology of knowledge seem to be changing the polarity of "inside" versus "outside." Rather, from this perspective there are no "outsiders" but only "insiders" in different communities. To be more specific, within the community of religion scholars we share a common vocabulary and an assumption that religions have played an important role in human cultures. We exhibit common practices such as classroom dialogue, disciplined reading, examinations, and professional conferences. If this enterprise of the study of religion is entered into with a sense of deliberate dedication to a task that is believed to be significantly valuable, then it is analogous to a religious community. At least the scholar is "inside" a particular committed community, not totally dissimilar in structure and function from a religious community.

To make the matter even more complicated, the scholar of religion who is "inside" the community of scholars dedicated to the study of religion may also be an "insider" in a particular traditional religion such as Judaism or Roman Catholic Christianity. As a committed member of two communities—that of the scholar and that of a person of traditional religious faith—he or she may find that the two communities enrich each other. The scholar's work, for example, may enhance religious life as it suggests new insights and hence aids in the deepening of religious faith. At the same time, the experience of being devoutly religious may give valuable data and suggest unique interpretations to the scholar's work.

On the other hand, these two aspects may clash seriously. The commitment, for example, to the God of the Bible may conflict with the commitment to philosophical scholarship that has led the person into serious doubts about Biblical theism. Or again, the process of demythologization, so characteristic of many scholars' work, may make participating in Jewish or Christian rituals seem a hollow sham. Conversely, the powerful tug of the mystery of the transcendent felt in traditional rituals and the coherent meaning offered by the worshiping and believing community may persuade the scholar to abandon the study of religion. Whenever these conflicts come, and they arise for most of us, we seek for ways to adjudicate the conflict. Otherwise we must give up being "inside" a traditional religion or give up being "inside" the community of scholars who study religion.

The approach that appears to offer promise of overcoming unnecessary conflict between authentic religiousness and the scholarly study of religion—the latter of which may be critical of religion, just as religion may stand in judgment against the absoluteness of any particular scholarly ideology—would appear to be located on the boundary between the two "inside" stances.

This proposed perspective is that of posturing ourselves where we are empathic to a particular religion or religious expression, seeking to understand it on its own terms. At the same time, we seek to reflect critically on the data of religion from "within" the framework of the scholarly enterprise. Sometimes we will actually be an "insider" in the religion being studied. Sometimes we will imagine ourselves being "inside" that community of faith. As scholars we will always be "inside" an inquiring community such as that of a sociologist or historian or philosopher investigating religion. At all times we will seek to remain at the boundary, in tension between two "inside" positions at the point where the two "circles" intersect, as shown in Figure 15-1.

If, then, a methodological stance seeks to do scholarly work at the overlapping boundary between being "inside" a religious community and "inside" the scholarly community, further exploration of the different "in-

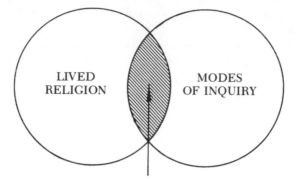

FIGURE 15-1. The boundary.

sides" is needed. For example, "inside" each religious tradition, or even in less formal and individualistic religiosity, there are a variety of sources that are believed to give knowledge about religion. Similarly, within the community of scholars there are many methods of inquiry. A brief commentary on several sources of knowledge may help move us toward a resolution of the problem of method in religious studies.

APPROACHES TO RELIGIOUS UNDERSTANDING WITHIN THE RELIGIONS

There is a tendency in all religions to assume that authentic information and interpretation are available from the experts or from some transcendent power that gives wisdom to special people. Within the various religions people have often looked to holy men, to the scriptures, and even to charismatic leaders to provide the authoritative word on all matters of crucial importance. In the Roman Catholic Church, for example, the Pope is believed to provide the truth whenever he speaks *ex cathedra* in matters of faith and morals. Or again, in orthodox Judaism the Torah, along with the oral tradition, are believed to be given by God and are authoritative for Judaism. No less authoritative is Muhammad's revelation for Muslims and Mary Baker Eddy's writing for Christian Scientists.

Authority as a basis of religious knowledge, however, appears to be ambiguous to the student of religion who is seeking to be on the boundary between religiousness and scholarship. Not only can individuals and scriptures be taken as authoritative, but tradition, personal feelings, falling stars, physical sensations, dreams, and even astrological signs may be considered as giving authority. For the more reflective people in a traditional religious community, however, the trustworthy sources of knowledge are usually more specifically identified than merely "authority" as discussed in the paragraphs that follow. Thus it seems appropriate to give a low priority to uncritical authority because it is so vague and can refer to anything and everything.

In every religion scripture provides a fundamental storehouse of knowledge (see Chapter 6). The *Bhagavad-Gita,* the Qur'an, the Buddhist Sutras, and the Bible, to name a few of the sacred scriptures of humanity, are sources of history, stories, ethical teachings, ritualistic prescriptions, and belief systems. It is difficult to imagine religious communities without scriptures, even though scholars usually assert that the scriptures have been produced *by* the religious communities. An example of the importance of scripture can be observed within the Protestant community. For the reformers, the scripture was the single authority for faith and practice. Modern Protestants, especially in conservative denominations, can be seen carrying their Bibles with them to Sunday services at their churches.

It seems obvious that those of us who are in the scholarly community will seek to understand the scriptures of every religion being studied. In so doing we will discover that people within a historical religion interpret their scriptures in different ways. Some claim that each word in the scripture is a direct revelation from the divine source and that the scripture is infallible—literally true. Others affirm that their scripture contains myth and story, that it is a symbol system unique to a particular culture, and that their sacred literature is unmatched in beauty and evocative power. As students of religion we will surely be interested in the different interpretations within the religious community being studied. Our task is, at minimum, to recognize and appreciate the depth of meaning that scripture has for the faithful.

In every religion and culture there seem to be people who have rare experiences that provide special kinds of knowledge. These experiences, called "mystical," are usually a result of spiritual discipline. Fasting, extensive periods of prayer, and meditation are common techniques leading to mystical awareness. As a result of discipline the mystic experiences an overpowering sense of awe, a conviction that there is a "oneness" to all reality and that the person experiencing the mystical state is in unity with the cosmic being—the divine.

Moreover, the mystic is convinced that he or she is in possession of knowledge that can be gained in no other way. Often mystics claim that the experience is ineffable (unexplainable in normal categories of thought). Nevertheless mysticism remains as one of the kinds of experience that are believed to provide religious knowledge.

Three brief illustrations may help explain the mystical experience as a way that is believed to lead to knowledge.

Acharya Sankara, an Indian spiritual leader of about 800 A.D., believed that genuine knowledge comes from the experience in which one has union with the divine.

It is . . . an awareness of identity with Brahman, and that as an "intuitus," a dawning of insight, our own clear-sighted realization of that which the scriptures taught. This awareness cannot be "produced." We cannot reason it out.[6]

St. John of the Cross (1542–1591) is a representative Christian mystic. This Spanish Carmelite monk not only described the mystical state but was able, through poetry, to express that which for others is inexpressable. For example, the following lines state the precondition of mystical awareness:

> In order to arrive at having pleasure in everything,
> Desire to have pleasure in nothing.
> In order to arrive at possessing everything,
> Desire to possess nothing.
> In order to arrive at being everything,
> Desire to be nothing.
> In order to arrive at knowing everything,
> Desire to know nothing.[7]

According to St. John of the Cross, the soul passes through a dark night in order to be unified with God. And this union with the divine light results in the happy bliss when

> I remain, lost in oblivion; My face I reclined on
>   the Beloved.
> All ceased and I abandoned myself, Leaving my cares
>   forgotten among the lilies.[8]

Within the tradition of Islam is the Sufi way. The term *way*, as used by the Sufis, suggests that the mystical "way" is different from the Law in Islam. Moreover, the esoteric path in the Sufi branch of Islam is grounded in the Qur'an and in the Prophet (Muhammad), to whom the scripture was revealed in a mystical experience. In fact submission to the will of Allah, the meaning of the word *Islam*, comes close to being a definition of mysticism.[9] And in the writings about Sufism this mystical way always seems to represent "the self-disclosure of God to man in his inmost self . . . The Sufi becomes, by the grace of God, one who lives and moves for, by, and in God."[10]

What, then, are we to think about the claim of the religious communities that mysticism is a path toward knowledge? As a student on the edge of a religious tradition looking in appreciatively, we cannot ignore the mystical claims. We may even believe that here is the center of religiousness. At least we must listen to the poetry and the metaphors spoken and written by the mystic, expecting to find authentic expressions of the depths of religious conviction.

APPROACHES TO RELIGIOUS UNDERSTANDING WITHIN THE SCHOLARLY COMMUNITY

If religious people claim to have distinctive sources of knowledge such as authority, scripture, and mystical experiences, the student of religion also has at his or her disposal ways of gaining, organizing, and testing knowledge that will be useful in understanding and interpreting religion.

The scholar, by definition, is one who uses all the intellectual tools available in the task of understanding the phenomena under investigation. Yet in utilizing the available methods the scholar is often in danger of falling into the fallacy of reductionism. That is, the data, in this case religion, may be reduced to fit into a single mode of inquiry.

In the perspective being developed here, however, we would seek to avoid such reductionism. We believe that the student can stand on the boundary between understanding empathically the religious life and being a rigorous scholar in one or more of the academic disciplines. It is possible, we believe, to avoid the dogma of methodological exclusiveness or reductionism on the one hand and religious naiveté on the other. What, then, are some of the methods open to the student of religion?

The physical and biological sciences provide a method that has grown in importance in this century. The scientific method includes the related procedures by which the scholar describes with precision data found in the objective world, proposes hypotheses for comprehensive interpretation of the data, and creates procedures for prediction and control of physical and biological phenomena. In so doing the scientist tests the validity of empirical statements. These procedures of the sciences are not totally irrelevant to the study of religion.

The scientific method as defined here, however, has only limited use in the study of religion in that the nature of most religious data is such that they do not lend themselves to the scientific method. Only in the areas of religion where an assertion is made about some empirical fact is the method of the sciences appropriate for the testing of such assertions. If, for example, the theory of the creation of the world is meant to be a literal statement, then the scientific method is a proper one for testing the truth of the proposition. But just as the method of studying physics is not the most useful approach for interpreting poetry, and mathematics is not the best academic discipline for studying human emotions, the sciences are of only limited value in the study of religion.

The methods of the social sciences, especially sociology, cultural anthropology, and psychology, are often used in religious studies. Sociology is the rigorous study of society with a concern for the origin and nature of society, as well as an inquiry into the forms and functions of human groups. Since sociologists seek information about all aspects of social living and wish to understand the way groups function, they will be concerned with religious communities. Questions, then, about religion as a social phenomena can and should be studied using the various sociological tools.

Cultural anthropology, while it draws upon biology, sociology, and geography, is the scholarly discipline that studies human beings within specific cultural contexts. With vast amounts of data having been gathered from every known civilization, cultural anthropologists are interested in understanding people and their life styles, physical anatomy, languages, and religious systems. We can surely expect that the cultural anthropologist whose specialization is South Asia will deal in depth with Hindu religion and culture. Such an academic approach is clearly relevant to the study of religion.

Another social science, psychology, provides methods that may be used for religious studies. Yet psychology is not a single area of inquiry with one method; it is a vast field with many schools of thought and an equally diverse group of methods of study. But whether psychology is concerned with a study of the psyche or the behavior patterns of rats, the approach of the various psychologies provides the scholarly community with important tools for the study of religion—both of the soul and of religious behavior.

The social scientists, as illustrated by the fields of sociology, cultural anthropology, and psychology, provide specific methods for the study of religion. Scholars who use those methods will, in fact, be "inside" the scholarly community even as they seek to be empathic to the data coming from "inside" another community—the religious community.

Someone has said that "everybody knows what history is until he begins to think about it. After that nobody knows."[11] Nonetheless, history is clearly a method useful in religious studies. Whether it is conceived as a chronological perspective on a given area or as specific interpretations of events, past and present, history does provide methods for the study of religion. So important is the historical method that a distinct category of "history of religions" has developed among scholars in the United States, providing specialized methods for the study of different religious traditions.

The rational mode of inquiry known as philosophy has long been applied to religious inquiry. Ancient Greek philosophers were both critics and supporters of religion. Classical philosophers through the centuries who were concerned with questions of metaphysics, epistemology, and axiology were inescapably involved with religious questions. Thus philosophy of religion became a discipline in which systems of religious belief were clarified, defended, and criticized. Later philosophers who have been influenced by scientific principles of verification have been less interested in religious questions. Nevertheless philosophy remains a discipline closely related to religious studies. When questions of meaning, value, and truth are being asked, then the philosophical methods are essential to the student of religion.

Another method that is of special interest to students of religion is called *phenomenology*. This branch of philosophy, utilized by people like Gerardus van der Leeuw, Joachim Wach, and Mircea Eliade, seeks to set aside all preconceptions about what is "real" or "true" and lets that which is being studied speak for itself. Eliade, in writing about the method, states that "a religious phenomenon will only be recognized as such if it is grasped at its own level, that is to say if it is studied as something religious." [12]

Recent scholars in the field of religion have developed newer methods of inquiry and interpretation. For example, comparative mythologists such as Joseph Campbell and David Miller have shown the interrelationship between ancient mythologies and archetypal images in the psyche, and through their constructive theories have given a distinctive mode of religious inquiry and interpretation. Moreover, Stanley Romaine Hopper, Nathan Scott, and Amos Wilder have shown the relevance of literary criticism to the task of understanding religious meaning.

A sketch of the academic disciplines clearly indicates, then, that there are many different methods of investigation. There is no a priori basis for repudiating any method. Rather, I propose that any method is useful if, in using it, the student can maintain the "boundary" stance. A person, for example, who as an anthropologist or a historian or a philosopher insists that from a particular "objective" perspective religion is nothing, but . . . is reducing religion to fit into limited methodological categories. On the other hand, any method that provides tools for inquiry into that which is "inside" religion and illuminates what is in religion, while avoiding distorting and reducing the data to its own categories, is surely useful as a method of study. The particular method to be chosen will depend on the data to be studied and the purpose of the investigation.

A RESOLUTION OF THE PROBLEM OF METHOD IN THE STUDY OF RELIGION

Thus far we have attempted to identify four aspects of the problem of method in the study of religion. First, we sketched the history of the field of study, placing the current study of religion in a secular and academic environment. Second, we tried to show the dilemma facing the student of religion. Namely, if we are simply on the "inside" of a religious tradition, it is difficult to gain a critical and comprehensive view of religion because we are too involved. If we are simply detached as an objective scholar, we may fail to grasp the essentials of religiousness because our intellectual tools too easily reduce religion to the limited scope of the particular method.

As a tentative solution to the second problem, we proposed that the student of religion is inevitably an "insider" in the scholarly community. The issue, then, is not one of being simply "inside" or "outsider." Rather, the scholar can function in the area where the "inside" of religion and "inside" of the scholarly world overlap—at the boundary of both. The danger is that we may fall off the thin edge into one camp or the other, negating the possibility of scholarship in religion.

Third, we discussed three sources of knowledge for religious people— authority, scripture, and mystical awareness. The data provided by these sources will be appreciatively and empathically examined by the student of religion. Fourth, we sketched various methods of inquiry that are available within the academic community. We proposed that all of these methods are useful. The particular method used at any one time will depend on the specific data under consideration and the purpose of the investigation.

We are now nearing a solution to the problem of method. Moreover, this solution has profound implications for a question we have thus far avoided: Is there one "true" religion, and do all questions within religion have one "true" answer? It is to the solution of the dual problem—the problem of method and the problem of religious truth—that we now turn.

If religious expressions are varied, as Part II of this book asserts and illustrates, and if there are many issues in religion, as Part III indicates, then we have a plethora of data and issues to examine as students of religion. Moreover, if there are many methods of inquiry, as suggested by the different academic disciplines, we have a rich variety of methods available for our study.

There seems to be no self-evident reason for claiming that one religious expression is more universally representative or valid than others. Nor is it self evident that one issue is more crucial to religious understanding than others. Nor does there appear to be any reason to hold that one scholarly method is always superior to all others. We seem to have many expressions, many issues, and many methods.

If we are to be serious students of religion, avoiding every kind of closed-mindedness and dogmatism, two demands will be made on us. First, we must be open in our observation and inquiry to all data in the various religions, whatever their claimed source—authority, scripture, mystical experience, or some other source. We will listen, observe, read, look, and let those data present themselves to us in their full power and on their own terms. Second, we may select whatever mode of inquiry is appropriate to our specific task and to the data being examined. We must be prepared to encourage others to use alternate methods, expecting their description and interpretation to be influenced by their method. With a plurality of data and with a variety of purposes for study, it seems to follow that we will use a plurality of methods.

If an adequate method is really a plurality of methods within the perspective of boundary line scholars, then we will be freed from the haunting question often placed to us: But what is the truth of religion or in religion? The fous of attention and the purpose of our inquiry will not be to find a single universal truth. Our goal, rather, will be to search for "adequate understanding," "broader visions of religious meaning," "significant interpretations," "more humane solutions to burning issues confronting religious people," and "intelligibility."

The implications of the epistemological pluralism being developed here do not necessarily lead to mere relativism. That is, we are not proposing that one idea, one method, one way of interpreting the data is just as good as another. Rather, we are asserting that all insights and conclusions are relative to the data being examined and the method of inquiry as well as the thoroughness of the study.

The approach proposed here demands empathic research, not excluding participation in a particular religion and, at the same time, rigorous scholarship in one or more secular methods. Such a posture leads to responsible scholarship and to confidence in the results of the study. For example, as scholars we can be convinced that our work is adequate in that we have been faithful to the data as well as to the demands of precise study. We can speak confidently about the human meaning and ultimate values conveyed in myth, belief, story, scripture, or art. We will be able to understand the pathos and pain of people who can find no resolution to the problem of God or evil or death, and we can also rejoice with those who are confident in their answers. But we may have to settle for truths (with a small *t*) rather than any absolute Truth. Such a conclusion, rather than discouraging the student of religion, may serve as a motivation for further study so that answers, partially found, may be clarified and ambiguities may become less clouded. Finally, we may discover, if slowly and painfully, what we cognitively and conatively affirm as unrestricted value.

If there is a single or universal "Truth," it will have to be apprehended, not in the scholar's den or through intellectual dialogue among scholars, but in the mystical experience which, even the mystics claim, is ineffable.

NOTES

1. Jacques Waardenburg, *Classical Approaches to the Study of Religion* (The Hague: Mouton, 1973), p. 14.
2. Given at Princeton University in 1968 at a conference honoring Professor George Thomas. Later printed as "Biblical Studies in the University," in Paul Ramsey and John F. Wilson, *The Study of Religion in Colleges and Universities* (Princeton, N.J.: Princeton University Press, 1970), p. 23.
3. Robert N. Bellah, "Religion in the University: Changing Consciousness, Changing Structures," in Claude Welch, *Religion in the Undergraduate Curriculum* (Washington, D.C.: Association of American Colleges, 1972), p. 14.
4. See H. Richard Niebuhr, *The Meaning of Revelation* (New York: Macmillan, 1941).
5. Michael Polanyi, *Science, Faith and Society* (Chicago: University of Chicago Press, 1946), chap. 2.
6. Rudolf Otto, *Mysticism East and West* (New York: Macmillan, 1932, 1960), p. 51.
7. St. John of the Cross, *Ascent of Mount Carmel*, trans. and ed. E. Allison Peers (Garden City, N.Y.: Image Books, 1958), p. 72.
8. Ibid., p. 12.
9. See Seyyed Hossein Nasr, *Ideals and Realities of Islam* (Boston: Beacon Press, 1964), chap. 5.
10. Frederick J. Streng, Charles L. Lloyd, Jr., and Jay T. Allen, *Ways of Being Religious* (Englewood Cliffs, N.J.: Prentice-Hall, 1973), p. 291.

11. *The World Book Encyclopedia* Chicago: Field Enterprises, 1961), VIII, 232.
12. Mircea Eliade, *Patterns in Comparative Religion* (New York: World, Meridan Books, 1958, 1972), p. xiii.

QUESTIONS FOR STUDY, REFLECTION, AND DISCUSSION

1. One of the most profound questions a person can ask is phrased in four words: *How do you know?* "How do you know the world is round?" "How do you know that John loves you?" "How do you know that the only way to know is by reason, or intuition, or empiricism?" "How do you know that 'there is no God but Allah and Muhammad is His prophet'?" After trying to respond to these questions, take some affirmation in religion that is meaningful to you. List all of the sources of knowledge available to you that have led you to your belief. Then list possible sources of knowledge that you have rejected.

2. If you are "inside" a particular religious community affirming that faith, how does this fact help and/or hinder your effort to study religion? If you are not "inside" any historical religion but are a secular person, in what ways does this help and/or hinder your effort to study religion?

3. Under what circumstances would you use a historical method to study religion? a psychological method? an anthropological method? sociological? philosophical? scientific? theological? some other method?

4. The convictions that you hold as a student may clash with the convictions that you hold as a religious person. Until that conflict is resolved you may have to either deny your desire to be a critical scholar or deny your religious faith. What are various ways in which you might seek to overcome the conflict and restore the possibility of being both a scholar and a believing Jew, Christian, or Hindu or a devout atheist?

PROJECTS

1. One mark of scholarly achievement is to be able to take a body of data and interpret it in a variety of ways. As a project, then, take some identifiable religious phenomenon such as a high-holiday ritual, an annual church business meeting, a wedding ceremony, an ancient myth, or a work of religious art. Describe and interpret it from a sociological perspective. Then describe and interpret it as though you were a Freudian psychologist. Do the same as an anthropologist, a historian, or a philosopher.

2. This chapter presents the point of view that the purpose of the study of

religion is not to arrive at "truth" but, rather, to gain "an adequate understanding," "broader visions of religious meaning," and so forth. Write an essay in which you take the position that there is one religious "truth" and that the task of the student of religion is to find that Truth. After writing the paper prepare an epilogue in which you critically evaluate the position you developed in the paper.

3. Along with a small group of people, become a participant observer in some religious event that is unfamiliar to all of you. This might be a Pentecostal service, a Catholic mass, a Zen meditation, a spiritualist seance, or a spiritual healing session. In a discussion with your own group following the experience, note the kinds of observations made by yourself and others. Are these observations philosophical (comments on the intellectual bases of beliefs)? Were the observations psychological (observing individual behavior or speculating on motivation)? Were the comments sociological (mentioning possible origins and functions of the group)? When you and the group have identified the various kinds of observations and interpretations made, see if you can agree on which method(s) was most helpful in interpreting the meaning of the event. Are there approaches that no one in the group used?

4. Plan a second field trip to a different religious event. Ask each person to write a description and interpretation of the event from a different methodological perspective. One will be a historian, another an anthropologist; still others will be sociologists, philosophers, psychologists, comparativists, physiologists, literary or art critics, and so forth. When the various interpretations have been written, collect the papers, have someone summarize each one, duplicate all of them, summarize them, and distribute the summaries to the members of the group. The papers should make an excellent basis for a discussion on the question, What really happened and what is its meaning for the members of the religious group and for the students reporting?

SELECTED BIBLIOGRAPHY

Allport, Gordon W. *The Individual and His Religion*. New York: Macmillan, 1962.

Banton, Michael, ed. *Anthropological Approaches to the Study of Religion*. New York: Barnes and Noble, 1968.

Berger, Peter L. *The Sacred Canopy: Elements of a Sociological Theory of Religion*. New York: Anchor Press, 1969.

Bettis, Joseph D., ed. *Phenomenology of Religion: Eight Modern Descriptions of the Essence of Religion*. New York: Harper & Row, 1969.

Capps, Walter H., ed. *Ways of Understanding Religion*. New York: Mcmillan, 1972.

Creel, Richard E. *Religion and Doubt: Toward a Faith of Your Own*. Englewood Cliffs, N.J.: Prentice-Hall, 1976.

Diamond, Malcolm L. *Contemporary Philosophy and Religious Thought: An Introduction to the Philosophy of Religion.* New York: McGraw-Hill, 1974.

Durkheim, Emile. *The Elementary Forms of Religious Life,* translated by Joseph W. Swain. New York: Free Press, 1954.

Eliade, Mircea. *Patterns in Comparative Religion.* New York: New American Library, 1958.

————. *The Quest: History and Meaning in Religion.* Chicago: University of Chicago Press, 1969.

————. *The Sacred and the Profane: The Nature of Religion,* translated by Willard R. Trask. New York: Harcourt Brace, Jovanovich, 1968.

————, and Joseph Kitagawa, eds. *History of Religions: Essays in Methodology.* Chicago: University of Chicago Press, 1959.

Evans-Pritchard, E. E. *Theories of Primitive Religion.* Oxford: Clarendon Press, 1965.

Frazer, Sir James. *The New Golden Bough,* revised and abridged by Theodor H. Gaster. New York: Mentor, 1975. Paperback.

Hick, John. *Philosophy of Religion.* Englewood Cliffs, N.J.: Prentice-Hall, 1973.

James, William. *The Varieties of Religious Experience.* New York: Macmillan, 1961.

Jung, Carl G. *Psychology and Religion.* Princeton, N.J.: Princeton University Press, Bollingen Series, vol. 20, 1970.

King, Winston L. *Introduction to Religion: A Phenomenological Approach.* New York: Harper & Row, 1968.

Lessa, W. A., and E. Z. Vogt, eds. *Reader in Comparative Religion: An Anthropological Approach.* New York: Harper & Row, 1972.

Magee, John B. *Religion and Modern Man.* New York: Harper & Row, 1967.

Maslow, Abraham H. *Religions, Values, and Peak-Experiences.* New York: Viking Press, 1970.

McClendon, James W., Jr. and James M. Smith, *Understanding Religious Convictions.* Notre Dame, Ind.: University of Notre Dame Press, 1975.

Moore, George Foot. History of Religions. New York: Scribner's, 1914–1919.

O'Dea, Thomas F. *The Sociology of Religion.* Englewood Cliffs, N.J.: Prentice-Hall, 1966.

Otto, Rudolf. *The Idea of the Holy.* New York: Oxford University Press, 1958.

Pye, Michael. *Comparative Religion: An Introduction Through Source Materials.* New York: Harper & Row, 1972.

Smart, Ninian. *The Phenomenon of Religion.* New York: Herder and Herder, 1973.

————, *The Religious Experience of Mankind,* rev. ed. New York: Scribner's, 1976.

Smith, Wilfred Cantwell. *The Faith of Other Men.* New York: Harper & Row, Harper Torchbooks, 1972.

————. *The Meaning and End of Religion.* New York: Harper & Row, 1978.

Starbuck, Edwin D. *The Psychology of Religion, An Empirical Study of the Growth of Religious Consciousness.* New York: Scribner's, 1903.

Streng, Frederick J., Charles L. Lloyd, and Jay T. Allen, eds. *Ways of Being Religious: Readings for a New Approach to Religion.* Englewood Cliffs, N.J.: Prentice-Hall, 1973.

Van Der Leeuw, G. *Religion in Essence and Manifestation.* New York: Harper & Row, 1963.

Wach, Joachim. *Comparative Study of Religions.* New York: Columbia University Press, 1958.

————. *Sociology of Religion.* Chicago: University of Chicago Press, 1962.

Weber, Max. *The Protestant Ethic and the Spirit of Capitalism.* New York: Scribner's, 1930.

Yinger, J. Milton. *Scientific Study of Religion.* New York: Macmillan, 1970.

Epilogue

You, the reader, have come a long way in the study of religion since you opened the first page of this book. With this intellectual adventure well begun, the authors hope that you will now possess intellectual tools for describing and interpreting religion wherever you find it—in Morocco, in an Indian tribe, or in yourself. We would like to think that you are now ready to investigate any area of religion with skill and confidence, since you have already done sustained reflection on the nature of religion and the variety of religious expressions, issues, and methods.

Recall for a moment the organization of this book: It has a logical progression, yet it is incomplete. Part I serves as an introduction to the term *religion* and to religion as a field of study. Part II follows with chapters on different forms of religious expression. It is clear now that myth, ritual, belief, scripture, and art are not the only forms of religious expression. Certainly moral acts to achieve justice are a religious expression. Institutions such as churches and synagogues are forms of religious expression as well. The list can go on and on, since expressions of religion are almost unending and the data for study are everywhere. In fact you are invited to make your own list of forms of religious expression and to explore their meaning.

In reviewing Part III, which is concerned with religious issues, it becomes evident that this book does not include all the issues. Moral conflicts regarding war and racism, issues like free will versus determinism, differences in doctrinal belief between religions and within the same tradition, as well as troublesome issues like "What is a Jew?" or "What is a Christian?" and issues surrounding various theories of the origin of religions, are all candidates for chapters in a book like this.

In full realization that this book is but an introduction, we hope that you have become enthusiastic about the study of religion and that you will pursue original and creative scholarship. If religion is "a varied and complex symbolic expression and appropriate response to what people deliberately affirm as being of unrestricted value for them" and if, as Whitehead said, religion is a "vision of something beyond, behind and within the passing flux of immediate things—something real, yet waiting to be realized," then this study can be of crucial significance for the life of learning. More personally, religious studies may open doors for your understanding, even embracing, of a dimension of life that is deeper than any intellectual enterprise—something that has the potential of moving even your existence away from banality and toward realization of the "vision." At the very least, this is a risk that must be taken by the student who is willing to reside at the boundary that is "inside" religion as well as "inside" the scholar's world.